GREAT TEACHERS

GREAT TEACHERS

PORTRAYED BY THOSE WHO STUDIED UNDER THEM

Edited with an Introduction by
HOUSTON PETERSON

New Brunswick
RUTGERS UNIVERSITY PRESS
MCMXLVI

To

ELLA B. PAYNE

For one term, teacher of the Eighth Grade,
Hoover Street Grammar School, Los Angeles

and

WILLIAM PEPPERELL MONTAGUE

Professor of Philosophy,
Columbia University

with gratitude

⤜⤜⤜·⤛⤛⤛

Acknowledgments

Much of my enjoyment in the preparation of this book came from the conversations with many friends who were generous with encouragement and suggestions. Here they are listed without titles or academic aura: John Bindrum, Julius Bloom, Boris Bogoslovsky, Lyman Bryson, Roger C. Carmien, Jr., Dorothy Clifford, Raymond Dowden, Mortimer Ehrlich, Weller Embler, George Funnell, Horsley Gantt, Leo and Ida Gershoy, William M. Hitzig, Julius Isaacs, Thomas L. Jeltrup, Gail Kennedy, I. Kandel, William H. Kilpatrick, Paul M. Kunz, Alvin Johnson, Louis Lasagna, William S. Lynch, Leslie Marchand, Frederic Meigs, Helen Moser, Lewis Mumford, Thomas Munro, Bonaro and Harry Overstreet, Patricia Reith, George Ritter, Mark Starr, and Henry W. Wells.

My special gratitude for continuous advice and assistance must go to L. K. Frank, Lorraine Carmien and Mitzi Peterson.

The editor is also indebted to the following:

To Doubleday, Doran and Company, Inc. for permission to reprint Chapters IV, V, and VI from *The Story of My Life* by Helen Keller, copyright 1902, 1903 by Doubleday, Doran and Company, Inc.; and also for permission to reprint a chapter from *Shaping Men and Women* by Stuart Sherman, copyright 1928 by Doubleday, Doran and Company, Inc.

To *The Nation* for permission to reprint from the article, "Professor Kittredge and the Teaching of English," by Stuart P. Sherman, which originally appeared in *The Nation* September 11, 1913.

To Harvard University Press for permission to reprint from *Freud: Master and Friend* by Hanns Sachs, copyright 1944 by Harvard University Press.

To The University Publishing Company for permission to reprint from *What Counted Most* by James William Crabtree, copyright 1937 by The University Publishing Company.

To The American Institute of Architects for permission to reprint from

The Autobiography of an Idea by Louis Henri Sullivan, copyright 1922 by The American Institute of Architects.

To H. G. Wells for permission to reprint from *The Story of a Great Schoolmaster* by H. G. Wells, copyright 1924.

To *The Sewanee Review* for permission to reprint the article, "Garman of Amherst," by Walter A. Dyer from Volume 43, page 146 of *The Sewanee Review*, The University of the South, Sewanee, Tennessee.

To Gabriella Shaler Webb for permission to reprint from *The Autobiography of Nathaniel S. Shaler*, copyright 1909.

To Little, Brown & Company and Atlantic Monthly Press for permission to reprint from *The Letters of William James*, edited by Henry James, copyright by Little, Brown & Company and Atlantic Monthly Press.

To Henry Holt and Company, Inc. for permission to reprint from "Frederick Jackson Turner," by Carl Lotus Becker in *American Masters of Social Sciences*, edited by Howard Odum, copyright 1927 by Henry Holt and Company, Inc.

To Dodd, Mead & Company for permission to reprint Chapter I, Part 3, from *Cesar Franck* by Vincent D'Indy, copyright 1910 by Dodd, Mead & Company.

To J. B. Lippincott Company for permission to reprint the chapter, "In Memoriam: Francis Barton Gummere," from *Plum Pudding* by Christopher Morley, copyright 1921 by J. B. Lippincott Company.

To The Bobbs-Merrill Company for permission to reprint the chapter, "Woodrow Wilson, Princeton Schoolmaster," from *Gods and Little Fishes* by Alfred Pearce Dennis, copyright 1931, and used by special permission of the publishers, The Bobbs-Merrill Company.

To Scott Nearing for permission to reprint from *Educational Frontiers* by Scott Nearing, copyright 1925 by Scott Nearing.

To Cornell University Press for permission to reprint from *George Lincoln Burr* by Roland H. Bainton, copyright 1943 by Cornell University Press.

To The Viking Press, Inc. for permission to reprint the material on John Dewey and others from *Philosopher's Holiday* by Irwin Edman, copyright 1938 by Irwin Edman.

To D. Appleton-Century Company, Inc. for permission to reprint from

ACKNOWLEDGMENTS

Leschetizky as I Knew Him by Ethel Newcomb, copyright 1921 by D. Apple-ton-Century Company, Inc.

To Charles Scribner's Sons for permission to reprint from *Heads and Tales* by Malvina Hoffman, copyright 1930 by Charles Scribner's Sons.

To the Whitney Museum of American Art for permission to reprint from *Robert Henri* by Helen Appleton Read, a publication of the Museum's American Artists Series; and to Margery Ryerson for permission to reprint miscellaneous notes culled from Robert Henri's criticisms and class talks as published in *The Art Spirit* by Robert Henri, copyright 1923, 1930 by J. B. Lippincott Company.

Contents

CONTENTS

Introductory

THIS IS A BOOK about teachers — teachers in action in the home, the class room, the seminar, the laboratory, the clinic, the lecture hall. It is not a series of new profiles but a collection of first-hand accounts already written by former students, written from the heart in order to acknowledge a profound debt and to share a privilege. Of course, there are great teachers in action at this moment but their portraits have not been painted and it did not seem fair to present them in hastily improvised sketches. I have had no thought of making a master list of "the greatest" in every field of education. That would indeed have been an end-less, a painful, and a pompous task. Rather I have tried to bring together some of the outstanding personalities who will interest almost any literate layman and kindle the mind of almost any honest teacher.

This means further that we are only incidentally concerned with educational theorists, famous scholars, and administrators. Many a theorist is ineffective in carrying out his own principles and many a scholar is slipshod about the teaching which inter-feres with his primary interest. As for the administrator, in his weak embodiment he is suspicious of first-rate teaching, if not actually hostile, because it arouses intellectual ferment and disturbs the academic calm. If there is trouble on a campus, it is likely that some teacher has done his work too well.

When such motion pictures as "Good-by, Mr. Chips" and "The Corn Is Green" are box office successes, when changes in college curricula are front page news, and when education is considered the ultimate key to world order, it seems hardly necessary to dwell on the importance of the teaching profession

—and yet, the point cannot be made too often or too em-
phatically. For "as long as people continue to believe absurdities, they will continue to commit atrocities" (to quote
the unforgettable sentence that Desmond MacCarthy has put
into the mouth of Voltaire), and no one has the same opportunity as the teacher to dispel absurdities, trifling, or terrible.
Day in and day out, he enlightens and strengthens, or poisons
and mutilates. "A parent gives life, but as parent gives no
more," said Henry Adams. "A murderer takes life, but his deed
stops there; a teacher affects eternity; he can never tell where
his influence stops."

In what autobiography is this fateful influence not underlined?
Recalling his two years at the College of William and Mary,
Thomas Jefferson wrote: "It was my good fortune, and what
probably fixed the destinies of my life, that Dr. Wm. Small of
Scotland was then Professor of Mathematics, a man profound
in most of the useful branches of science, with a happy talent of
communication, and an enlarged and liberal mind." In recount-
ing his Cambridge education, Charles Darwin said: "I have not
yet mentioned a circumstance which influenced my whole career
more than any other. This was my friendship with Professor
Henslow. . . . I became known as the man who walks with
Henslow." How much more we would like to know of that
shadowy frontier figure, Mentor Graham, who taught grammar
and surveying and a little law to Abraham Lincoln.

On the other hand, we must recoil from the graveyard of
books and authors killed by inept pedagogy. Who has not had
an entire subject, such as history or mathematics, ruined for him?
Who has not been driven permanently away from Shakespeare or
Wordsworth or Emerson by heavy-handed scholarship or mis-
guided dissection? The epithets of crime are not inappropriate
here, for again and again one hears students speak of being
"robbed" by one professor, or of having a subject "killed" by
another. Even the austere Professor Whitehead has grown violent in this connection: "The great English Universities, under

xvi

whose direct authority school-children are examined in plays of Shakespeare, to the certain destruction of their enjoyment, should be prosecuted for soul-murder." And in another passage: "Wordsworth talks of men of science who 'murder to dissect.' In the past, classical scholars have been veritable assassins compared to them." And in consequence Greek and Latin have been pushed aside more rapidly and fully than necessary. Sir William Osler, in the final address of his career before the Classical Association at Oxford, discussed "The Old Humanities and the New Science" and pointed out innumerable opportunities for keeping the classics alive—but the warning seems to have come too late.

All this is merely symbolic of the troubles and tragedies of education which are bemoaned in every critical period and with special intensity in our own. Curriculum changes are now being made or demanded on every side—broad comprehensive courses of study covering the major areas of human experience in place of the cafeteria confusion of the unrestrained elective system. Methods of teaching every subject in the catalogue are rationally or recklessly defended, as the keys to our educational difficulties. But the best possible curriculum or the best possible method, drawn from the latest findings of psychology, will suffer fatally in the hands of a dull, unimaginative teacher. For as William James said: "Psychology is a science, and teaching is an art; and sciences never generate arts directly out of themselves. An intermediary inventive mind must make the application, by using its originality." And so we are about to see some inventive minds at work—perhaps to acquire a little of their inventiveness or at least a little of their courage.

This is no plea for slavish imitation, which paralyzes spontaneity, or for absurdly high standards which only a few can approach. "The illusions created by the exceptional teacher, in the effort to determine practicable aims and effective methods" (to use the heavy but precise phrasing of David Snedden) have driven many a person to melancholy or cynicism. But we of moderate abilities can get a distinct lift from a consideration of the exceptional teacher, and rise imperceptibly to new planes of energy and value.

No more is this a plea for "campus personalities" lacking both scholarship and discipline. Teachers of that sort often do more harm than good although they are features remembered by many an alumnus. Fine teachers are usually colorful but it is color operating through a subject matter and with a method. An empty cry for "great personalities," without other considerations, is, as Robert Hutchins says, "the formula for educational futilitarianism."

Although the Chinese walls between departments are crumbling in many places, they are still sufficiently thick and strong — buttressed by professional vested interests, and members of each department tend to stick to the techniques of their own specialty. Teachers of history will read books on "the teaching of history," teachers of science will read books on "the teaching of science," and so on. Yet there is a common spirit in all good teaching, and those from different fields might learn much from one another, if they had the chance. It is not only the musician who can profit from overhearing a lesson by César Franck or Leschetizky. It is not only the philosopher who will be heartened by the Socratic spirit of Mark Hopkins or Charles Garman. Why may not the primary and secondary school teachers have hints for the college professor — and vice versa? A little book of extracts on Louis Agassiz's method of instruction was prepared by Professor Lane Cooper, not for young zoologists but for students of "those organic forms which we call forms of literature and works of art."

Undoubtedly some of the most effective teachers in American schools and colleges are to be found in the gymnasium and on the athletic fields. They have a clarity of aim, a measurement of achievement, that many of their bookish colleagues must envy. While others engage in heated pedagogical debate, they put into practice the slogan of "learning by doing" and work out concretely the connection between "interest and effort." By insisting that "form" is the key to speed and power, they sometimes convey more of a sense of aesthetic principles than do abstruse professors of art appreciation; for almost always effective athletic form is the beautiful, well co-ordinated way of doing things. But alas, fine athletes do not ordinarily become able writers — and I can find no persuasive portrait in this field. We must follow Socrates to the Gymnasium.

As there is contagion in the study of great teachers in action, there is also amusement and consolation in discovering that our anxieties are not unique. We are not the first to be profoundly worried about the burning issues of general and special education, of traditional and progressive methods, of the "Olympian and earthly" phases of teaching. We are not the first to weigh the comparative merits of the lecture and the discussion, or to see the difference between the problems of undergraduate and graduate teaching. How many illustrations should be used to bring out a principle? How much repetition is necessary? What if the argument must follow into the carefully guarded territory of a sovereign colleague? It is valuable, I believe, to encounter such questions in a dramatic context and to realize again that there is no easy formal answer to them. It is enlarging to share not only the enthusiasm of Mark Hopkins but also his agony in the face of an unresponsive class.

But how arrange this series of portraits? The obvious pattern, at first thought, was chronological according to teachers. After deciding to start with James Mill (1773–1836), the father and teacher of John Stuart Mill (1806–1873), it would have been a simple matter to proceed step by step to such present-day teachers as John Dewey and John Erskine. But the result would have been a curious educational encyclopedia with little plot or direction, with an elementary teacher suddenly followed by a teacher of philosophy or musical theory. There would have been the same result if a chronological arrangement by students had been followed.

Why not follow a typical college catalogue and classify the teachers by departments or divisions, with the well recognized "separation of learning into the three areas of natural science, social studies and the humanities?" But this solution would have simply underlined the differences between specialties and obscured our emphasis on the basic art to which all teachers contribute. "Apart from what is technical," said Lord Acton, "method is only the reduplication of common sense, and is best acquired by observing its use by the ablest men in every variety of intellectual employment."

Well, then, why not some arrangement according to teaching techniques such as the formal and the informal, the mechanical, and the imaginative; the lecture, the discussion, and the tutorial, et cetera? However convenient these distinctions may be, they are ignored by the able teacher when he uses several approaches to his students in the same hour or at different times in a term. In any case, for the purposes of this book, it seemed better to bring up such questions tentatively at the end, rather than have them arbitrarily answered in the table of contents.

After these considerations, it seemed best to start with teachers of young children and end with teachers of adults. From two strange homes, we will pass into a country school and two high schools; then to a number of college classrooms; to a laboratory, through seminars, to an epoch-marking clinic. But as we began with the child and teacher, face to face, we will come, full circle, to find advanced students of the arts face to face with their masters. Finally we will see the greatest of American teachers speaking to people of all ages and from all walks of life.

At an early stage of this manuscript, my good friend and former student, Louis Lasagna, wrote me concerning Helen Keller's account of her teacher, Anne Mansfield Sullivan:

"The more I think about it, the better this seems as the opening essay. Does it seem too far fetched to picture the young Helen Keller as the symbol par excellence of every student that

ever lived? We are all Helen Kellers in some degree — vision be-
clouded, ears undiscriminating, speech uncertain and untrue.
We have all needed at one time or another, to have TRUTH
spelled out slowly for us, to have our capabilities redefined and
revaluated, and the limitations of our sensations and perceptions
suggested. It is no mean epitaph for any teacher to have it said
of him that 'He rendered all whom he taught less deaf, less
dumb, less blind.' "

HOUSTON PETERSON

GREAT TEACHERS

Anne Mansfield Sullivan

⇒ 1866 – 1936 ⇐

MORE than anyone can intimate or estimate, the story of Helen Keller is the story of Anne Mansfield Sullivan. This is not said to minimize the heroic achievements of the one, but to do justice to the intelligent, affectionate, and courageous devotion of the other.

Only Dickens at his darkest could describe the early years of Anne Sullivan. One of four children brought up near Springfield, Massachusetts, in the utterly poverty-stricken home of immigrant, Irish parents, she saw her five-year-old sister die of a malignant fever, her brother afflicted with a tubercular hip, her father a decaying drunkard, her mother wasting away from disease and hunger, and she herself—half blind with trachoma. At ten, she and her brother Jimmie were wards of the sovereign state—in the squalor of the public almshouse at Tewksbury, near Boston. There Jimmie died and Anne endured for most of five harrowing years. No, the famous teacher of Helen Keller was not a Boston blue blood who took up social work as a career.

At last, through her own rebellious initiative, she was transferred from Tewksbury to the Perkins Institution and Massachusetts Asylum for the Blind where the great work of Dr. Samuel Gridley Howe was now being carried on by his son-in-law, Michael Anagnos. In his first trip to the United States in 1842, Dickens had found many things to admire, and some to detest, but he was most deeply touched by what Dr. Howe had done for Laura Bridgman, and to Dr. Howe's report on her he gave ten pages of American Notes. "There she was before me," wrote Dickens, "built up, as it were, in a marble cell, impervious to any ray of light, or particle of sound; with her poor white hand peeping through a chink in the

3

wall, beckoning to some good man for help, that an immortal soul might be awakened.

"Long before I looked upon her, the help had come. Her face was radiant with intelligence and pleasure . . . From this mournful ruin of such bereavement, there had slowly risen up this gentle, tender, guileless, grateful-hearted being."

Within two years after Anne Sullivan had settled at the Perkins Institution, operations on her eyes brought back her sight, however imperfectly, but she remained at the school as student and helper, graduating as valedictorian of her class, at the age of twenty. Meanwhile, she had learned the manual alphabet and spent many hours chatting with Laura Bridgman. But her future was quite indefinite that summer after graduation while she vacationed with her friend and benefactor, Mrs. Laurence Hutton, on Cape Cod. Then, out of the blue, came a letter from Mr. Anagnos, asking her if she would like to become the teacher of a blind, deaf and mute child in Alabama!

In the little town of Tuscumbia, a sorrowing mother held to one ray of hope because she recalled Dickens's account of Laura Bridgman. Her sprightly daughter Helen, at nineteen months, had been suddenly stricken with what the doctors called "acute congestion of stomach and brain." The fever passed as quickly as it had come — but Helen was completely blind and deaf and the few words she had begun to use were soon lost. Several heavy years passed for Captain and Mrs. Keller and then they went to Baltimore where an oculist convinced them that Helen's eyes were beyond treatment but sent them for further advice to Dr. Alexander Graham Bell, in Washington. It was Dr. Bell who suggested that they get in touch with Michael Anagnos.

When Anne Sullivan received Anagnos's letter about the opportunity in Alabama, she decided to accept, but in order to prepare herself she returned to the Institute for the winter to study the minute records that Dr. Howe and his assistants had kept in their work with Laura Bridgman. Then, without waiting for her eyes to heal from a new operation, she started on the long trip south. The rest is history.

Out of the Dark

HELEN KELLER

->>>·<<<-

THE MOST IMPORTANT DAY I remember in all my life is the one on which my teacher, Anne Mansfield Sullivan, came to me. I am filled with wonder when I consider the immeasurable contrast between the two lives which it connects. It was the third of March, 1887, three months before I was seven years old.

On the afternoon of that eventful day, I stood on the porch, dumb, expectant. I guessed vaguely from my mother's signs and from the hurrying to and fro in the house that something unusual was about to happen, so I went to the door and waited on the steps. The afternoon sun penetrated the mass of honeysuckle that covered the porch, and fell on my upturned face. My fingers lingered almost unconsciously on the familiar leaves and blossoms which had just come forth to greet the sweet southern spring. I did not know what the future held of marvel or surprise for me. Anger and bitterness had preyed upon me continually for weeks and a deep languor had succeeded this passionate struggle.

Have you ever been at sea in a dense fog, when it seemed as if a tangible white darkness shut you in, and the great ship, tense and anxious, groped her way toward the shore with plummet and sounding line, and you waited with beating heart for something to happen? I was like that ship before my education began, only I was without compass or sounding line, and had no way of knowing how near the harbour was. "Light! give me light!"

was the wordless cry of my soul, and the light of love shone on me in that very hour.

I felt approaching footsteps. I stretched out my hand as I supposed to my mother. Some one took it, and I was caught up and held close in the arms of her who had come to reveal all things to me, and more than all things else, to love me.

The morning after my teacher came she led me into her room and gave me a doll. The little blind children at the Perkins Institution had sent it and Laura Bridgman had dressed it; but I did not know this until afterward. When I had played with it a little while, Miss Sullivan slowly spelled into my hand the word "d-o-l-l." I was at once interested in this finger play and tried to imitate it. When I finally succeeded in making the letters correctly I was flushed with childish pleasure and pride. Running downstairs to my mother I held up my hand and made the letters for doll. I did not know that I was spelling a word or even that words existed; I was simply making my fingers go in monkey-like imitation. In the days that followed I learned to spell in this uncomprehending way a great many words, among them *pin*, *hat*, *cup*, and a few verbs like *sit*, *stand*, and *walk*. But my teacher had been with me several weeks before I understood that everything has a name.

One day while I was playing with my new doll, Miss Sullivan put my big rag doll into my lap also, spelled "d-o-l-l" and tried to make me understand that "d-o-l-l" applied to both. Earlier in the day we had had a tussle over the words "m-u-g" and "w-a-t-e-r." Miss Sullivan had tried to impress it upon me that "m-u-g" is *mug* and that "w-a-t-e-r" is *water*, but I was persistent in confounding the two. In despair she had dropped the subject for the time, only to renew it at the first opportunity. I became impatient at her repeated attempts and, seizing the new doll, I dashed it upon the floor. I was keenly delighted when I felt the fragments of the broken doll at my feet. Neither sorrow nor regret followed my passionate outburst. I had not loved the doll. In the still, dark world in which I lived there was no strong sentiment or tenderness. I felt my teacher sweep the fragments to one side of the hearth, and I had a sense of satisfaction that the cause of my discomfort was removed. She brought me my hat, and I knew I was going out into the warm sunshine. This thought, if a wordless sensation may be called a thought, made me hop and skip with pleasure.

We walked down the path to the well house, attracted by the fragrance of the honeysuckle with which it was covered. Some one was drawing water and my teacher placed my hand under the spout. As the cool stream gushed over one hand she spelled into the other the word *water*, first slowly, then rapidly. I stood still, my whole attention fixed upon the motions of her fingers. Suddenly I felt a misty consciousness as of something forgotten — a thrill of returning thought; and somehow the mystery of language was revealed to me. I knew then that "w-a-t-e-r" meant the wonderful cool something that was flowing over my hand. That living word awakened my soul, gave it light, hope, joy, set it free! There were barriers still, it is true, but barriers that could in time be swept away.

I left the well house eager to learn. Everything had a name, and each name gave birth to a new thought. As we returned to the house every object which I touched seemed to quiver with life. That was because I saw everything with the strange, new sight that had come to me. On entering the door I remembered the doll I had broken. I felt my way to the hearth and picked up the pieces. I tried vainly to put them together. Then my eyes filled with tears; for I realized what I had done, and for the first time I felt repentance and sorrow.

I learned a great many new words that day. I do not remember what they all were; but I do know that *mother, father, sister, teacher* were among them — words that were to make the world blossom for me, "like Aaron's rod, with flowers." It would have been difficult to find a happier child than I was as I

7

lay in my crib at the close of that eventful day and lived over the joys it had brought me, and for the first time longed for a new day to come.

.   .   .   .

I recall many incidents of the summer of 1887 that followed my soul's sudden awakening. I did nothing but explore with my hands and learn the name of every object that I touched; and the more I handled things and learned their names and uses, the more joyous and confident grew my sense of kinship with the rest of the world.

When the time of daisies and buttercups came Miss Sullivan took me by the hand across the fields, where men were preparing the earth for the seed, to the banks of the Tennessee River, and there, sitting on the warm grass, I had my first lessons in the beneficence of nature. I learned how the sun and the rain make to grow out of the ground every tree that is pleasant to the sight and good for food, how birds build their nests and live and thrive from land to land, how the squirrel, the deer, the lion, and every other creature finds food and shelter. As my knowledge of things grew I felt more and more the delight of the world I was in. Long before I learned to do a sum in arithmetic or describe the shape of the earth, Miss Sullivan had taught me to find beauty in the fragrant woods, in every blade of grass, and in the curves and dimples of my baby sister's hand. She linked my earliest thoughts with nature, and made me feel that "birds and flowers and I were happy peers."

But about this time I had an experience which taught me that nature is not always kind. One day my teacher and I were returning from a long ramble. The morning had been fine, but it was growing warm and sultry when at last we turned our faces homeward. Two or three times we stopped to rest under a tree by the wayside. Our last halt was under a wild cherry tree a short distance from the house. The shade was grateful, and the tree was so easy to climb that with my teacher's as-

ANNE MANSFIELD SULLIVAN

sistance I was able to scramble to a seat in the branches. It was so cool up in the tree that Miss Sullivan proposed that we have our luncheon there. I promised to keep still while she went to the house to fetch it.

Suddenly a change passed over the tree. All the sun's warmth left the air. I knew that the sky was black, because all the heat, which meant light to me, had died out of the atmosphere. A strange odor came up from the earth. I knew it, it was the odor that always precedes a thunderstorm, and a nameless fear clutched at my heart. I felt absolutely alone, cut off from my friends and the firm earth. The immense, the unknown, enfolded me. I remained still and expectant; a chilling terror crept over me. I longed for my teacher's return; but above all things I wanted to get down from that tree.

There was a moment of sinister silence, then a multitudinous stirring of the leaves. A shiver ran through the tree, and the wind sent forth a blast that would have knocked me off had I not clung to the branch with might and main. The tree swayed and strained. The small twigs snapped and fell about me in showers. A wild impulse to jump seized me, but terror held me fast. I crouched down in the fork of the tree. The branches lashed about me. I felt the intermittent jarring that came now and then, as if something heavy had fallen and the shock had traveled up till it reached the limb I sat on. It worked my suspense up to the highest point, and just as I was thinking the tree and I should fall together, my teacher seized my hand and helped me down. I clung to her, trembling with joy to feel the earth under my feet once more. I had learned a new lesson — that nature "wages open war against her children, and under softest touch hides treacherous claws."

After this experience it was a long time before I climbed another tree. The mere thought filled me with terror. It was the sweet allurement of the mimosa tree in full bloom that finally overcame my fears. One beautiful spring morning when I was alone in the summerhouse, reading, I became aware of a

wonderful subtle fragrance in the air. I started up and instinctively stretched out my hands. It seemed as if the spirit of
spring had passed through the summerhouse. "What is it?" I
asked, and the next minute I recognized the odour of the mimosa
blossom-laden branches almost touching the long grass. Was
there ever anything so exquisitely beautiful in the world before!
Its delicate blossoms shrank from the slightest earthly touch; it
seemed as if a tree of paradise had been transplanted to earth. I
made my way through a shower of petals to the great trunk and
for one minute stood irresolute; then, putting my foot in the
broad space between the forked branches, I pulled myself up
into the tree. I had some difficulty in holding on, for the branches
were very large and the bark hurt my hands. But I had a delicious
sense that I was doing something unusual and wonderful, so I
kept on climbing higher and higher, until I reached a little seat
which somebody had built there so long ago that it had grown
part of the tree itself. I sat there for a long, long time, feeling
like a fairy on a rosy cloud. After that I spent many happy hours
in my tree of paradise, thinking fair thoughts and dreaming
bright dreams.

.   .   .   .

I had now the key to all language, and I was eager to learn to
use it. Children who hear acquire language without any particular effort; the words that fall from others' lips they catch
on the wing, as it were, delightedly, while the little deaf
child must trap them by a slow, and often painful process. But
whatever the process, the result is wonderful. Gradually from
naming an object we advance step by step until we have trav-
ersed the vast distance between our first stammered syllable
and the sweep of thought in a line of Shakespeare.

At first, when my teacher told me about a new thing I asked
very few questions. My ideas were vague, and my vocabulary
was inadequate; but as my knowledge of things grew, and I
learned more and more words, my field of inquiry broadened,

and I would return again and again to the same subject, eager for further information. Sometimes a new word revived an image that some earlier experience had engraved on my brain.

I remember the morning that I first asked the meaning of the word, "love." This was before I knew many words. I had found a few early violets in the garden and brought them to my teacher. She tried to kiss me; but at that time I did not like to have any one kiss me except my mother. Miss Sullivan put her arm gently round me and spelled into my hand, "I love Helen."

"What is love?" I asked.

She drew me closer to her and said, "It is here," pointing to my heart, whose beats I was conscious of for the first time. Her words puzzled me very much because I did not then understand anything unless I touched it.

I smelt the violets in her hand and asked, half in words, half in signs, a question which meant, "Is love the sweetness of flowers?"

"No," said my teacher.

Again I thought. The warm sun was shining on us.

"Is this not love?" I asked, pointing in the direction from which the heat came, "Is this not love?"

It seemed to me that there could be nothing more beautiful than the sun, whose warmth makes all things grow. But Miss Sullivan shook her head, and I was greatly puzzled and disappointed. I thought it strange that my teacher could not show me love.

A day or two afterward I was stringing beads of different sizes in symmetrical groups — two large beads, three small ones, and so on. I had made many mistakes, and Miss Sullivan had pointed them out again and again with gentle patience. Finally I noticed a very obvious error in the sequence and for an instant I concentrated my attention on the lesson and tried to think how I should have arranged the beads. Miss Sullivan touched my forehead and spelled with decided emphasis, "Think."

In a flash I knew that the word was the name of the process

that was going on in my head. This was my first conscious perception of an abstract idea.

For a long time I was still—I was not thinking of the beads in my lap, but trying to find a meaning for "love" in the light of this new idea. The sun had been under a cloud all day, and there had been brief showers; but suddenly the sun broke forth in all its southern splendour.

Again I asked my teacher, "Is this not love?"

"Love is something like the clouds that were in the sky before the sun came out," she replied. Then in simpler words than these, which at that time I could not have understood, she explained: "You cannot touch the clouds, you know; but you feel the rain and know how glad the flowers and the thirsty earth are to have it after a hot day. You cannot touch love either; but you feel the sweetness that it pours into everything. Without love you would not be happy or want to play."

The beautiful truth burst upon my mind—I felt that there were invisible lines stretched between my spirit and the spirits of others.

James Mill

>>> 1773 – 1836 <<<

I F THE EDUCATION of Helen Keller was a ceaseless exercise in tenderness and tact, the education of John Stuart Mill by his father James Mill was a ruthless experiment in intellectual discipline — the most remarkable case of acceleration in history which well may have given him "an advantage of a quarter of a century over his contemporaries."

A dour Scotchman, indeed, James Mill was a tireless social reformer, the spearhead of the then radical Benthamite movement in a period of general reaction, when the British ruling class seemed bent on "promoting the greatest happiness of the smallest number." Thanks largely to him, Bentham became a convinced democrat and Benthamism became an immediate power instead of an endless series of provocative manuscripts. In his views of life, James Mill "partook of the character of the Stoic, the Epicurean, and the Cynic, not in the modern but the ancient sense of the word," said the son. "In his personal qualities the Stoic predominated. His standard of morals was Epicurean, inasmuch as it was utilitarian, taking as the exclusive test of right and wrong, the tendency of actions to produce pleasure or pain . . . He was not insensible to pleasures; but he deemed very few of them worth the price which, at least, in the present state of society, must be paid for them.

"The element which was chiefly deficient in his moral relation to his children was that of tenderness. I do not believe that this deficiency lay in his own nature. I believe that he had much more feeling than he habitually showed, and much greater capacities of feeling than were ever developed. He resembled most Englishmen in being ashamed of the signs of feeling, and by the absence of demonstration, starving the feelings themselves."

13

However, it was not only the severe character of James Mill that determined the severe education that he gave to his son. Coupled with that character was the British empiricist theory of the human mind as "a blank tablet" on which almost anything can be written, the theory that human nature is almost infinitely "pliable," the ever recurring theory that human nurture is far more important than nature. Why not then take a normal, healthy child, and by endless patience, turn him into a perfect Benthamite, to carry on the good work?

In essential agreement with this point of view even in his later years, John Stuart Mill actually considered himself "rather below than above par" in quickness of apprehension, retentive memory and strength of character — and thus his unusual achievements must have been due to his unusual education. But we may suspect that he was a "gifted child" to begin with.

"No other record of the early development of an eminent man is more complete," writes Catherine Morris Cox in her Genetic Studies of Genius, *adding that on the basis of that record, John Stuart Mill's I.Q. has been rated at 190.*

Unwasted Years

JOHN STUART MILL

—»»·«««—

IT SEEMS PROPER that I should prefix to the following bio-
graphical sketch, some mention of the reasons which have
made me think it desirable that I should leave behind me
such a memorial of so uneventful a life as mine. I do not for a
moment imagine that any part of what I have to relate can be
interesting to the public as a narrative, or as being connected
with myself. But I have thought that in an age in which education, and its improvement, are the subject of more, if not of
profounder study than at any former period of English history,
it may be useful that there should be some record of an education
which was unusual and remarkable, and which, whatever else
it may have done, has proved how much more than is commonly
supposed may be taught, and well taught, in those early years
which, in the common modes of what is called instruction, are
little better than wasted. It has also seemed to me that in an
age of transition in opinions, there may be somewhat both of
interest and of benefit in noting the successive phases of any
mind which was always pressing forward, equally ready to
learn and to unlearn either from its own thoughts or from those
of others. But a motive which weighs more with me than either
of these, is a desire to make acknowledgment of the debts
which my intellectual and moral development owes to other
persons; some of them of recognized eminence, others less known
than they deserve to be, and the one to whom most of all is due,
one whom the world had no opportunity of knowing. The

15

reader whom these things do not interest, has only himself to blame if he reads farther, and I do not desire any other indulgence from him than that of bearing in mind, that for him these pages were not written.

I was born in London, on the 20th of May, 1806, and was the eldest son of James Mill, the author of the *History of British India*. My father, the son of a petty tradesman and (I believe) small farmer, at Northwater Bridge, in the county of Angus, was, when a boy, recommended by his abilities to the notice of Sir John Stuart, of Fettercairn, one of the Barons of the Exchequer in Scotland, and was, in consequence, sent to the University of Edinburgh, at the expense of a fund established by Lady Jane Stuart (the wife of Sir John Stuart) and some other ladies for educating young men for the Scottish Church. He there went through the usual course of study, and was licensed as a preacher, but never followed the profession; having satisfied himself that he could not believe the doctrines of that or any other Church. For a few years he was a private tutor in various families in Scotland, among others that of the Marquis of Tweeddale, but ended by taking up his residence in London, and devoting himself to authorship. Nor had he any other means of support until 1819, when he obtained an appointment in the India House.

In this period of my father's life there are two things which it is impossible not to be struck with: one of them unfortunately a very common circumstance, the other a most uncommon one. The first is, that in his position, with no resource but the precarious one of writing in periodicals, he married and had a large family; conduct than which nothing could be more opposed, both as a matter of good sense and of duty, to the opinions which, at least at a later period of life, he strenuously upheld. The other circumstance is the extraordinary energy which was required to lead the life he led, with the disadvantages under which he labored from the first, and with those which he brought upon himself by his marriage. It would have been no

16

small thing, had he done no more than to support himself and his family during so many years by writing, without ever being in debt, or in any pecuniary difficulty; holding, as he did, opinions, both in politics and in religion, which were more odious to all persons of influence, and to the common run of prosperous Englishmen in that generation than either before or since; and being not only a man whom nothing would have induced to write against his convictions, but one who invariably threw into everything he wrote, as much of his convictions as he thought the circumstances would in any way permit: being, it must also be said, one who never did anything negligently; never undertook any task, literary or other, on which he did not conscientiously bestow all the labor necessary for performing it adequately. But he, with these burdens on him, planned, commenced, and completed, the *History of India*; and this in the course of about ten years, a shorter time than has been occupied (even by writers who had no other employment) in the production of almost any other historical work of equal bulk, and of anything approaching to the same amount of reading and research. And to this is to be added, that during the whole period, a considerable part of almost every day was employed in the instruction of his children: in the case of one of whom, myself, he exerted an amount of labor, care, and perseverance rarely, if ever, employed for a similar purpose, in endeavouring to give, according to his own conception, the highest order of intellectual education.

A man who, in his own practice, so vigorously acted up to the principle of losing no time, was likely to adhere to the same rule in the instruction of his pupil. I have no remembrance of the time when I began to learn Greek; I have been told that it was when I was three years old. My earliest recollection on the subject, is that of committing to memory what my father termed vocables, being lists of common Greek words, with their signification in English, which he wrote out for me on cards. Of grammar, until some years later, I learnt no more

17

than the inflexions of the nouns and verbs, but, after a course of vocables, proceeded at once to translation; and I faintly remember going through *Æsop's Fables*, the first Greek book which I read. The *Anabasis*, which I remember better, was the second. I learnt no Latin until my eighth year. At that time I had read, under my father's tuition, a number of Greek prose authors, among whom I remember the whole of Herodotus, and of Xenophon's *Cyropaedia* and *Memorials of Socrates*; some of the lives of the philosophers by Diogenes Laertius; part of Lucian, and *Isocrates ad Demonicum* and *Ad Nicoclem*. I also read, in 1813, the first six dialogues (in the common arrangement) of Plato, from the *Euthyphron* to the *Theoctetus* inclusive: which last dialogue, I venture to think, would have been better omitted, as it was totally impossible I should understand it. But my father, in all his teaching, demanded of me not only the utmost that I could do, but much that I could by no possibility have done. What he was himself willing to undergo for the sake of my instruction, may be judged from the fact that I went through the whole process of preparing my Greek lessons in the same room and at the same table at which he was writing: and as in those days Greek and English lexicons were not, and I could make no more use of a Greek and Latin lexicon than could be made without having yet begun to learn Latin, I was forced to have recourse to him for the meaning of every word which I did not know. This incessant interruption, he, one of the most impatient of men, submitted to, and wrote under that interruption several volumes of his *History* and all else that he had to write during those years.

The only thing besides Greek, that I learnt as a lesson in this part of my childhood, was arithmetic: this also my father taught me: it was the task of the evenings, and I well remember its disagreeableness. But the lessons were only a part of the daily instruction I received. Much of it consisted in the books I read by myself, and my father's discourses to me, chiefly during our walks. From 1810 to the end of 1813 we were living in Newington Green, then an almost rustic neighborhood. My father's health required considerable and constant exercise, and he walked habitually before breakfast, generally in the green lanes toward Hornsey. In these walks I always accompanied him, and with my earliest recollections of green fields and wild flowers is mingled that of the account I gave him daily of what I had read the day before. To the best of my remembrance, this was a voluntary rather than a prescribed exercise. I made notes on slips of paper while reading, and from these in the morning walks, I told the story to him; for the books were chiefly histories, of which I read in this manner a great number: Robertson's histories, Hume, Gibbon; but my greatest delight, then and for long afterwards, was Watson's *Philip the Second and Third*. The heroic defence of the Knights of Malta against the Turks, and of the revolted Provinces of the Netherlands against Spain, excited in me an intense and lasting interest. Next to Watson, my favorite historical reading was Hooke's *History of Rome*. Of Greece I had seen at that time no regular history, except school abridgements, and the last two or three volumes of a translation of Rollin's *Ancient History*, beginning with Philip of Macedon. But I read with great delight Langhorne's translation of Plutarch. In English history, beyond the time at which Hume leaves off, I remember reading Burnet's *History of his Own Time*, though I cared little for anything in it except the wars and battles; and the historical part of the *Annual Register*, from the beginning to about 1788, where the volumes my father borrowed for me from Mr. Bentham left off. I felt a lively interest in Frederic of Prussia during his difficulties, and in Paoli, the Corsican patriot; but when I came to the American war, I took my part, like a child as I was (until set right by my father) on the wrong side, because it was called the English side. In these frequent talks about the books I read, he used, as opportunity offered, to give me explanations and ideas respecting civilization, government, morality, mental cultivation, which he required me afterward to restate to him in my own words. He also made me read, and give him a verbal account of, many books which would not have interested me sufficiently to induce me to read them of myself: among others, Millar's *Historical View of the English Government*, a book of great merit for its time, and which he highly valued; Mosheim's *Ecclesiastical History*, McCrie's *Life of John Knox*, and even Sewell and Rutty's *Histories of the Quakers*. He was fond of putting into my hands books which exhibited men of energy and resource in unusual circumstances, struggling against difficulties and overcoming them: of such works I remember Beaver's *African Memoranda*, and Collins's *Account of the First Settlement of New South Wales*. Two books which I never wearied of reading were Anson's *Voyages*, so delightful to most young persons, and a collection (Hawkesworth's, I believe) of *Voyages Round the World*, in four volumes, beginning with Drake and ending with Cook and Bougainville. Of children's books, any more than of playthings, I had scarcely any, except an occasional gift from a relation or acquaintance: among those I had, *Robinson Crusoe* was pre-eminent, and continued to delight me through all my boyhood. It was no part, however, of my father's system to exclude books of amusement, though he allowed them very sparingly. Of such books he possessed at that time next to none, but he borrowed several for me; those which I remember are the *Arabian Nights*, Cazotte's *Arabian Tales*, *Don Quixote*, Miss Edgeworth's *Popular Tales*, and a book of some reputation in its day, Brooke's *Fool of Quality*.

In my eighth year I commenced learning Latin, in conjunction with a younger sister, to whom I taught it as I went on, and who afterward repeated the lessons to my father: and from this time, other sisters and brothers being successively added as pupils, a considerable part of my day's work consisted of this preparatory teaching. It was a part which I greatly disliked; the more so, as I was held responsible for the lessons of my pupils, in almost as full a sense as for my own: I, however, derived from this discipline the great advantage of learning more thoroughly and retaining more lastingly the things which I was set to teach: perhaps, too, the practice it afforded in explaining difficulties to others, may even at that age have been useful. In other respects, the experience of my boyhood is not favorable to the plan of teaching children by means of one another. The teaching, I am sure, is very inefficient as teaching, and I well know that the relation between teacher and taught is not a good moral discipline to either. I went in this manner through the Latin grammar, and a considerable part of *Cornelius Nepos* and Caesar's *Commentaries*, but afterward added to the superintendence of these lessons, much longer ones of my own.

In the same year in which I began Latin, I made my first commencement in the Greek poets with the *Iliad*. After I had made some progress in this, my father put Pope's translation into my hands. It was the first English verse I had cared to read, and it became one of the books in which for many years I most delighted: I think I must have read it from twenty to thirty times through. I should not have thought it worth while to mention a taste apparently so natural to boyhood, if I had not, as I think, observed that the keen enjoyment of this brilliant specimen of narrative and versification is not so universal with boys, as I should have expected both *a priori* and from my individual experience. Soon after this time I commenced Euclid, and somewhat later, Algebra, still under my father's tuition.

From my eighth to my twelfth year, the Latin books which I remember reading were, the *Bucolics* of Virgil, and the first six books of the *Æneid*; all Horace, except the *Epodes*; the *Fables* of Phaedrus; the first five books of Livy (to which from my love of the subject I voluntarily added, in my hours of leisure, the remainder of the first decade); all Sallust; a considerable part of Ovid's *Metamorphoses*; some plays of Terence; two or three books of Lucretius; several of the Orations of Cicero, and of his writings on oratory; also his letters to Atticus, my father taking the trouble to translate to me from the French the historical explanations in Mingault's notes. In

Greek I read the *Iliad* and *Odyssey* through; one or two plays of Sophocles, Euripides, and Aristophanes, though by these I profited little; all Thucydides; the *Hellenics* of Xenophon; a great part of Demosthenes, Æschines, and Lysias; Theocritus; Anacreon; part of the *Anthology*; a little of Dionysius; several books of Polybius; and lastly Aristotle's *Rhetoric*, which, as the first expressly scientific treatise on any moral or psychological subject which I had read, and containing many of the best observations of the ancients on human nature and life, my father made me study with peculiar care, and throw the matter of it into synoptic tables. During the same years I learnt elementary geometry and algebra thoroughly, the differential calculus, and other portions of the higher mathematics far from thoroughly: for my father, not having kept up this part of his early acquired knowledge, could not spare time to qualify himself for removing my difficulties, and left me to deal with them, with little other aid than that of books: while I was continually incurring his displeasure by my inability to solve difficult problems for which he did not see that I had not the necessary previous knowledge.

As to my private reading, I can only speak of what I remember. History continued to be my strongest predilection, and most of all ancient history. Mitford's *Greece* I read continually; my father had put me on my guard against the Tory prejudices of this writer, and his perversions of facts for the whitewashing of despots, and blackening of popular institutions. These points he discoursed on, exemplifying them from the Greek orators and historians, with such effect that in reading Mitford my sympathies were always on the contrary side to those of the author, and I could, to some extent, have argued the point against him: yet this did not diminish the ever new pleasure with which I read the book. Roman history, both in my old favorite, Hooke, and in Ferguson, continued to delight me. A book which, in spite of what is called the dryness of its style, I took great pleasure in, was the *Ancient Universal History*, through the incessant reading of which, I had my head full of historical details concerning the obscurest ancient people, while about modern history, except detached passages, such as the Dutch War of Independence, I knew and cared comparatively little. A voluntary exercise, to which throughout my boyhood I was much addicted, was what I called writing histories. I successively composed a Roman history, picked out of Hooke; an abridgement of the *Ancient Universal History*; a *History of Holland*, from my favorite Watson and from an anonymous compilation; and in my eleventh and twelfth year I occupied myself with writing what I flattered myself was something serious. This was no less than a *History of the Roman Government*, compiled (with the assistance of Hooke) from Livy and Dionysius: of which I wrote as much as would have made an octavo volume, extending to the epoch of the Licinian Laws. It was, in fact, an account of the struggles between the patricians and plebeians, which now engrossed all the interest in my mind which I had previously felt in the mere wars and conquests of the Romans. I discussed all the constitutional points as they arose: though quite ignorant of Niebuhr's researches, I, by such lights as my father had given me, vindicated the Agrarian Laws on the evidence of Livy, and upheld, to the best of my ability, the Roman Democratic party. A few years later, in my contempt of my childish efforts, I destroyed all these papers, not then anticipating that I could ever feel any curiosity about my first attempts at writing and reasoning. My father encouraged me in this useful amusement, though, as I think judiciously, he never asked to see what I wrote; so that I did not feel that in writing it I was accountable to any one, nor had the chilling sensation of being under a critical eye.

But though these exercises in history were never a compulsory lesson, there was another kind of composition which was so, namely, writing verses, and it was one of the most disagreeable of my tasks. Greek and Latin verses I did not write, nor learnt the prosody of those languages. My father, thinking this not worth the time it required, contented himself with making me read aloud to him, and correcting false quantities. I never composed at all in Greek, even in prose, and but little in Latin. Not that my father could be indifferent to the value of this practice, in giving a thorough knowledge of these languages, but because there really was not time for it. The verses I was required to write were English. When I first read Pope's *Homer*, I ambitiously attempted to compose something of the same kind, and achieved as much as one book of a continuation of the *Iliad*. There, probably, the spontaneous promptings of my poetical ambition would have stopped; but the exercise, begun from choice, was continued by command. Conformably to my father's usual practice of explaining to me, as far as possible, the reasons for what he required me to do, he gave me, for this, as I well remember, two reasons highly characteristic of him: one was, that some things could be expressed better and more forcibly in verse than in prose: this, he said, was a real advantage. The other was, that people in general attached more value to verse than it deserved, and the power of writing it, was, on this account, worth acquiring. He generally left me to choose my own subjects, which, as far as I remember, were mostly addresses to some mythological personage or allegorical abstraction; but he made me translate into English verse many of Horace's shorter poems: I also remember his giving me Thomson's *Winter* to read, and afterwards making me attempt (without book) to write something myself on the same subject. The verses I wrote were, of course, the merest rubbish, nor did I ever attain any facility of versification, but the practice may have been useful in making it easier for me, at a later period, to acquire readiness of expression.

In a subsequent stage of boyhood, when these exercises had ceased to be compulsory, like most youthful writers I wrote tragedies; under the inspiration not so much of Shakespeare as of Joanna Baillie, whose *Constantine Paleologus* in particular appeared to me one of the most glorious of human compositions. I still think it one of the best dramas of the last two centuries.

I had read, up to this time, very little English poetry. Shakespeare my father had put into my hands, chiefly for the sake of the historical plays, from which, however, I went on to the others. My father never was a great admirer of Shakespeare, the English idolatry of whom he used to attack with some severity. He cared little for any English poetry except Milton (for whom he had the highest admiration), Goldsmith, Burns, and Gray's *Bard* which he preferred to his *Elegy*: perhaps I may add Cowper and Beattie. He had some value for Spenser, and I remember his reading to me (unlike his usual practice of making me read to him), the first book of the *Faerie Queene*; but I took little pleasure in it. The poetry of the present century he saw scarcely any merit in, and I hardly became acquainted with any of it till I was grown up to manhood, except the metrical romances of Walter Scott, which I read at his recommendation and was intensely delighted with; as I always was with animated narrative. Dryden's poems were among my father's books, and many of these he made me read, but I never cared for any of them except *Alexander's Feast*, which, as well as many of the songs in Walter Scott, I used to sing internally, to a music of my own: to some of the latter, indeed, I went so far as to compose airs, which I still remember. Cowper's short poems I read with some pleasure, but never got far into the longer ones; and nothing in the two volumes interested me like the prose account of his three hares. In my thirteenth year I met with Campbell's poems, among which *Lochiel*, *Hohenlinden*, the *Exile of Erin*, and some others, gave me sensations I had never before experienced from poetry. Here, too, I made nothing of the longer poems, except the striking opening of *Gertrude of Wyoming*, which long kept its place in my feelings as the perfection of pathos.

During this part of my childhood, one of my greatest amusements was experimental science; in the theoretical, however, not the practical sense of the word; not trying experiments — a kind of discipline which I have often regretted not having had —

nor even seeing, but merely reading about them. I never remember being so wrapt up in any book, as I was in Joyce's *Scientific Dialogues*; and I was rather recalcitrant to my father's criticisms of the bad reasoning respecting the first principles of physics, which abounds in the early part of that work. I devoured treatises on chemistry, especially that of my father's early friend and schoolfellow, Dr. Thomson, for years before I attended a lecture or saw an experiment.

From about the age of twelve, I entered into another and more advanced stage in my course of instruction; in which the main object was no longer the aids and appliances of thought, but the thoughts themselves. This commenced with Logic, in which I began at once with the *Organon*, and read it to the *Analytics* inclusive, but profited little by the *Posterior Analytics*, which belong to a branch of speculation I was not yet ripe for. Contemporaneously with the *Organon*, my father made me read the whole or parts of several of the Latin treatises on the scholastic logic; giving each day to him, in our walks, a minute account of what I had read, and answering his numerous and searching questions. After this, I went in a similar manner, through the *Computatio sive Logica* of Hobbes, a work of a much higher order of thought than the books of the school logicians, and which he estimated very highly; in my own opinion beyond its merits, great as these are. It was his invariable practice, whatever studies he exacted from me, to make me as far as possible understand and feel the utility of them: and this he deemed peculiarly fitting in the case of the syllogistic logic, the usefulness of which had been impugned by so many writers of authority. I well remember how, and in what particular walk, in the neighborhood of Bagshot Heath (where we were on a visit to his old friend, Mr. Wallace, then one of the Mathematical Professors at Sandhurst) he first attempted by questions to make me think on the subject, and frame some conception of what constituted the utility of the syllogistic logic, and when I had failed in this, to make me understand it by explanations. The explanations did not make the matter at all clear to me at the time; but they were not therefore useless; they remained as a nucleus for my observations and reflections to crystallize upon; the import of his general remarks being interpreted to me, by the particular instances which came under my notice afterward. My own consciousness and experience ultimately led me to appreciate quite as highly as he did, the value of an early practical familiarity with the school logic. I know of nothing, in my education, to which I think myself more indebted for whatever capacity of thinking I have attained. The first intellectual operation in which I arrived at any proficiency, was dissecting a bad argument, and finding in what part the fallacy lay: and though whatever capacity of this sort I attained, was due to the fact that it was an intellectual exercise in which I was most perseveringly drilled by my father, yet it is also true that the school logic, and the mental habits acquired in studying it, were among the principal instruments of this drilling. I am persuaded that nothing, in modern education, tends so much, when properly used, to form exact thinkers, who attach a precise meaning to words and propositions, and are not imposed on by vague, loose, or ambiguous terms. The boasted influence of mathematical studies is nothing to it; for in mathematical processes, none of the real difficulties of correct ratiocination occur. It is also a study peculiarly adapted to an early stage in the education of philosophical students, since it does not presuppose the slow process of acquiring, by experience and reflection, valuable thoughts of their own. They may become capable of disentangling the intricacies of confused and self-contradictory thought, before their own thinking faculties are much advanced; a power which, for want of some such discipline, many otherwise able men altogether lack; and when they have to answer opponents, only endeavor, by such arguments as they can command, to support the opposite conclusion,

27

scarcely even attempting to confute the reasonings of their antagonists; and, therefore, at the utmost, leaving the question, as far as it depends on argument, a balanced one.

During this time, the Latin and Greek books which I continued to read with my father were chiefly such as were worth studying, not for the language merely, but also for the thoughts. This included much of the orators, and especially Demosthenes, some of whose principal orations I read several times over, and wrote out, by way of exercise, a full analysis of them. My father's comments on these orations when I read them to him were very instructive to me. He not only drew my attention to the insight they afforded into Athenian institutions, and the principles of legislation and government which they often illustrated, but pointed out the skill and art of the orator — how everything important to his purpose was said at the exact moment when he had brought the minds of his audience into the state most fitted to receive it; how he made steal into their minds, gradually and by insinuation, thoughts which, if expressed in a more direct manner would have roused their opposition. Most of these reflections were beyond my capacity of full comprehension at the time; but they left seed behind, which germinated in due season. At this time I also read the whole of Tacitus, Juvenal, and Quintilian. The latter, owing to his obscure style and to the scholastic details of which many parts of his treatise are made up, is little read, and seldom sufficiently appreciated. His book is a kind of encyclopedia of the thoughts of the ancients on the whole field of education and culture; and I have retained through life many valuable ideas which I can distinctly trace to my reading of him, even at that early age. It was at this period that I read, for the first time, some of the most important dialogues of Plato, in particular the *Gorgias*, the *Protagoras*, and the *Republic*. There is no author to whom my father thought himself more indebted for his own mental culture, than Plato, or whom he more frequently recommended to young students. I can bear similar testimony in regard to myself. The Socratic method, of which the Platonic dialogues are the chief example, is unsurpassed as a discipline for correcting the errors, and clearing up the confusions incident to the *intellectus sibi permissus*, the understanding which has made up all its bundles of associations under the guidance of popular phraseology. The close, searching elenchus by which the man of vague generalities is constrained either to express his meaning to himself in definite terms, or to confess that he does not know what he is talking about; the perpetual testing of all general statements by particular instances; the siege in form which is laid to the meaning of large abstract terms, by fixing upon some still larger class name which includes that and more, and dividing down to the thing sought — marking out its limits and definition by a series of accurately drawn distinctions between it and each of the cognate objects which are successively parted off from it — all this, as an education for precise thinking, is inestimable, and all this, even at that age, took such hold of me that it became part of my own mind. I have felt ever since that the title of Platonist belongs by far better right to those who have been nourished in, and have endeavored to practise Plato's mode of investigation, than to those who are distinguished only by the adoption of certain dogmatical conclusions, drawn mostly from the least intelligible of his works, and which the character of his mind and writings makes it uncertain whether he himself regarded as anything more than poetic fancies, or philosophic conjectures.

In going through Plato and Demosthenes, since I could now read these authors, as far as the language was concerned, with perfect ease, I was not required to construe them sentence by sentence, but to read them aloud to my father, answering questions when asked: but the particular attention which he paid to elocution (in which his own excellence was remarkable) made this reading aloud to him a most painful task. Of all things which he required me to do, there was none which I did so constantly ill, or in which he so perpetually lost his temper with me. He had thought much on the principles of the art of reading, especially the most neglected part of it, the inflections of the voice, or modulation as writers on elocution call it (in contrast with articulation on the one side, and expression on the other), and had reduced it to rules, grounded on the logical analysis of a sentence. These rules he strongly impressed upon me, and took me severely to task for every violation of them: but I even then remarked (though I did not venture to make the remark to him) that though he reproached me when I read a sentence ill, and told me how I ought to have read it, he never, by reading it himself, showed me how it ought to be read. A defect running through his otherwise admirable modes of instruction, as it did through all his modes of thought, was that of trusting too much to the intelligibleness of the abstract, when not embodied in the concrete. It was at a much later period of my youth, when practising elocution by myself, or with companions of my own age, that I for the first time understood the object of his rules, and saw the psychological grounds of them. At that time I and others followed out the subject into its ramifications and could have composed a very useful treatise, grounded on my father's principles. He himself left those principles and rules unwritten. I regret that when my mind was full of the subject, from systematic practice, I did not put them, and our improvements of them, into a formal shape.

A book which contributed largely to my education, in the best sense of the term, was my father's *History of India*. It was published in the beginning of 1818. During the year previous, while it was passing through the press, I used to read the proof sheets to him; or rather, I read the manuscript to him while he corrected the proofs. The number of new ideas which I received from this remarkable book, and the impulse and stimulus as well as guidance given to my thoughts by its criticisms and disquisitions on society and civilization in the Hindoo part, on institutions and the acts of governments in the English part, made my early familiarity with it eminently useful to my subsequent progress. And though I can perceive deficiencies in it now as compared with a perfect standard, I still think it, if not the most, one of the most instructive histories ever written, and one of the books from which most benefit may be derived by a mind in the course of making up its opinions.

The Preface, among the most characteristic of my father's writings, as well as the richest in materials of thought, gives a picture which may be entirely depended on, of the sentiments and expectations with which he wrote the *History*. Saturated as the book is with the opinions and modes of judgment of a democratic radicalism then regarded as extreme; and treating with a severity, at that time most unusual, the English Constitution, the English law, and all parties and classes who possessed any considerable influence in the country; he may have expected reputation, but certainly not advancement in life, from its publication; nor could he have supposed that it would raise up anything but enemies for him in powerful quarters: least of all could he have expected favor from the East India Company, to whose commercial privileges he was unqualifiedly hostile, and on the acts of whose government he had made so many severe comments: though, in various parts of his book, he bore a testimony in their favour, which he felt to be their just due, namely, that no government had on the whole given so much proof, to the extent of its lights, of good intention toward its subjects; and that if the acts of any other government had the light of publicity as completely let in upon them, they would, in all probability, still less bear scrutiny.

On learning, however, in the spring of 1819, about a year after the publication of the History, that the East India Directors desired to strengthen the part of their home establishment which was employed in carrying on the correspondence with India, my father declared himself a candidate for that employment, and, to the credit of the Directors, successfully. He was appointed one of the Assistants of the Examiner of India Correspondence; officers whose duty it was to prepare drafts of despatches to India, for consideration by the Directors, in the principal departments of administration. In this office, and in that of Examiner, which he subsequently attained, the influence which his talents, his reputation, and his decision of character gave him, with superiors who really desired the good government of India, enabled him to a great extent to throw into his drafts of despatches, and to carry through the ordeal of the Court of Directors and Board of Control, without having their force much weakened, his real opinions on Indian subjects. In his History he had set forth, for the first time, many of the true principles of Indian administration: and his despatches, following his History, did more than had ever been done before to promote the improvement of India, and teach Indian officials to understand their business. If a selection of them were published, they would, I am convinced, place his character as a practical statesman fully on a level with his eminence as a speculative writer.

This new employment of his time caused no relaxation in his attention to my education. It was in this same year, 1819, that he took me through a complete course of political economy. His loved and intimate friend, Ricardo, had shortly before published the book which formed so great an epoch in political economy; a book which never would have been published or written, but for the entreaty and strong encouragement of my father; for Ricardo, the most modest of men, though firmly convinced of the truth of his doctrines, deemed himself so little capable of doing them justice in exposition and expression, that he shrank from the idea of publicity. The same friendly encouragement induced Ricardo, a year or two later, to become a member of the House of Commons; where, during the few remaining years of his life, unhappily cut short in the full vigor of his intellect, he rendered so much service to his and my father's opinions both on political economy and on other subjects.

Though Ricardo's great work was already in print, no didactic treatise embodying its doctrines, in a manner fit for learners, had yet appeared. My father, therefore, commenced instructing me in the science by a sort of lectures, which he delivered to me in our walks. He expounded each day a portion of the subject, and I gave him next day a written account of it, which he made me rewrite over and over again until it was clear, precise, and tolerably complete. In this manner I went through the whole extent of the science; and the written outline of it which resulted from my daily *compte rendu*, served him afterward as notes from which to write his *Elements of Political Economy*. After this I read Ricardo, giving an account daily of what I read, and discussing, in the best manner I could, the collateral points which offered themselves in our progress.

On Money, as the most intricate part of the subject, he made me read in the same manner Ricardo's admirable pamphlets, written during what was called the Bullion Controversy; to these succeeded Adam Smith; and in this reading it was one of my father's main objects to make me apply to Smith's more superficial view of political economy, the superior lights of Ricardo, and detect what was fallacious in Smith's arguments, or erroneous in any of his conclusions. Such a mode of instruction was excellently calculated to form a thinker; but it required to be worked by a thinker, as close and vigorous as my father. The path was a thorny one, even to him, and I am sure it was so to me, notwithstanding the strong interest I took in the subject. He was often, and much beyond reason, provoked by my failures in cases where success could not have been expected; but in the main his method was right, and it succeeded. I do not believe that any scientific teaching ever was more thorough, or better fitted for training the faculties, than the mode in which logic and political economy were taught to me by my father. Striving, even in an exaggerated degree, to call forth the activity of my faculties, by making me find out everything for myself, he gave his explanations not before, but after, I had felt the full force of the difficulties; and not only gave me an accurate knowledge of these two great subjects, as far as they were then understood, but made me a thinker on both. I thought for myself almost from the first, and occasionally thought differently from him, though for a long time only on minor points, and making his opinion the ultimate standard. At a later period I even occasionally convinced him, and altered his opinion on some points of detail: which I state to his honor, not my own. It at once exemplifies his perfect candor, and the real worth of his method of teaching.

At this point concluded what can properly be called my lessons: when I was about fourteen I left England for more than a year; and after my return, though my studies went on under my father's general direction, he was no longer my schoolmaster. I shall therefore pause here, and turn back to matters of a more general nature connected with the part of my life and education included in the preceding reminiscences.

In the course of instruction which I have partially retraced, the point most superficially apparent is the great effort to give, during the years of childhood an amount of knowledge in what are considered the higher branches of education, which is seldom acquired (if acquired at all) until the age of manhood. The result of the experiment shows the ease with which this may be done, and places in a strong light the wretched waste of so many precious years as are spent in acquiring the modicum of Latin and Greek commonly taught to schoolboys; a waste which has led so many educational reformers to entertain the ill-judged proposal of discarding these languages altogether from general education. If I had been by nature extremely quick of apprehension, or had possessed a very accurate and retentive memory, or were of a remarkably active and energetic character, the trial would not be conclusive; but in all these natural gifts I am rather below than above par; what I could do, could assuredly be done by any boy or girl of average capacity and healthy physical constitution: and if I have accomplished anything, I owe it, among other fortunate circumstances, to the fact that through the early training bestowed on me by my father, I started, I may fairly say, with an advantage of a quarter of a century over my contemporaries.

There was one cardinal point in this training, of which I have already given some indication, and which, more than any-thing else, was the cause of whatever good it effected. Most boys or youths who have had much knowledge drilled into them, have their mental capacities not strengthened, but over-laid by it. They are crammed with mere facts, and with the opinions or phrases of other people, and these are accepted as a substitute for the power to form opinions of their own: and thus the sons of eminent fathers, who have spared no pains in their education, so often grow up mere parroters of what they have learnt, incapable of using their minds except in the furrows traced for them. Mine, however, was not an education of cram. My father never permitted anything which I learnt to degenerate into a mere exercise of memory. He strove to make the under-standing not only go along with every step of the teaching, but, if possible, precede it. Anything which could be found out by thinking I never was told, until I had exhausted my efforts to find it out for myself. As far as I can trust my remembrance, I acquitted myself very lamely in this department; my recollec-tion of such matters is almost wholly of failures, hardly ever of success. It is true the failures were often in things in which success in so early a stage of my progress, was almost im-possible. I remember at some time in my thirteenth year, on my happening to use the word idea, he asked me what an idea was; and expressed some displeasure at my ineffectual efforts to define the word: I recollect also his indignation at my using the common expression that something was true in theory but re-quired correction in practice; and how, after making me vainly strive to define the word theory, he explained its meaning, and showed the fallacy of the vulgar form of speech which I had used; leaving me fully persuaded that in being unable to give a correct definition of Theory, and in speaking of it as something which might be at variance with practice, I had shown unparalleled ignorance. In this he seems, and perhaps was, very unreasonable; but I think only in being angry at my failure. A pupil from whom nothing is ever demanded which he cannot do, never does all he can.

One of the evils most liable to attend on any sort of early proficiency, and which often fatally blights its promise, my father most anxiously guarded against. This was self-conceit. He kept me, with extreme vigilance, out of the way of hearing myself praised, or of being led to make self-flattering comparisons between myself and others. From his own intercourse with me I could derive none but a very humble opinion of myself; and the standard of comparison he always held up to me, was not what other people did, but what a man could and ought to do. He completely succeeded in preserving me from the sort of influences he so much dreaded. I was not at all aware that my attainments were anything unusual at my age. If I accidentally had my attention drawn to the fact that some other boy knew less than myself—which happened less often than might be imagined—I concluded, not that I knew much, but that he, for some reason or other, knew little, or that his knowledge was of a different kind from mine. My state of mind was not humility, but neither was it arrogance. I never thought of saying to myself, I am, or I can do, so and so. I neither estimated myself highly nor lowly: I did not estimate myself at all. If I thought anything about myself, it was that I was rather backward in my studies, since I always found myself so, in comparison with what my father expected from me. I assert this with confidence, though it was not the impression of various persons who saw me in my childhood. They, as I have since found, thought me greatly and disagreeably self-conceited; probably because I was disputatious, and did not scruple to give direct contradictions to things which I heard said. I suppose I acquired this bad habit from having been encouraged in an unusual degree to talk on matters beyond my age, and with grown persons, while I never had inculcated on me the usual respect for them. My father did

not correct this ill-breeding and impertinence, probably from
not being aware of it, for I was always too much in awe of him
to be otherwise than extremely subdued and quiet in his
presence. Yet with all this I had no notion of any superiority
in myself; and well was it for me that I had not. I remember the
very place in Hyde Park where, in my fourteenth year, on the eve
of leaving my father's house for a long absence, he told me that
I should find, as I got acquainted with new people, that I had
been taught many things which youths of my age did not commonly know; and that many persons would be disposed to talk
to me of this, and to compliment me upon it. What other things
he said on this topic I remember very imperfectly; but he wound
up by saying, that whatever I knew more than others, could not
be ascribed to any merit in me, but to the very unusual advantage which had fallen to my lot, of having a father who was able
to teach me, and willing to give the necessary trouble and time;
that it was no matter of praise to me, if I knew more than those
who had not had a similar advantage, but the deepest disgrace
to me if I did not. I have a distinct remembrance, that the suggestions thus for the first time made to me, that I knew more
than any other youths who were considered well educated, was
to me a piece of information, to which, as to all other things
which my father told me, I gave implicit credence, but which
did not at all impress me as a personal matter. I felt no disposition to glorify myself upon the circumstance that there were
other persons who did not know what I knew; nor had I ever
flattered myself that my acquirements, whatever they might be,
were any merit of mine: but, now when my attention was
called to the subject, I felt that what my father had said respecting my peculiar advantages was exactly the truth and common
sense of the matter, and it fixed my opinion and feeling from
that time forward.

It is evident that this, among many other of the purposes of
my father's scheme of education, could not have been accomplished if he had not carefully kept me from having any

great amount of intercourse with other boys. He was earnestly
bent upon my escaping not only the corrupting influence which
boys exercise over boys, but the contagion of vulgar modes of
thought and feeling; and for this he was willing that I should
pay the price of inferiority in the accomplishments which schoolboys in all countries chiefly cultivate. The deficiencies in my
education were principally in the things which boys learn from
being turned out to shift for themselves, and from being brought
together in large numbers. From temperance and much walking,
I grew up healthy and hardy, though not muscular; but I could
do no feats of skill or physical strength, and I knew none of the
ordinary bodily exercises. It was not that play, or time for it,
was refused me. Though no holidays were allowed, lest the
habit of work should be broken, and a taste for idleness acquired, I had ample leisure in every day to amuse myself; but as
I had no boy companions, and the animal need of physical
activity was satisfied by walking, my amusements, which were
mostly solitary, were in general, of a quiet, if not a bookish
turn, and gave little stimulus to any other kind even of mental
activity than that which was already called forth by my studies:
I consequently remained long, and in a less degree have always
remained, inexpert in anything requiring manual dexterity; my
mind, as well as my hands, did its work very lamely when it
was applied, or ought to have been applied, to the practical
details which, as they are the chief interest of life to the majority of men, are also the things in which whatever mental
capacity they have, chiefly shows itself: I was constantly
meriting reproof by inattention, inobservance, and general
slackness of mind in matters of daily life. My father was the
extreme opposite in these particulars: his senses and mental
faculties were always on the alert; he carried decision and
energy of character in his whole manner and into every action of
life: and this, as much as his talents, contributed to the strong
impression which he always made upon those with whom he
came into personal contact. But the children of energetic

38

parents, frequently grow up unenergetic, because they lean on their parents, and the parents are energetic for them. The education which my father gave me, was in itself much more fitted for training me to know than to do. Not that he was unaware of my deficiencies; both as a boy and as a youth I was incessantly smarting under his severe admonitions on the subject. There was anything but insensibility or tolerance on his part towards such shortcomings: but, while he saved me from the demoralizing effects of school life, he made no effort to provide me with any sufficient substitute for its practicalizing influences. Whatever qualities he himself, probably, had acquired without difficulty or special training, he seems to have supposed that I ought to acquire as easily. He had not, I think, bestowed the same amount of thought and attention on this, as on most other branches of education; and here, as well (as) in some other points of my tuition, he seems to have expected effects without causes.

Lizzie Moore

≫ 1843 – 1915 ≪

JOHN STUART MILL and Helen Keller may be considered the two extreme examples of students — the one with almost every possible advantage, the other with almost every possible handicap, yet each with a single dedicated mentor. It is time to turn to more typical situations — the eternal class room with its teacher and group of pupils.

As we grow older, we are apt to forget our earlier and often ablest teachers who kindled our minds and hearts in the first grade, or the sixth or the tenth. Modest people with modest salaries, overburdened with an endless succession of classes, their very names are lost in the shadows of the past. But not so with some of our college and university professors who are closer to us in time. These we are apt to remember with exaggerated praise, especially if they have been successful authors or conspicuous in some other way.

Every now and then, however, the balance is righted somewhat by the appearance of a vignette or an article on some primary or secondary school teacher who has won the gratitude of thousands. There was Fred C. Kelley's picture of Miss Jean B. Elwell who taught for nearly fifty years in the public schools of Xenia, Ohio. There was Dorothy Walworth's picture of little Miss Hungerford who taught for fifty years at Cornwall, New York, and was the life-long inspiration of the great naval engineer, Sir Stephen Pigott. There was Richard Lockridge's recollection of Miss Fox, "The Grammarian." Such little pieces send the mind back to our own Miss Hungerfords gratefully — and justly.

Our picture is of a country school teacher seventy-five years ago. She had few pedagogical theories, few audiovisual aids, but she had imagina-

41

tion—and McGuffey's Readers. The selections from McGuffey give some notion of an overwhelmingly successful series of grammar school textbooks (total sale of the six readers and speller estimated at one hundred and twenty-two million copies) that rivalled the Bible in shaping our John Does and Henry Fords through three-fourths of a century.

One of the pupils of Lizzie Moore was James William Crabtree, who was brought up in Ohio and Nebraska and was graduated from the State Normal School at Peru, Nebraska. After teaching in rural schools for six years, and serving as a principal and state high school inspector, he became president of the Peru State Normal School (1904–1910) and later president of the River Falls (Wisconsin) State Teachers College (1911–1917)—in each case a vigorous and beloved leader. But his great moment came in 1917 when he was made secretary of the rather feeble National Education Association, with headquarters at Washington. By the time he had retired in 1935 the membership of the Association had risen from seventy-three hundred to two hundred and sixteen thousand! His unpretentious, homey little autobiography, What Counted Most, is an American document.

Progressive Educator

JAMES WILLIAM CRABTREE

→≫·≪←

I AM NOT PLANNING to relate incidents in chronological order. I am placing them under general headings which carry me back and forth as to dates. But I wish, near the very beginning, to pay my respects to Lizzie Moore from whom I have drawn inspiration all my life. Her name must be near the head of the list of "Things That Counted Most" in my life. She was my teacher when I was seven or eight years old in a country school in southern Ohio—still known as the Pleasant Valley School.

I heard my father tell a neighbor that Lizzie Moore was a born teacher and that the more ragged the child the more she loved him. It looked to me as if that were true. I often saw her divide her lunch with hungry children. She was certainly an ideal teacher for that poverty-stricken community in the terrible depression of the seventies. She had a delightful personality. She made herself a part of the community. She put the schoolhouse in good condition for revival meetings. She had to scrub the floor the morning after evening services to clear away the results of a lot of tobacco chewing.

Miss Moore learned all she could about the animals, birds, and snakes, common to that timbered country in order to talk our language better and in order to tell us more than we knew about the fox, the raccoon, and the hoot owl. She questioned us and our parents about them. She let us bring our rabbits, raccoons, and other pets to school on special occasions.

As you know, those were the days when people believed in

43

the adage, "spare the rod and spoil the child;" even Miss Moore
felt bound to act in harmony with public sentiment.

She found it necessary on one occasion to keep me after school
and to use the switch on me for disobedience. Some of us boys
had decided we would not cry however hard the whipping. I
withstood the tinge of pain bravely enough, but the real punishment came when she laid the switch on the desk and with tears
in her eyes said, "You are not such a bad boy. You are not bad
at heart. You are really a good boy, and you know it. I don't
want you to act that way any more. Won't you please promise
me? I just can't stand it to whip. I am almost sick now."

As she spoke, her feelings gave way. She took the chair,
placed her face in her hands, and sobbed audibly for a few
moments before she could get control of her voice. I then joined
in the crying act, made promises, swept the floor, and said,
"Good-by, Miss Moore," two or three times as I was leaving.
After that, I was at school early each day to build the fire and to
clean off the blackboard. Two of us gave a third boy a good
trouncing later on for talking back to Miss Moore. My parents
observed that I was a "changed boy" after that experience.

I did more than my share in decorating the schoolhouse for
Christmas. We brought sprigs of pine, branches of laurel, and
little bunches of mountain tea with its scented leaves and its
little red berries. Miss Moore advised us to decorate our own
homes in the same way. She advised against buying presents.
She suggested little plays and things to do rather than things to
buy. She knew only too well of the poverty-stricken families
with whose children she labored.

The few toys and presents in the homes were inexpensive
but we had our parents and brothers and sisters. The decorations
were about all we had at school except that there we had our
Lizzie Moore and our little friends. I doubt whether as much as
twenty-five dollars was spent for Christmas presents in the
entire district and yet, in all the years of plenty since that time,

LIZZIE MOORE

I have never seen a more joyful Christmas than that particular one.

When I read Bess Streeter Aldrich's *The Woman Who Was Forgotten*, I could not help thinking of beautiful Lizzie Moore. Recently, and just fifty years after leaving the old school to go out West, I returned to Scioto County, Ohio, to see the house in which I was born, the schoolhouse in which I got my start, and the few relatives and friends yet to be found. I inquired about Lizzie Moore. To my surprise no one knew what had become of her. Surely some of the older citizens would know. Then I began to realize my lack of real appreciation of that woman who had been a source of inspiration to me for half a century. She had taught the school only one year but she had given a score of boys and girls in that neighborhood higher ideals.

She had filled boys and girls with worthy ambitions. She made a man of me. A wonderful woman — but forgotten!

I wonder whether she ever knew how much her pupils in that district owed to her. I wonder whether she ever knew of anything beyond their devotion to her at the time. She must have known of the appreciation of parents, but I fear she never realized how much she put into the lives of children in that school and in the other schools in which she taught.

Today, we would say that Lizzie Moore was a progressive teacher. The neighbors in that district said at the time that she was "different." Some said that she had common sense because she didn't like to wait until the children had mastered all words of one, two, and three syllables in the spelling book before taking up reading, and she didn't like to teach the a-b-ab's and the e-b-eb's because so many of these "words" had no meaning.

On Friday afternoons, Lizzie Moore picked out a few poems for the entire school to learn to recite in concert. She attached importance to those that taught valuable lessons in life. I remember especially one which she got from *McGuffey's Third Reader*, "Try, Try Again." She said that when we became men and women we would be glad we had learned that poem in school. She hoped we would often think of it through life. She said it was as true as it was beautiful.

She taught us "Harry and the Guidepost" to give us courage, and "Try, Try Again" to give us perseverance. Hundreds of times I have thought of these poems at the right time.

I am using these two poems and the story of *The Seven Sticks* from *McGuffey's Third Reader.*

TRY, TRY AGAIN

'T is a lesson you should heed,
  Try, try again;
If at first you don't succeed,
  Try, try again;

Then your courage should appear,
For, if you will persevere,
You will conquer, never fear;
  Try, try again.

Once or twice though you should fail,
  Try, try again;
If you would, at last, prevail,
  Try, try again;
If we strive, 't is no disgrace,
Though we may not win the race;
What should you do in the case?
  Try, try again.

If you find your task is hard,
  Try, try again;
Time will bring you your reward,
  Try, try again.

All that other folks can do,
Why, with patience, should not you?
Only keep this rule in view:
  Try, try again.

— T. H. PALMER

When I was ten, I had gone on an errand to the home of an uncle, who lived about half a mile away, and stayed until after dark. The path home went up over a ridge and through some timber. I claimed not to be afraid but I was at least alert and could run if necessary. Just as I was reaching the top of the ridge, I saw between me and the sky a great giant figure bending over the path. My limbs almost refused to move. I shall never forget how real and how black that figure ahead looked. I halted for only a moment and, thinking of "Harry and the Guidepost," I gathered courage to move on.

As I approached the giant, I saw it was only a tree full of dry leaves, but the rattling of the leaves and a flock of birds flying away made a frightful noise. In spite of the revelation, I found myself hurrying on over the hill and down home. I was almost too tired to tell the story. The family was proud of my bravery. As foolish as it may seem, I must admit that *Harry and the Guidepost* gave me both conscious and unconscious support many times thereafter.

HARRY AND THE GUIDEPOST

The night was dark, the sun was hid
  Beneath the mountain gray,
And not a single star appeared
  To shoot a silver ray.

Across the heath the owlet flew,
  And screamed along the blast;
And onward, with a quickened step,
  Benighted Harry passed.

Now, in thickest darkness plunged,
    He groped his way to find;
And now, he thought he saw beyond,
    A form of horrid kind.

In deadly white it upward rose,
    Of cloak and mantle bare,
And held its naked arms across,
    To catch him by the hair.

Poor Harry felt his blood run cold,
    At what before him stood;
But then, thought he, no harm, I'm sure,
    Can happen to the good.

So, calling all his courage up,
    He to the monster went;
And eager through the dismal gloom
    His piercing eyes he bent.

And when he came well nigh the ghost
    That gave him such affright,
He clapped his hands upon his side,
    And loudly laughed outright.

For 'twas a friendly guidepost stood,
    His wandering steps to guide;
And thus he found that to the good,
    No evil could betide.

Ah well, thought he, one thing I've learned,
    Nor shall I soon forget;
Whatever frightens me again,
    I'll march straight up to it.

> And when I hear an idle tale,
>   Of monster or of ghost,
> I'll tell of this, my lonely walk,
>   And one tall, white guidepost.

A story that Miss Moore often called attention to was that of *The Seven Sticks* also in the *McGuffey Third Reader*. I heard a man of international reputation use this story the other day to illustrate a point in an address. I have heard it used to good effect scores of times. I almost regret that children of today do not get more of those character building stories such as Mr. McGuffey used in his *Readers*. I wish that children had more teachers like Lizzie Moore to plant the principle of the story in their minds and to make it a part of their lives.

This story of *The Seven Sticks* aided in lessening the heat of little arguments in our family and doubtless led all pupils of that day to recognize more fully the value of teamwork in their later work. It helps me to see more clearly today the need of teamwork in our own organized profession. I take pleasure in repeating the story.

THE SEVEN STICKS

A man had seven sons, who were always quarreling. They left their studies and work, to quarrel among themselves. Some bad men were looking forward to the death of their father, to cheat them out of their property by making them quarrel about it.

The good old man, one day, called his sons around him. He laid before them seven sticks, which were bound together. He said, "I will pay a hundred dollars to the one who can break this bundle."

Each one strained every nerve to break the bundle. After a long but vain trial, they all said that it could not be done.

"And yet, my boys," said the father, "nothing is easier to do." He then untied the bundle and broke the sticks, one by one, with perfect ease.

"Ah!" said his sons, "it is easy enough to do it so; anybody could do it in that way."

49

Their father replied, "As it is with these sticks, so is it with you, my sons. So long as you hold fast together and aid each other, you will prosper, and none can injure you.

"But if the bond of union be broken, it will happen to you just as it has to these sticks, which lie here broken on the ground."

Next to the help which came from my parents was that which I received from Lizzie Moore. Perhaps next to that was what I received from Jim Blackburn when I was fourteen, and from J. M. McKenzie when I was eighteen. These were classroom teachers. I owe very, very much to other friends along the way, but these names stand out. In relating my experiences, I have given essentially your own experience and that of leading citizens everywhere. I see among the teachers of today many a Lizzie Moore. There never has been a better type of devotion among teachers than at the present time. Since that experience in losing Lizzie Moore, I have written other favorite teachers to express appreciation.

One of the saddest thoughts of my life is that I failed to keep track of her and to let her know what I owed to her.

.   .   .   .

I told this Lizzie Moore story over the radio in 1933. It caught the imagination of the radio audience. Scores of leading citizens wrote in asking for copies of the address. Many a one said that he sent a Christmas message to his Lizzie Moore; a few had made trips to see her.

The Commander of the American Legion made a trip, immediately, across two states to visit the teacher to whom he owed much. The interest aroused was greater because of its being a true story and because nearly every man and woman has had just such a teacher. A number of my radio friends undertook to help me find her. I soon had heard of six Lizzie Moores of the sixties and seventies in Ohio. Could we learn which of the six had taught at Pleasant Valley? We finally found out about her but not until after she had passed on. Mr. Bonner, now teacher at Pleasant Valley, got track of her ninety-nine-year-old sister, Mrs. Jennie F. Snook, at Williamsburg, Ohio, and from her we got the complete story.

Soon after Lizzie Moore taught our school, she was married to a Presbyterian minister in Western Pennsylvania. You will be pleased to learn that she was a leader in the church and in the community, living an exceedingly useful life. Both she and her husband, the Reverend E. Z. Thomas, were held in high esteem. They were socially prominent. Together, they devoted themselves to years of helpful service and outstanding good.

Of five children, two have passed on. The husband died a number of years ago and Lizzie Moore Thomas died in 1915 at Leechburg, Pennsylvania, at the age of seventy-two. Of course, I shall always blame myself for not having found her before it was too late.

Moses Woolson

⇶ 1821 – 1896 ⇷

IN HIS AUTOBIOGRAPHY, Frank Lloyd Wright *frequently refers to Louis Henri Sullivan, "the master for whose influence, affection, and comradeship" he has never ceased to feel gratitude. If our debt to Wright is great, our debt to Sullivan is even greater, for it was largely he who made "form follows function" the battle cry of the modern architect; and we can watch that basic principle evolve in his Autobiography of An Idea.*

The article on Sullivan in the Dictionary of American Biography refers to the influence on him of "a certain Moses Woolson"; but the phrase "a certain," when applied to a person, usually indicates complete uncertainty and leaves us with little more than a proper name.

However, we do know that Moses Woolson was principal of the Portland (Me.) High School for Girls and that in 1856 he did a daring thing; he married a member of his graduating class, a Miss Abba Louisa Goold, who was seventeen years his junior. In 1868 they settled in Boston where he became a first year teacher in the English High School—not as famous as the Latin High School where George Santayana and so many other notables studied—but with its own distinguished record.

Mr. Clarence Carter, one of the three surviving alumni of the class of 1873, reports in a personal communication that Moses Woolson "soon proved himself absolutely unfitted for general teaching and discipline there.

"His knowledge of botany, mineralogy and English Literature was excellent but he was only medium in French (our only foreign language of that day) and an absolute failure in mathematics.

53

"He had an ungovernable temper, was especially harsh and violent in his treatment of some of the smaller boys of the class, if they lacked influential fathers or sponsors, and by the end of our school year (1870–71) he had shown that his assertions could not be relied upon and were sometimes inspired by his desires for personal advancement or to impair the standing or reputation of his associates. His last year or two in the school were passed in continued friction, and, in 1874, he was formally dismissed from the Boston school system.

"Louis Henri Sullivan and I were fellow, and friendly, classmates during his short attendance at E. H. S. and in later years became warm friends. . . ."

Yet the two classmates give diametrically opposite characterizations of the same teacher. Perhaps much further information would help explain the mystery but to a less extreme degree such different reactions are common enough. The temperament that will attract and inspire one pupil will repel or discourage another. Evidently Moses Woolson was just what Louis Sullivan needed in 1870 — and just what Clarence Carter didn't need — or didn't want!

Taskmaster

LOUIS HENRI SULLIVAN

>>>·<<<

Louis still had time to brush up rapidly for the high school examinations. He had chosen the English High rather than the Latin High. He was accustomed to thinking and acting for himself, seldom asking advice. His thoughts in mass were directed ever toward his chosen career; and he believed that the study of Latin would be a waste of time for him; the time element was present always as a concomitant of his ambitions. He wished always to advance in the shortest time compatible with sure results. He had no objection to Latin as such, but believed its study suitable only to those who might have use for it in afterlife. He had a keen gift for separating out what he deemed essential for himself.

On September third, his birthday, he received a letter from Utica, filled with delicate sentiments, encouraging phrases, and concluding with an assurance that the writer would be with him in spirit through his high school days.

The English and Latin High Schools, in those days, were housed in a single building, rather old and dingy, on the south side of Bedford Street; a partition wall separating them, a single roof covering them. The street front was of granite, the side walls of brick. There were brick-paved yards for the recess half-hour with overflow to the street and a nearby bakery. It was a barn-like, repellant structure fronting on a lane as narrow as the prevailing New England mind of its day.

Louis passed the examinations and his name was entered in the year book 1870–71.

He was among those—about forty in all—assigned to a room on the second floor, presided over by a "master" named Moses Woolson. This room was dingy rather than gloomy. The individual desks were in rows facing north, the light came from windows in the west and south walls. The master's platform and desk were at the west wall; on the opposite wall was a long blackboard. The entrance door was at the north, and in the southwest corner were two large glass-paneled cabinets, one containing a collection of minerals, the other carefully prepared specimens of wood from all parts of the world.

The new class was assembled and seated by a monitor, while the master sat at his desk picking his right ear. Louis felt as one entering upon a new adventure, the outcome of which he could not forecast, but surmised would be momentous.

Seated at last, Louis glanced at the master, whose appearance and make-up suggested, in a measure, a farmer of the hardy, spare, weather-beaten, penurious, successful type—apparently a man of forty or under. When silence had settled over the mob, the master rose and began an harangue to his raw recruits; indeed he plunged into it without a word of welcome. He was a man above medium height, very scant beard, shocky hair; his movements were panther-like, his features, in action, were set as with authority and pugnacity, like those of a first mate taking on a fresh crew.

He was tense, and did not swagger—a man of passion. He said, in substance: "Boys, you don't know me, but you soon will. The discipline here will be rigid. You have come here to learn and I'll see that you do. I will not only do my share but I will make you do yours. You are here under my care; no other man shall interfere with you. I rule here—I am master here— as you will soon discover. You are here as wards in my charge; I accept that charge as sacred; I accept the responsibility involved as a high, exacting duty I owe to myself and equally to you. I will give to you all that I have; you shall give to me all that you have. But mark you: The first rule of discipline shall

56

be SILENCE. Not a desk-top shall be raised, not a book touched, no shuffling of feet, no whispering, no sloppy movements, no rustling. I do not use the rod, I believe it the instrument of barbarous minds and weak wills, but I will shake the daylight out of any boy who transgresses, after one warning. The second rule shall be STRICT ATTENTION. You are here to learn, to think, to concentrate on the matter in hand, to hold your minds steady. The third rule shall cover ALERTNESS. You shall be awake all the time—body and brain; you shall cultivate promptness, speed, nimbleness, dexterity of mind. The fourth rule: You shall learn to LISTEN; to listen in silence with the whole mind, not part of it; to listen with your whole heart, not part of it, for sound listening is a basis for sound thinking; sympathetic listening is a basis for sympathetic, worth-while, thinking; accurate listening is a basis of accurate thinking. Finally you are to learn to OB-SERVE, to REFLECT, to DISCRIMINATE. But this subject is of such high importance, so much above your present understanding, that I will not comment upon it now; it is not to be approached without due preparation. I shall not start with you with a jerk, but tighten the lines bit by bit until I have you firmly in hand at the most spirited pace you can go." As he said this last saying, a dangerous smile went back and forth over his grim set face. As to the rest, he outlined the curriculum and his plan of procedure for the coming school year. He stressed matters of hygiene; and stated that a raised hand would always have attention. Lessons were then marked off in the various books—all were to be "home lessons"—and the class was dismissed for the day.

Louis was amazed, thunderstruck, dumbfounded, overjoyed! He had caught and weighed every word as it fell from the lips of the master; to each thrilling word he had vibrated in open-eyed, amazed response. He knew now that through the years his thoughts, his emotions, his dreams, his feelings, his romances, his visions, had been formless and chaotic; now in this man's utterances, they were voiced in explosive condensation, in a flash they became defined, living, real. A pathway had been shown him, a wholly novel plan revealed that he grasped as a banner in his hand, as homeward bound he cried within, "At last a Man!"

Louis felt the hour of freedom was at hand. He saw, with inward glowing, that true freedom could come only through discipline of power, and he translated the master's word of discipline into its true intent: SELF DISCIPLINE OF SELF POWER. His eager life was to condense now in a focusing of powers: What had the words meant — "silence," "attention," "promptness," "speed," "accurate," "observe," "reflect," "discriminate," but powers of his own, obscurely mingled, un-co-ordinated, and, thus far, vain to create? Now, in the master's plan, which he saw as a ground plan, he beheld that for which, in the darkness of broad daylight, he had yearned so desperately in vain; that for which, as it were with empty, outstretched hands, he had grasped, vaguely groping; as one seeing through a film, that for which he had hungered with an aching heart as empty as his hands. He had not known, surely, what it was he wished to find, but when the master breathed the words that Louis felt to be inspired: "You are here as wards in my charge; I accept that charge as sacred; I accept the responsibility involved as a high exacting duty I owe to myself and equally to you. I will give to you all that I have, you shall give me all that you have," — a veil was parted, as it were by magic, and behold! there stood forth not alone a man but a TEACHER of the young.

On board the train for Wakefield, Louis took account of himself; he viewed the long, loop-like journey he had but recently completed, still fresh and free in memory's hold. He had gathered in, as though he had flung and drawn a huge lassoo, the Berkshires, the Mohawk and its valley, Little Falls, the Black River, the Moose River, the primeval forest, and the Falls, the Hudson, the Catskills, the Palisades, New York

58

Harbor, Long Island Sound; he had voyaged by rail, by river, and by sea. All these things, these acts, with their inspiring thoughts and emotions and reveries he had drawn into himself and shaped as one single imposing drama, ushering in a new and greater life. Or, in a sense, reversed his "child-domain," holding, within the encircling woods, his ravine, his rivulet, his dam, his lovely marsh, his great green field, his tall, beauteous, slender elm; land of his delight, paradise of his earth-love, sequestered temple of his nature-worship, sanctuary of his visions and his dreams, had seemed at first, and hopefully, to extend itself progressively into a larger world as far as Newburyport and Boston, there, however, to stop, to remain fixed and bound up for seven long years, held as by a sinister unseen dam, the larger, urgently growing Louis, held also back within it, impatient, repressed, confined, dreaming of power, storing up ambition, searching for what lies behind the face of things, agitated and at times morose, malignant. When, of a sudden, the dam gives way, the child-domain so far enlarged, rushes forth, spreading over the earth, carrying with it the invisible living presence of Louis's ardent soul, pouring its power of giving and receiving far and wide over land and sea, encompassing mountains and broad valleys, great rivers, turbulent waterfalls, a solemn boundless forest enfolding a lustrous lake, and again a noble river mountain-banked, an amazing harbor, and the great salt waves of the sea itself.

Thus were the boundaries extended; thus were the power and splendor of Mother Earth revealed in part; thus was provided deep and sound foundation for the masterful free spirit, striding in power, in the open, as the genius of the race of purblind, groping, striving, ever hoping, ever dreaming, illusioned mankind.

And thus it seemed to Louis that he was becoming stronger and surer of himself. Reverting to the words of the master, he dared affirm that this very power was within him, as a ward in his charge; that he must accept that charge as sacred; that he must accept the responsibility involved as a high exacting duty he owed to himself and equally to it; that he must give to it his all, to insure that it might give to him its all.

And Louis now saw clearly, and in wonder, that a whim of his Grandpa, not the Rice Grammar School, had prepared him to meet Moses Woolson on fair terms. With confident assurance he awaited the beginning of what he foresaw was to be a long and arduous disciplinary training, which he knew he needed, and now welcomed.

That evening he told Grandpa what he thought of Moses Woolson and his plan; and Grandpa, with inward seeing eyes, smiled indulgence at his grandson seated on his knee, one hand about his neck, as he mused aloud: "My dear child, allowing for the rosy mist of romance through which an adolescent like yourself sees all things glorified, I will say that in the whole wide world it is true there may be found a few such men as you portray; but as a venerable and prudent Grandpa I shall reserve the right to wait awhile that we may see how the ideal and the real agree. But you go at it just the same, regardless of what may be passing in the back of my bald head." And Louis laughed, and kissed and hugged his Grandpa, and settled to his lessons, as Grandma knitted by the student lamp, as Uncle Julius thrummed away on a helpless guitar and sang the melancholy sentimental ditties of the day, and as Grandpa, in slippers, gazed with incredulity at a boy on the floor oblivious of them all.

As it has but little import in this story, we shall pass over the breaking-in period of Moses Woolson's class, and begin an exposition of Moses Woolson's plan and method, and Louis's responses thereto at that period the master himself had forecast as "when I have you firmly in hand at the most spirited pace you can go." Suffice it to say that with great skill in intensive training he had brought them to this point within three months.

The ground work of his plan was set forth in his opening

address, and is now to be revealed in its workings in detail.

The studies on which Louis set the highest value were algebra, geometry, English literature, botany, mineralogy, and French language. All these subjects were to him revelations. Algebra had startled him; for, through its portal, he entered an unsuspected world of symbols. To him the symbol X flashed at once as a key to the unknown but ascertainable. Standing alone, he viewed this X in surprise as a mystic spirit in a land of enchantment, opening vistas so deep he could not see the end, and his vivid imagination saw at once that this X, expanded in its latent power, might prove the key to turn a lock in a door within a wall which shut out the truth he was seeking — the truth which might dissolve for him the mystery that lay behind appearances. For this X, he saw, was manipulated by means of things unknown.

Thus he saw far ahead; looking toward the time when he would be mature. Geometry delighted him because of its nicety, its exactitude of relationships, its weird surprises — all like fairy tales, fairy tales which could be proved, and then you said: Q.E.D. He began to see what was meant by a theorem, a postulate, a problem, and that proof was a reasoned process based on certain facts or assertions. It was well for him, at the time, that he did not perceive the Euclidian rigidity, in the sense that he had noted the fluency of Algebra. As to Botany, had he not always seen trees and shrubs and vines and flowers of the field, the orchard and the garden?

Now he was learning their true story, their most secret intimacies, and the organization of their world. He loved them all the more for this. Mineralogy was new and revealing, the common stones had begun as it were, to talk to him in their own words. Concerning French he was ardent, for he had France in view. English literature opened to him the great world of words, of ordered speech, the marvelous vehicle whereby were conveyed every human thought and feeling from mind to mind, from heart to heart, from soul to soul, from imagination to imagination, from thought to thought; and to his ever widening view, it soon arose before him as a vast treasure house wherein was stored, in huge accumulation, a record of the thoughts, the deeds, the hopes, the joys, the sorrows, and the triumphs of mankind.

Moses Woolson was not a deep thinker, nor was Moses Woolson erudite or scholarly, or polished in manners, or sedate. Rather was he a blend of wild man and of poet. But of a surety he had the art of teaching at his fingers tips and his plan of procedure was scientific to a degree, so far beyond the pedagogic attainments of his day that he stood unique, and was cordially hated by his craft as lambs might fear and hate a wolf. Today men would speak of such a man as a "human dynamo," a man ninety-nine per cent "efficient." His one weakness was a temper he all too often let escape him, but his high strung, nervous make-up may be averred in part extenuation, for this very make-up was the source of his accomplishment and power: he surely gave in abundance, with overflowing hands, all that he had of the best to give.

His plan of procedure was simple in idea, and therefore possible of high elaboration in the steady course of its unfolding into action and results. For convenience it may be divided into three daily phases seemingly consecutive, but really inter-blended; first came severe memory drill, particularly in geometry, algebra, French grammar and in exact English; this work first done at home, and tested out next day in the school room. Second, (first, next day) a period of recitation in which memory discipline and every aspect of alertness were carried at high tension. At the end of this period came the customary half-hour recess for fresh air and easing up. After recess came nature study with open book. Chief among them Gray's *School and Field Book of Botany*—Louis's playground; then came a closing lecture by the Master.

Thus it may be said, there was a period of high tension, followed by a period of reduced tension, and this in turn by a closing period of semi- or complete relaxation, as the master reeled off in easy, entertaining talk, one of his delightful lectures. It was in the nature studies, and in these closing lectures, particularly those in which he dwelt upon the great out-of-doors, and upon the glories of English literature, that the deep enthusiasms of the man's nature came forth undisguised and unrestrained, rising often to the heights of impassioned eloquence, and beauteous awakening imagery. These lectures, or rather, informal talks covered a wide range of subjects, most of them lying beyond the boundaries of the school curriculum.

Thus, in a sense, Moses Woolson's school room partook of the nature of a university—quite impressively so when Professor Asa Gray of Harvard came occasionally to talk botany to the boys. He did this out of regard for Moses Woolson's love of the science. The unfailing peroration of these lectures— every one of them, was an exhortation in favor of "Women's Rights," as the movement was called at the time; for Moses Woolson was a sincere and ardent champion of womankind. On this topic he spoke in true nobility of spirit.

But the talks that gripped Louis the hardest were those on English literature. Here the master was completely at his ease. Here, indeed, he revelled, as it were, in the careful analysis and lucid exposition of every phase of his subject, copious in quotation, delightfully critical in taking apart a passage, a single line, explaining the value of each word in respect of action, rhythm, color, quality, texture, fitness, then putting these elements together in a renewed recital of the passage which now became a living, moving utterance. Impartial in judgment, fertile in illustration and expedient, clear in statement, he opened to view a new world, a new land of enchantment.

One day, to Louis's amazement, he announced that the best existing history of English literature was written by a Frenchman, one Hyppolite Taine by name. This phenomenon he ex-

63

plained by stating that the fine French mind possessed a quality and power of detachment unknown to the English; that Monsieur Taine further possessed that spiritual aspect of sympathy, that vision, which enabled him to view, to enter freely and to comprehend a work of art regardless yet regardful of its origin in time or place; and he rounded an antithesis of French and English culture in such wise as to arouse Louis's keenest attention, for the word culture had hitherto possessed no significance for him; it was merely a word! Now his thoughts, his whole being, floated o'er the sea to distant France, whereupon he arose from his seat and asked Moses Woolson what culture really meant, and was told it signified the genius of a people, of a race. And what was meant by the genius of a people? It signified their innate qualities and powers of heart and mind; that therefore their culture was their own expression of their inmost selves, as individuals, as a people, as a race. Louis was magnificently bewildered by this high concentration. He seemed to be in a flood of light which hid everything from view; he made some sheepish rejoinder, whereupon Moses Woolson saw his own mistake.

He came down from his high perch to which he had climbed unwittingly, for it was dead against his theory and practice to talk above the heads of his boys. He thereupon diluted the prior statement with a simply worded illustration, and Louis was glad to find his own feet still on the ground. Then Louis put the two aspects of the statement side by side again, and "culture" became for him a living word — a sheer veil through which, at first, he could but dimly see; but living word and sheer living veil had come from without to abide with him. It seemed indeed as though Moses Woolson had passed on to him a wand of enchantment which he must learn to use to unveil the face of things. Thus Louis dreamed.

By the end of the school year Moses Woolson, through genius as a teacher, had turned a crudely promising boy into, so to speak, a mental athlete. He had brought order out of disorder, definition out of what was vague, superb alertness out of mere boyish ardor; had nurtured and concentrated all that was best in the boy; had made him consciously courageous and independent; had focussed his powers of thought, feeling and action; had confirmed Louis's love of the great out-of-doors, as a source of inspiration; and had climaxed all by parting a great veil which opened to the view of this same boy, the wonderland of poetry.

Thus with great skill he made of Louis a compacted personality, ready to act on his own initiative, in an intelligent purposeful way. Louis had the same capacity to absorb, and to value discipline, that Moses Woolson had to impart it, and Louis was not a brilliant or showy scholar. He stood well up in his class and that was enough. His purpose was not to give out, but to receive, to acquire. He was adept in the art of listening and was therefore rather silent of mood. His object was to get every ounce of treasure out of Moses Woolson. And yet for Moses Woolson, the master and the man, he felt neither love nor affection, and it is quite likely that the master felt much the same toward him. What he felt toward the man was a vast admiration, he felt the power and the vigor of his intense and prodigal personality. It is scarcely likely that the master really knew, to the full extent, what he was doing for this boy, but Louis knew it; and there came gradually over him a cumulative reciprocity which, at the end, when he had fully realized the nature of the gift, burst forth into a sense of obligation and of gratitude so heartfelt, so profound, that it has remained with him in constancy throughout the years. There may have been teachers and teachers, but for Louis Sullivan there was and could be only one. And now, in all too feeble utterance he pleads this token, remembrance, to the memory of that ONE long since passed on.

Frederick William Sanderson

⋙ 1857 – 1922 ⋘

THE HEADMASTER of Oundle had completed his address on "The Duty and Service of Science in the New Era" to several hundred members of the National Union of Scientific Workers. Before asking for questions, the chairman, Mr. H. G. Wells, remarked: "I think you will agree with me that you have heard not only one of the most interesting and suggestive but the most curious discourses you have ever heard. It is not always easy to follow Mr. Sanderson, but he is worth following into the remotest corner. He has a style of discourse which I can only compare with some of the modern practices in painting . . ." At this Sanderson chuckled, slid from his chair and died almost instantly, perhaps the greatest of all English headmasters.

Thirty years before he had taken over a small decaying public school ("private school," to Americans) dominated by the classics, and transformed it into a flourishing young commonwealth. "The modern school is not made by the very simple and easy method of abandoning Greek," he said in that last speech. And he had not tried to eliminate Greek or Latin from Oundle; but he had added science and engineering, to be taught as group enterprises and not in the spirit of individual competition. The result was a new order of young men in England, thousands of them, not merely gentlemen, but citizens with an equal concern for science and society.

Yet "one of the most characteristic memories that every Oundle boy carried away with him was that of the headmaster's Divinity lesson at twelve o'clock on Sundays." These were sometimes taken down verbatim by the boys, often parodied gaily in the studies — but always listened to

67

with deep interest. In The Story of a Great Schoolmaster, H. G. Wells, who admired Sanderson more than any man he ever knew, has included one of those Scripture lessons as recorded by "X and Y." Even without the ruddy and jolly face, the flashing spectacles, the living voice, these notes help us to understand the affection in which Sanderson was held.

Do we make the most of our Chapel meetings, our school assemblies, our convocations? Do they have the drama, the excitement, the warmth, that make students look back on them with delight, with nostalgia? All too often one sees a student body move lazily into an auditorium or a gymnasium and come away an hour later, blanketed with boredom, or discussing anything but the subject they have just confronted. But bring them a sensitive speaker, or a panel of speakers, and involve them actively in the give and take of ideas—and a convocation can become an oasis furnishing living water for the dullest class rooms on the campus.

"Boys have only one characteristic in common, their dislike to any change," said Sanderson—but he didn't mean it.

Sanderson of Oundle

X AND Y (AND H. G. WELLS)

->>>·<<<-

"SCRIPTURE LESSON

"*Delivered by F. W. Sanderson on Sunday, 25th May 1919, and taken down word for word by X and Y, and subsequently written up by them.*

"*Limitations of space and time have prevented them from including all the lesson. Omissions have been indicated. They apologise for the lapses of the speaker into inaudibility, which were not their fault. They do not hold themselves in any way responsible for the opinions expressed herein.*

"ANALYSIS

"OF THE PORTIONS COPIED.

"Characteristic portions in the Gospel of St. Matthew.

"Obstinacy of the Oxford and Cambridge Schools Examination Board.

"Character of the devil, according to some modern writers.

"First act of our Lord on beginning the Galilean Ministry.

"Empire Day.

"*Subject of the Scripture lesson:*—St. Matthew, *chaps. iv and v.*

"(The Temptations, the commencement of the Galilean Ministry, the first portion of the Sermon on the Mount.)

"(The headmaster enters, worries his gown, sits down, adjusts his waistcoat, and coughs once.)

"The—um—er—I am taking you through the Gospel of St. Matthew. I think, as a matter of fact, we got to the end of the third chapter. We won't spend much time over the fourth. The fourth, I think, is the—er—er—Temptations, which I have already taken with you—a rather—er—very interesting—ah—very interesting—er—survival. That the Temptation Narrative should have survived shows that there is probably something of value in it or I do not think it would have survived. There are two incidents of very similar character of—er—very—er—similar character and—ah—different to a certain extent from everything else—er—ah—There is a boy in that corner not listening to me. Who is that boy in the corner there? No, not you—two rows in front. I will come down to you later, my boy. There are two incidents in the Gospel Narrative which are similar in—er—character and which I have for the moment called Survivals—very characteristic, namely, the somewhat surprising narrative of the Temptation of our Lord, and the other the account of the Transfiguration. These are different in form and character from other narratives, just in the same way as the account of our Lord sending messages to the Baptist differs from others. Er—yes—that last one. I should put them together as coming from a similar source (lapse into inaudibility—bow wow wow—Somewhat subtle—bow wow). One remarks that the Temptations are always looked at from the personal point of view, which I have put down in my synopsis. Has anybody here got my synopsis? Lend it to me a moment. I don't think the personal significance of the Gospel stories has importance nowadays. We needn't consider it. That's what I think about things in general. Personal importance giving place to universal needs. We are not so much concerned with whether boys do *evil* or not. Of course it annoys me if I find a boy doing evil. Leading others astray. Shockingly annoying. Oughtn't to be. Like continuous mathematics not enabling a boy to pass in arithmetic—bow wow wow—screw loose. See what I mean, K___? Not referring to you, my boy (laughter). Hunt me up something in Plato about all these things. During the last generation—

"(Half a page omitted.)

"Just in the same way from another point of view shall we live for our own advancement, which we are continually tempted to do? It's awfully annoying if you do certain things and people won't recognise them. I was pretty heftily annoyed myself at a meeting of the Oxford and Cambridge Board. Professor Barker — great man — I nearly always agree with him. Professor Barker. They had made science compulsory for the school certificate. Bow wow wow. I don't want boys turned aside from their main purpose to have to get up scraps and snippets of science. Literary pursuits and so on. I wouldn't have it at any price. Bow wow wow. Modern languages are compulsory too. By looking at a boy's French set I can tell whether he can pass or not. Bow wow. Professor Barker proposed that science should be voluntary. I seconded him, but I said that languages should be voluntary as well. He didn't see that at all. Isn't it enough to make a man angry?

"(Half a dozen lines omitted from our notes as incomprehensible.)

"Now I am inclined to think that Satan in this Gospel is not intended to be the Satan of our minds — the prince of evil. He is intended to be more like the Satan in the book of Job. He is the devil's advocate. He argues for the other side. For the opposition. He is put up to create opposition. This may in itself be a valuable thing. I don't know that I need go further into it. I would just like to tell you this, boys. Some modern writers, especially Bernard Shaw, have a very high esteem for the devil. He prefers hell to heaven. So he says. Of course he hasn't been there, so he can't tell. So he is voted a dangerous personage because, dear souls, they don't know what he means. What *he* means is that heaven as it has been run down to and God as *He* has been run down to — everything placid and simple and inactive and non-creative and sleepy. People don't worship God. They worship (burble, burble). They don't disturb their minds and think about things. That's what he means. Yes. Man and Superman. Activity of intellect. That's more or less what he has in mind. He prefers people doing something outrageously wrong than doing nothing at all. I don't know if it's true; it's all expressed in Greek thought.

"(Four pages omitted on running with the tide, Lloyd George, the importance of French in examinations, and the correct way of getting a true national spirit.)

"Well, our Lord now proceeded to found His Galilean Ministry. And what was the first thing He did, L____? It's quite obvious. What did He do? Obvious. Were you thinking of what I said just now? No, sir. My stream of words goes over you, not through you. Obvious. Now what was the first thing He did? What is obviously the first thing He did? Why, it's painfully obvious, even to L____. What was it? What? Where are we, L____? L____ has lost the place. Which paragraph do I mean, L____? Read the paragraph I mean. No. I have finished that. Next one. Obvious. What is it about? Yes, what is it about? What is it about? Two or four? Yes, four! Now what is obvious? Obvious! Now you've just got it, and you're ten minutes behind. Of course. The first obvious thing He had to do was to get a band of faithful disciples. Very first thing He did. What did He call them to be? To be what? Fishers of Men. Obvious.

"(Five pages omitted on Empire Day, Medical Study, and Cancer.)

"Now the—er—the Sermon on the Mount. You have heard this ever since you were on your mother's knee. At least I hope so. Beyond the historical times of your memory. For you, the Sermon on the Mount is as old as the ages. And yet I dare trespass on the Sermon on the Mount. "I've heard of it before," you say. "I'm tired of it. Do something fresh." Boys, you must go and read old things and breathe into them the new Spirit of Life. Now what is that chapter in Ezekiel, boys? Do you know the number of the page, and the paragraph, and the chapter? No. What am I talking about? Why, the valley of dry bones. Never heard of it! No. Is it in Jeremiah, Ezekiel, or where, or

Habakkuk? Is it in Ezekiel 1? No. 36? No. 37? Yes. Dry Bones. Bones. Yes. That's what. I am going to take you to a valley of dry bones. Dry Bones. Bones. It is your business to go into the dry bones of the past and cover them with flesh, and breathe into them the new Spirit. I often read the Sermon on the Mount. It never bores me. I have more excuse to be bored than you. I learned it, gracious goodness, how long ago! Beyond Historic times. I loved it as a boy. Dry Bones.

"(Three pages on the Sermon on the Mount.)

"Now yesterday was Empire Day. Why did you want me to put the flag up? Rule Britannia! Britannia rules the waves! Is not that it? (Yes, sir.) Dear boys! I wouldn't throw cold water on it for worlds. Well, you had your flag. It didn't fly. There was no wind behind it. There was no devil to blow it. Dear boys, you wanted that flag for a reason I think a shade wrong. It wouldn't be within the—what's the word I want?—suited for our modern gauges. The new world won't come until we give up the idea of Conquest and Extension of Empire—no new kingdom until its members are imbued with the principles that competition is wrong, that conquest is wrong, that co-operativeness is right, and sacrifice a law of nature. Now, how do the seven Beatitudes read with *Rule Britannia?* Now you say you believe in your Bibles. You say you are Christians. Pious Christians. You would be most annoyed if I called you heathens. Well, if so, you believe that these are right:—

"Blessed are the poor in spirit, for theirs is the kingdom of heaven. Rule Britannia!

"Blessed are they that mourn, for they shall be comforted. Rule Britannia!

"Blessed are the meek, for they shall inherit the earth. Rule Britannia!

"Blessed are they that hunger and thirst after righteousness, for they shall be filled. Britannia rules the waves!

"Blessed are the merciful, for they shall obtain mercy. Rule Britannia!

73

"Blessed are the pure in heart, for they shall see all that is worth seeing and living for. Wave your flag! Rule Britannia!

"Blessed are the peacemakers, for they shall be called sons of God. Rule Britannia!

"Blessed are they that have been persecuted for righteousness sake. Rule Britannia! It is incongruous. . . .

"Dear souls! My dear souls! I wouldn't lead you astray for anything. I can't explain it . . . this national spirit of yours. Beneath it all there is a spirit of great righteousness. I wouldn't tamper with it for thousands of pounds. But you must just see the other side. . . .

"(Starts on the Salt of the Earth, but is interrupted by time. Sets a heavy prep., and goes.)"

Mark Hopkins

⇒ 1802 – 1887 ⇐

W HO HAS NOT HEARD OF "Mark Hopkins on one end of a
log and a student on the other?" That is the most mis-
quoted and misused text in the annals of educational gossip. One
might think that Mark Hopkins was a backwoods teacher of surveying or the sole occupant of the old red school house, instead of being professor of philosophy at Williams College for over fifty years and president
for thirty-six. The origin of the famous remark was a speech by General,
later President, Garfield at a dinner of the Williams College Alumni,
at Delmonico's on December 28, 1871. What Garfield did say seems
to have been as follows: "I am not willing that this discussion should
close without mention of the value of a true teacher. Give me a log hut,
with only a simple bench, Mark Hopkins at one end and I on the other,
and you may have all the buildings, apparatus and libraries without
him."

Not as an administrator or author, not as a scholar or original thinker,
does Mark Hopkins come down to us, but solely as a great teacher whose
fame and influence were vastly out of proportion to the little stage — a
classroom for seniors — on which he did his main work. No doubt he was a
"born teacher" but he had the advantage of a medical education after his
graduation from Williams. However inadequate the little Berkshire
Medical College at Pittsfield, Massachusetts, may have been, it gave
Hopkins a mass of concrete information, an understanding of the concrete
human being, that is not possessed by the typical academic philosopher.
"Godlike," said Hippocrates, "is the philosopher who is also a physician."

75

Several of Hopkins' former students tried to recapture in print his spirit and method: John B. Bascom, the celebrated President of the University of Wisconsin; Arthur Latham Perry, Professor at Williams and author of influential textbooks and articles in economics; Franklin Carter, the sixth President of Williams, and Leverett Wilson Spring, clergyman, teacher and historian. There are also illuminating passages about Hopkins in that charming autobiography, And Gladly Teach by Bliss Perry (son of A. L. Perry) and in the Life and Confessions of a Psychologist by G. Stanley Hall.

After serving in the Congregational ministry in Massachusetts and Kansas for thirteen years, Spring became Professor of belles-lettres and English Literature at the University of Kansas, at Lawrence. There he wrote a pioneer, well-documented work on Kansas: Prelude to the War for the Union. In 1886 he returned to Williams as Professor of Rhetoric, where he remained until his retirement in 1909. His booklet, Mark Hopkins, Teacher, published in 1888, is valuable not only as a graphic account of the old master himself but as an essay on the whole subject of the art of teaching.

In his final estimate of Hopkins, G. Stanley Hall said: "While I should now differ with him widely on almost every point, he did give us a precious set of attitudes and apercus in the highest study of mankind, which is man. I believe that my own interests have had a wider range because of him, and although so much that he taught is more or less obsolete today, there is no need so great as that of a man of his synthetic and apodictic type and with a range no less wide to introduce young people to these subjects."

Socratic Yankee

LEVERETT WILSON SPRING

→»·«←

T HE RELATIONS OF Mark Hopkins to education were almost
exclusively of the personal sort. He confined himself for
the most part to a single department of it, and was concerned very slightly with what might lie outside of its limits.
The voluminous professional literature that has accumulated
about the subject did not attract him. I do not know whether
he concurred with Professor Rosenkranz in the opinion that the
books devoted to education "abound more in shallowness than
any other literature," but at all events he was careful to let
them alone. He never investigated the science of pedagogics, nor
the influence of educational institutions on the course of civilization. And if he had made explorations in these directions, if a
passion for erudition . . . had possessed him, he would have
realized from it small benefit for his pains.

Though Dr. Hopkins had little interest in the pedagogical
theories and speculations which are found in books, it is not to
be supposed by any means that he failed to consider the general
subject of education. In one of his public utterances — the address delivered on the fiftieth anniversary of his election as
President of Williams College — he spoke at length on educational ideals. "The outcome of a college training ought to be,"
he said, "a sound body, a disciplined mind, a liberal education,
a right character." Forty-five years before he urged the same
ideas in an oration at Mount Holyoke Seminary. They present
nothing that is novel or exceptional. In the more notable defini-

tions of education, they are the chief factors, whether we say with Richter that the ideal is "the harmonious maximum of all individual qualities taken together;" or with Matthew Arnold that it is that training which carries us "to a knowledge of ourselves and the world;" or with Rosenkranz that it "consists in the development in man of his inborn theoretical and practical rationality," the special elements of which he classifies as the physical, the intellectual, and the practical. What is more, these four points upon which Dr. Hopkins dwelt indicate lines along which great historic experiences have run. Their theatre has been national as well as individual.

Nor did Dr. Hopkins have any perceptible influence upon public schools. Little of that practical ability, that satisfaction in affairs, which characterized Dr. Arnold and Horace Mann, appear in him. They possessed a strain of executive genius — were eager to tear down that they might rebuild on better models. The prediction before the election of Arnold to the mastership of Rugby that if he should get the appointment, he would change the face of public education in England, was fulfilled abundantly. And the twelve years during which Horace Mann was secretary of the Board of Education made an epoch in the schools of Massachusetts. To the vocation of agitator Dr. Hopkins was not suited. The clearness and coolness of his thinking, the large comprehensive views which were characteristic of him, held in check the emotional intensity requisite for any notable success in it. Few men weighed things more dispassionately. Wholesale condemnation is seldom the language of the broadest philosophy, and crusades have an affinity with somewhat of blindness if not of narrowness. Dr. Hopkins believed in zeal — he devoted one of his later baccalaureate sermons to this subject — but he would have a care that it should be mixed properly with intellect. In existing educational institutions he saw more good and less evil than professional reformers would allow.

Unlike Arnold, who took up the calling of teacher as a

matter of course, Dr. Hopkins was without prevision of his future. No inner light gave early intimations of what his work should be—no articulate voice cried to him in imperative tones, "This is the way, walk ye in it!"

He was not a man of premonitions; he had no prophetic instinct which transported him beyond this ignorant present and felt the future in the instant. The recognition of his genius came first from without, not from within. He did not seek the profession of teacher; what is more, there was not at the outset any considerable personal gravitation toward it. It was his intention to become a physician and with that object in view he completed a course of medical study. Some men are born with aptitudes so unmistakable, with prepossessions so strong and definite that the questions of work and place are settled in advance. It would have required, certainly, an extraordinary combination of unfriendly circumstances to shut Charles Darwin out of the field of natural history. A boy who at the age of seven years paints portraits with a brush made of hairs plucked from the back of the house cat will become an artist in spite of obstacles. But there are other men, possessed as their subsequent careers amply demonstrate, of the highest ability who find serious difficulty in deciphering their commission to the world. It often requires a series of uncomfortable experiments to clear up the matter—to adjust the inward talent to the outward environment. The great educators have encountered as much difficulty as any other class of men in determining for what they were made. Pestalozzi tried his hand at theology, at law, and at farming before he found his niche as school master. In Dr. Hopkins' case, I think this unconsciousness resulted from the remarkable equilibrium of his intellectual capacities. His genius was not monochromatic. It might have been turned with results almost equally happy into several different channels. I am sure he would have made his mark as a physician if his original plans had been carried out. To the profession of law his mental equipment was even more signally adapted. It may not be worth while to speak of what might have been, but I believe our country has seen no greater jurist than the possible judge that lay in Mark Hopkins. And in this poise of a genius, capable of many and diverse activities, it is not surprising that premonitions were mostly absent, or that chance should have some part, apparently, in determining the particular field of its work.

This unconsciousness is no doubt the more remarkable when we remember that Dr. Hopkins realized as a teacher the old fable of Minerva who sprang full-armed from the brain of Jupiter. The usual stages of experiment, modification, progress, with their alternations of failure and success, do not appear in his tuition. His earliest essays at it exhibit scarcely less power than his meridian work; he began with full strength. In 1830 he was as extraordinary a teacher as in 1860. The modifications of time and experience affected incidentals rather than essentials. While precocity, that touches an individual capacity, that is confined to the field of a single power, must involve self-consciousness to a greater or lesser degree, yet in the more complicated and balanced instances of it we readily see that the tendency would be to obscure if not obliterate self-consciousness.

But the students of the early days were not insensible to the presence of a great man among them, and it was they who elected him President of Williams College. The health of Dr. Griffin, who held the position from 1821 to 1836, began to break down toward the close of this period, and it became evident that at no distant day a successor must be chosen.

Dr. Hopkins did not seek the place, nor did he regard himself as especially qualified for it. The executive duties which it involved, the inevitable attention to multitudinous details, were never altogether agreeable to him. Some one asked him who among the candidates possible or suggested ought in his judgment to be elected. "John Morgan is the man," he replied — John Morgan of the class of 1826 who was professor of Biblical

Literature at Oberlin for more than forty years. The class of 1836, which happened to be one of unusual ability, has the honor of choosing the successor of Dr. Griffin. There was opposition in the Board of Trustees to the candidacy of the Professor of Moral Philosophy and Rhetoric — the chair which Dr. Hopkins occupied at that time. So far as I can learn this opposition revolved around the fact that his age was insufficient. To us it seems a trivial cause for hesitation. It did not appear so, however, to our grandfathers. In the selection of presidents, college trustees of two generations ago had a decided partiality for middle-aged or old men with established reputations. At young men they looked askance, whatever their promise might be. While the board was in session for the purpose of choosing Dr. Griffin's successor, it received a letter from the class of 1836 setting forth the profound impression which the instruction of Professor Hopkins had produced, and formally thanking the gentlemen for the privilege of sitting at his feet, which their wisdom had made possible. The letter was read before the board and produced great excitement — "If the boys want him," old Dr. Shepherd finally said, "let them have him." They did want him and they had him.

.   .   .   .

The elements of his power were many and diverse. Among those which the most cursory and superficial observation could not miss was his personal appearance. He had a magnificent physical frame. The enthusiastic words of Theodore Parker in reference to Daniel Webster might be transferred to him, and those who knew the man will hesitate before they bring charges of exaggeration. "Since Charlemagne I think there has not been such a grand figure in Christendom." Large-framed; with a massive, well-poised head of strikingly intellectual mould; benignant and winsome in countenance, seasoning his words with a gracious voice, he commanded respect, conciliated affection, kindled enthusiasm by his presence. The physical element has been a powerful factor in the success of oratory. Not infrequently voice and person have outdone intellect and imagination in effective service. With an insignificant body and a feeble elocution there could have been no Mirabeau or Daniel O'Connell. It is true that men whose personal presence was weak have succeeded as public speakers, but such success has been exceptional. Though the vocations of orator and teachers differ in some obvious particulars, yet they have much in common, and the physical equation is about as large in the one case as in the other. And young men are keenly sensitive to the attractions of a noble presence. When Dr. Hopkins entered the classroom every student felt a sudden change in the atmosphere. He felt that the humanity in it had received a signal and fascinating re-enforcement.

Then I put enthusiasm as second in the list of his salient qualities. Dr. Hopkins himself in one of his public addresses emphasized strongly the necessity of it. "He who carries the torchlight into the recesses of science," he said, "and shows the gems that are sparkling there, must not be a mere hired conductor, who is to bow in one company, and bow out another, and show what is to be seen with a heartless indifference, but must have an ever-living fountain of emotion that will flow afresh as he contemplates anew the works of God and the great principles of truth and duty."

In all memorable educational achievements enthusiasm has borne a distinguished part. There are not wanting instances of them in which it was the capital source of power — in which but for its inspiration and contagion overwhelming failure must have ensued. Pestalozzi not only did not succeed in the practical management of his schools, but his theories are somewhat incoherent and unintelligible. They are confused; they lack clear-cut and definite outlines. Different disciples report conflicting versions of them. And yet few men have a more assured and permanent place in the history of education, and the fact must be ascribed chiefly to his pathetic humanitarianism. He had an unconquerable passion to minister to the lower classes of his country, to shelter and elevate the vagrant, homeless uncared-for-children who swarmed in his neighborhood, for whom he was ready to yield himself up a living sacrifice, and his philanthropic, self-denying labors laid the foundation of modern popular education. Though indebted to Rousseau for impulse and suggestion, he may justly claim the honor of inaugurating, half unconsciously it may be, the great movement, which is so conspicuous a feature in the civilization of our times, to extend the moral and intellectual stimulus of education to the entire community—a movement which some dreamers affect to believe will rid us by and by of "the dirty, hungry, ignorant, awkward, thankless and will-less mass devoted alone to animal existence."

If the enthusiasm which burned in Dr. Hopkins' soul was different, it was not less real. It continued for three score years with no abatement—at least I could discover none during the last weeks of his work, when after an absence of a quarter of a century I visited his class-room. It was the same gracious, and magnificent personality that I had known and revered as a student. When I looked at him I could see in the deeper furrows that crossed his brow, in the greater deliberation of his movements, in the slight deafness that at times made it difficult for him to catch the answers of the class, that time had touched him, though but tenderly. Yet if I closed my eyes the old days seemed to have returned. The ear reported that things were as they used to be. He was then eighty-five years old, but his intellectual powers appeared to be as brilliant as ever, and his interest as keen in questions which he had discussed with six generations of students. The old man, braving all weathers, met his class eight hours weekly for more than half the winter months. "I missed only one day last year," he said just before the end came, "and then the young men sent a committee asking me not to venture out, since the great storm that was raging made the streets nearly impassable." There was no distemper in this enthusiasm. It had nothing of the demonstrative, passionate, ill-regulated element which we see in Pestalozzi; nothing of the sentimentality, the posing and waywardness which cast shadows upon Rousseau's career—it was a fine, subtile, rational intensity such as became a great philosopher who viewed life broadly and profoundly. In a nature where intellectual qualities are so remarkable, intensity of a purely emotional cast, fervor that has its seat principally in the heart, must of necessity have occupied a subordinate position. Yet there was no lack of emotional elements in his nature. Friends who knew him intimately discovered depths of sentiment in his soul, shy and furtive tenderness which ordinary acquaintances would not suspect. A native reserve inclined him to silence touching the whole world of his inner and spiritual self. In some respects he was a solitary man shut up with himself and his God. It was easier, more natural for him to speak of his thoughts than of his feelings. But though he may have been silent it does not follow that the feelings were absent. I remember that on one occasion near the close of his life, conversation turned upon the poetry of Robert Browning. He said that it did not attract him; that he liked clearness and had little patience with obscure, cloudy verse, in which one must beat about painfully to find the meaning. "But," he continued and a profound look came over his face, a spiritual and illuminated expression, which seemed the reflex of a far-gazing vision into the unseen and eternal, "but I too am a mystic." It will be a surprise to many that this man of sun-bright intellect, who seemed to have little commerce with cloud-land or dream-land, should claim kindred with Thomas á Kempis and Bernard of Clairvaux. Intellectual voices may have rung loudest in this self-contained yet powerful enthusiasm, but there was also in it a deep undertone of the spiritual.

Again, Dr. Hopkins knew where to begin in teaching—a matter of the first importance. I recollect hearing some one quote, in illustration of this point, the reply of Grimm to a scholar who asked him for the heads of an Icelandic grammar. "You might as well ask me," said Grimm, "to write the book. When these heads are decided upon, when the outlines of the treatise are fixed, the most formidable difficulties will be overcome. What remains will be mostly detail and can be managed without difficulty." Probably no teacher ever understood better than Dr. Hopkins the eligible approaches to ethical and philosophical subjects. He followed nature and natural methods in the best sense of those much abused terms. "Beginning with the elements," to quote substantially his own words spoken in 1843, "he constructed together with his pupils, so that they felt that they aided in it, the fair fabric of a science with which they became familiar from foundation to the topstone." These words intimate what in his judgment the teacher of philosophy ought to attempt, and he certainly reached his own ideal. A right beginning facilitated a successful construction. Teacher and student proceeded in company from the lower to the higher, from the conditioned to the conditioning, "tracing relations and carrying out principles, and (finally) taking a wide and comprehensive survey of the whole subject." With some qualifications and limitations it may be called a process of rediscovery. It has a remote kinship with the theories of Rousseau and Herbert Spencer, who would discard books, set aside history which records the experiences of the past, assume that everything is unknown, that what is behind us is not worthy of our attention, and attempt to solve the riddle of the universe by retracing anew the experiences of humanity. This theory of education has attractive aspects, and has led astray some of the ablest writers on the subject. It would be easy to pick holes in it—to show that at least in this extravagant form it is utterly impracticable. Dr. Hopkins scouted the idea of going back of experience in his instruction, and of attempting to reenact the mingled drama of human history. He put a large value upon the lessons of experience, and in his rediscoveries he simply laid hold of the rudiments of philosophy, rebuilt them in the presence of his pupils and with their help, into forms more complicated and intricate. In spirit and method it was original work, and brought his department into line with modern science. While it might not be the absolute and unqualified truth to say that he antici- pated what is known as physiological psychology, yet his habit of viewing man as a whole, of beginning with the body, and of studying it in relation to the intellectual and moral faculties, was an authentic forerunner of it.

The range of his work was extensive. For many years he had eleven exercises weekly with the senior class. Two-thirds of the instruction of that class fell upon him. What he attempted to do for it in the line of investigation, what fields of thought and research he explored with them, is briefly summarised in one of his baccalaureate sermons. He undertook to investigate man; to discover his place in nature; to exhibit the systems that com- pose his body; to explore the mazes of mental science and the "misty regions of metaphysics that lie beyond;" to examine the grounds of obligation and of belief in the being of God; to trace the analogies between reason and revelation, as well as to sur- vey the doctrines and mysteries of Christianity. It was a comprehensive scheme, and touched most of the great intel- lectual and spiritual problems of humanity.

Eminent instructors have their own way of handling classes, and the individuality of their work is no less positive and determinate than that of painters or musicians. Niebuhr found lectures a satisfactory organ of instruction. "He read word for word from his manuscript," says Rosenkranz, "and what a teacher was he!"

It has been said of Dr. Wayland, who made a strong im- pression upon many of his pupils, that "he was an educating force rather than a great or inspiring teacher." His success was not so much the triumph of skill and address as of sheer strength. With sufficient opportunity for reflection he analysed subjects clearly and illustrated them forcibly, but he lacked celerity in mental processes. He had little of the swift intuition which

86

penetrates character at a glance and as quickly shapes instruction to the occasion.

I have spoken already of Dr. Arnold — of the changes which he effected in the public schools of England and of the early and unquestioning instinct, the bent of mind that no combination of circumstances would be likely to overbear, which led him into the vocation of teacher. His methods of work took form and color, on the one hand, from his evangelistic fervor, his earnest desire that "to the enquiring love of truth" his pupils should add "the divine love of goodness"; his absorbing ambition to compass an education which "was not (according to the popular phrase) based upon religion, but was itself religious"; and on the other, from the fact that he dealt mostly with boys in the preparatory stage. To a considerable extent he was their companion and entered with zest into their games and recreations. He diffused among them, however, a spirit of seriousness, led them to self-respect and to a conviction that some honorable toil awaited them in the world. Whatever their peculiar bent might be, in whatever direction their abilities might lie, they felt sure of his sympathy, and that gave them confidence in themselves and in their work.

> "To us thou wast still
>   Cheerful and helpful and firm!
> Therefore to thee it was given
>   Many to save with thyself."

While Arnold's "unhasting, unresting" labors have borne much religious fruit, it is not to be supposed that they lacked intellectuality, though that was not their predominent feature. He believed the union between moral and intellectual excellence to be very intimate. His habit was, not to drench his pupils with information, but to stimulate independence of investigation by questions and suggestions. Yet after all it was the personal element that told most effectively, for many of his contemporaries were his equals in intellect and his superiors in scholarship—the personal element which it is so difficult to characterize and so impossible to measure. "The system is lost in the man," says Dean Stanley, "the recollections of the headmaster of Rugby are inseparable from the recollections of the personal guide and friend of his scholars."

Another great teacher of yet different mould belongs to our generation—Agassiz. He also was a man of unique and engaging personality. The Gallic power of pleasing appeared in him to an exceptional degree. So intense and comprehensive was his enthusiasm for his specialties, that, if it had not been held in check by a steadiness of discrimination that lurked beneath all the glow and fervor, he must have become a fanatic, and his intensity was linked with fascinating gifts of speech. Such a mental equipment led of necessity to a lecture system of teaching—to oratory adjusted to the classroom. Agassiz trained his students in the use of their senses; he set them at tasks of observation and comparison. Natural science cannot be taught successfully without resort to this sort of drill. That the methods which it demands are not wholly applicable to philosophy is obvious enough. Yet, after all the appropriate qualifications have been made, it remains that the salient, individualizing element in Agassiz's teaching was his luminous and persuasive talk.

But no one of these eminent men was as great an artist in the classroom, no one of them carried instruction to such a consummate pitch of spiritual power as Dr. Hopkins. His art was as natural and unstudied as the lyric gifts of Robert Burns. Yet it was art of the first order, though I presume he would have been the last man in the world to claim any such thing. It was worth a journey across the continent to see him manage a class. He fathomed students by a flash of intuition. If they ever deceived him, it was an unusual occurrence. To know them, to penetrate beneath the surface and discover what may be found there, to recognize possibilities as well as actualities, are cardi-

nal points in an ideal teacher, and he had them in rare perfection. With this knowledge of human nature he could walk
firmly and confidently. "It is far easier," he once said, "to
generalize a class and give it a lesson to get by rote and hear it
said and let it pass than it is to watch the progress of the individual mind and awaken interest and answer objections and
explore tendencies." He never generalized a class. Of course
in every considerable number of students there are some whom
it is impossible to touch; whom the resources of the most accomplished instructor are powerless to rouse out of their
sluggishness and indifference. To carry forward a class of in-
genuous youth, watching them as they conquer new positions
and gain broader views filled him, Dr. Hopkins says, with some
such ecstasy as Wordsworth felt when he beheld a rainbow in
the sky. But if, as will sometimes happen, he has an insensitive,
unimpressionable class; if his words fall dead and there is no
interest, the depression will be correspondingly great. He has
spoken strongly on this point and his words are worth quoting.
In this absence of enthusiasm the instructor alone, he said, "can
know the anxiety, I had almost said agony with which, as the
prophet of old on the dead body of the child, he once and again
as it were puts his mouth to its mouth, and his eyes to its eyes
and stretches himself upon the class, and finds no life come.
And he alone knows how cheerless and hopeless and slavish is
the dull routine of his labors after that. There are, it seems to
me, few modes of gaining a living short of actual villainy, which
a man of sensibility would not prefer to it!"

Dr. Hopkins understood "the worth and significance of
personality." It was a conception that underlay the whole
economy of his teaching. He had reached substantially the same
doctrine as that which Mulford enunciates in his *Republic of God*.
All dogmatic methods of teaching—methods which would
sacrifice the independence of the student in the interest of some
system of philosophy—are in so far inimical to personality
which involves its own freedom and self-determination; which

89

"is impaired in the same measure in which it is determined from without." It is a doctrine the importance of which many distinguished teachers have failed to realize. They have been more zealous to make converts to their theories than to develop individuality. In not a few instances their partizanship reached the pitch of intolerance. What they thought and felt they would have their students think and feel. To dissent subjected the pupil to suspicions that something was wrong in mind or heart. The truth is placed before him for acceptance, not for investigation and criticism. Perhaps it is unnecessary that I should cite examples in illustration of this method of teaching. It would not be difficult to do so, as they are sufficiently numerous. There was a strain of the dogmatic in Sir William Hamilton for whom Dr. Hopkins had a hearty admiration, though he did not fully accept his philosophy. Hamilton won the love and admiration of his pupils, yet he took dissent from his opinions impatiently; his ardent and imperious temper chafed under opposition; the atmosphere of his lecture room certainly put no premium upon independence of thinking. In Dr. Hopkins there was absolutely no trace of the dogmatic spirit. When students adopted his opinions doubtless he was gratified, but he considered it of vastly higher importance to establish habits of self-reliance. For this reason he encouraged freedom of inquiry. "You have been trained," he said in his Baccalaureate Sermon before the class of 1867, "to regard the freest discussion not only as a right but as a duty. You will bear me witness that you have been called unto liberty." And the young men were called unto this liberty, that, through the exercise of it they might attain a noble personality. He dwelt somewhat at large upon this theme in the Baccalaureate for 1859. "Bring out your own individuality," he said, "it is your own. As such, respect and cherish it; only avoid all affected singularity; you will, I think, allow that individuality has been respected in your course of instruction here; that the object has been not to put upon you the earmark of any system, but to bring your individuality out

90

under the inspiration of a love of truth. If it be different from that of others, do not be troubled. It ought to be. Bring it out in its simplicity anywhere within the broad light and expanse of the one perfect example. . . . And while I thus call upon you to bring out your own individuality, let me say to you, also, respect that of others; and not only so, appreciate it and rejoice in its manifestation."

Let no one suppose that this encouragement of freedom grew out of indifference: that his own personal convictions sat lightly upon him; that he held them with a loose grasp. Liberality has limits. Whatever the intellect may do, the sensibility, the spiritual consciousness, draw lines. There is an incident related in Dr. Hopkins' last book, *The Scriptural Idea of Man*, which discloses an intensity of feeling and a peremptoriness of action quite unexpected in one who so justly stands as an exponent of all that is generous and liberal. "It is now nearly forty years," he remarks, "since the first volume of Emerson's essays was published. That volume I bought and read with pleasure. The second volume I also bought when that appeared, but before reading it much, if at all, I happened to open to this passage, "Jesus would absorb the race; but Tom Paine, or the coarsest blasphemer helps humanity by resisting this exuberance of power." I immediately closed the book and did not open it again till after the death of Emerson. It seemed to me so dreadful that "the coarsest blasphemer" should be welcomed as a benefactor of the race if he could only limit the influence of Him who was and is, to me, the Redeemer of the race, the second Adam, the man, and whose influence was, for me, the hope of the race."

It was not as an auxiliary to mental gymnastics merely that he valued freedom. The acquisition of knowledge and of intellectual acuteness never satisfied him; he never rested in them as the end of instruction, but looked upon them as means for realizing noble conceptions of life. Liberty and discussion shall be stepping stones to loftier ideals. His views of what is possible were broad and inspiring. He saw life whole — saw a complete and rounded humanity, not one in which reason usurps the functions of other faculties; in which the inner voices of mysticism silence the testimony of the external world, nor in which the senses have undue authority and cast discredit on spiritual things, but he believed devoutly in a trinity of spirit, soul and body. As we have seen he sought to put men in possession of their best self. He rejected everything that savored of dogmatism. With a system like Fenelon's, which tends to transform the pupil into an image of the master, he had no patience. He held with Richter that "it is only mediocrity that seeks to supplant the individuality of others by its own." In what he attempted to do we have the opposite pole of the earliest forms of education. They were national and purposed to place on every man an unmistakable stamp of nationality. Each member of the family or tribe must be fashioned after the race type, and differences reduced to the lowest point. But he preached and practiced a gospel of emancipation, which broke down all artificial restrictions and prepared the individual to become "a member of the spiritual world of humanity."

Dr. Hopkins' mind worked with great rapidity in the classroom. Apparently emergencies did not surprise, much less disconcert him. "It was no uncommon thing," some one has said, "for a bright or audacious student to pose Dr. Wayland by a sudden question." Neither bright nor audacious students, if they ever made the attempt, and I do not recall anything of the sort during my college course, had much success with Dr. Hopkins. In general his movements were deliberate. He liked to brood over things, to take time for maturing his thought. Under ordinary conditions he did not write rapidly. Most of his literary work was done slowly. I understand that his famous Baccalaureates were composed with a good deal of deliberation and revision. Yet in case of necessity he could accomplish great tasks in a brief time. That admirable volume — *The Evidences of Christianity* was thrown off in a few weeks. It was delivered as a series of lectures during the month of January 1844 before the Lowell Institute. The preceding commencement took place late in the summer, and nothing had been done upon the lectures. They were to be prepared in the vacation but when it came the Doctor found that his mind would not work. He could not think, or hold his attention to the subject. "I knew enough about myself and about medicine," he said to the writer, "to understand that I must stop. I had been doing the work of three men. If my physical strength had not been great, so that I was able to carry heavy burdens, I do not see how the college could have lived at all. The vacation was short and when the term opened in the autumn my duties would be exacting. But I dropped everything and went into the woods for three weeks. That saved me. I came back and wrote the lectures." Yet in the classroom this mental celerity was always present. There he had wings.

Dr. Hopkins' method was Socratic. Of him as well as of the old Greek it may be said that he had a genius of interrogation. It was a keen, skillful, kindly questioning, not without accompaniment of quaint and humorous remarks. In later years it was seldom that much irony came to the surface. I have been told that in his earlier work he was somewhat addicted to its use. He had a rare and subtle quality of it. To style it sarcasm would be too gross, so refined and delicate it was, yet so effective. I should not call it the irony of intellectual scorn, such as abounds in the books of Matthew Arnold. Nor is it to be classed with the lofty and tragic irony of Isaiah and Sophocles. It resembles, rather, that of Maurice or of Cardinal Newman, in which there is less of the broadsword than of the Damascus blade, in which the desire heroically to cut men out of their conceits or stupidities prevails over all considerations of scorn. Whether Dr. Hopkins came to regard irony as "the language of the devil" and therefore to be renounced, I am not wholly certain, but it seemed to disappear gradually from his teaching. If he employed it at all in the later days it was on those exceptional occasions which will now and then arise when nothing but caustics are effective. The general temper of his classroom was that of absolute candor and fairness. No one ever had occasion to complain in this particular. He had no disposition to confound a student for the sake of enjoying his confusion. A gladiator of his rank won victories with ease. Yet, though he would assuredly point out to the pupil the exact bearings of any position he may have taken, and bring him to appreciate the precise contents of his words — a process which sometimes subjected him to the discomfort of finding that he had been talking nonsense — not a trace of intellectual pride appeared. "I hear that you cornered several men this morning," a friend once remarked to him. "I never do that; I never corner men," was the almost indignant reply.

The Socratic method is not applicable to all circumstances, and even under the most favorable conditions must be supplemented by exposition and general didactic comment. Dr. Hopkins was a master in this sphere as well as in the arts of dialogue, though he rarely delivered formal lectures inasmuch as he thought students could be put to better uses than to convert them into writing machines. The mental discipline of copying discourses he did not rate very high. His expositions were characterized by clearness and definiteness. He laid great stress upon lucidity. With the use of obscure terms he had scarcely more patience than Jonathan Swift who pronounced it an inexcusable mistake. "I believe in no transcendental metaphysics," he said in his lectures at the Lowell Institute in 1873, "which is not capable of being communicated in good English, and of being understood by any man of good common sense." He recurred to the same thought, ten years afterward, in a course of lectures at Princeton Theological Seminary. "My object has been to aid you, gentlemen, in your studies by presenting for your consideration a simpler and more definite working apparatus than the one generally adopted." Then his analysis was thorough and penetrating and he had abundance of illustrative material

94

at hand. Among his books the volume which affords the best example of his didactic method, which will bring up most vividly to his pupils the scenes of his classroom, is *The Outline Study of Man*. As is commonly the case, there was a sensible difference between his written and his spoken style, though the same great fundamental qualities appear in both. His published works — I do not include among them his sermons which exhibit marked oratorical features — are an admirable example of philosophical or didactic prose in which lucidity, breadth and thoroughness of grasp, dignity of movement and large mental insight are noticeable. It may be said of them, as it has been of Macaulay's works, that they do not contain an obscure sentence. Their style has much of the charm which attracts us in what the critics call natural English — the English of John Bunyan and William Cobbett. But he cultivated assiduously the habit of extempore speech. "I saw very soon after I took up the work here," he said to me, "that I must learn to think and talk on my feet. Otherwise I could not carry on the institution; since in addition to the general care of the college and a large amount of teaching — I had in charge for a number of years the department of rhetoric as well as of philosophy — I must preach every Sunday morning. To write a sermon each week was out of the question, so I was driven to speaking without notes." He came to have a great facility in utterance. It was never voluble but befitted the man, and was germane to the subjects with which he dealt. And in the presence of his classes, where his natural reserve loosened and he spoke with more than usual freedom, this power of talk was seen at its best, abounding in words and phrases richly marked with character. While his tuition included much that did not and could not get into his books, *The Outline Study of Man*, has caught something of the clearness and simplicity, the profundity, and fascination of his talk.

Dr. Hopkins' methods remained substantially unchanged during his long career as a teacher. I think, however, that he himself supposed they had undergone considerable modification.

Indeed he said something to that effect on the only occasion when I remember to have heard him refer to them. I spoke of his classroom work in 1862–63 as I recalled it. "Things are different now" — it was in the winter of 1885–86 — he replied. "I have changed my ways of teaching since you were here." The innovation which he had in mind was the use of the blackboard. He employed it successfully in his lectures at the Lowell Institute to illustrate his system of philosophy, and this experience led him to have analyses and summaries of the lessons written upon it for the use of the pupils. But I am confident that he overrated the importance of this innovation — that in reality it brought with it very slight modification of method.

What Dr. Hopkins' attitude toward truth was and must have been is plain from what has been said. It was the catholic attitude of a large-molded philosopher, who, while he clings to the old, is ready also to welcome the new. Such men stand between the past and the present performing offices of mediation. They see very clearly the relations and interdependences of things. And thus they escape both extravagant theorizing and blind dogmatism. There were strains of a decidedly conservative order in Dr. Hopkins' character, yet he was heartily in sympathy with the fresher phases of truth. In an address delivered at Andover in 1837 before the Porter Rhetorical Society, he urged the scientific study of Christianity as adapted to secure that "true liberality of mind," which consists "in seeing the extent and connections of truth and in giving everything its place." He was a rationalist in the best meaning of that word. Whether this rationalizing habit was the real motive that caused the ministerial association, before which he appeared to obtain a license for preaching, to look a little doubtfully upon him, I am not quite certain. That they hesitated to grant him the license is well known, and also that they gave a different reason for their reluctance. "The ministers had a mind not to let me have my papers," the Doctor told a friend on his return from the association. "They said that I hadn't been through a theological seminary." But lack of theological training did not disqualify him from conducting for more than half a century his famous weekly exercise in the Assembly's Catechism, though it is probably true that the philosopher appeared more prominently in it than the divine. This exercise was not distinguished by any marked departure from his ordinary methods. It was simply an application of them to theology. And marvelous were the resources which he brought to bear upon the great mysteries of Christianity. Occasionally he would ignore the particular phase of doctrine which the manual propounded and spend his strength upon some principle that was vitally related to it, the exposition of which removed objections, cleared up obscurities and prepared the mind for its reception. Suppose the topic for the day to be the Trinity. How shall it be managed? Shall there be recourse to theological disquisitions and metaphysical subtleties? They might be proper for a divinity school, but they would be out of place before a miscellaneous college class. Now, instead of a direct discussion of the doctrine, the Doctor would probably execute a flank movement by expounding the law of mystery which prevails throughout the universe, and which, it is reasonable to suppose, would be displayed signally in the constitution of the divine being. "Clouds and darkness," he said in his master's oration delivered in 1827, "must still rest upon the existence, creative energy and attributes of the Great Cause uncaused, and the darkness of excessive bright forever compass his throne." If the student got little technical theology, he got what is better an insight into the rationale of it.

Another characteristic of Dr. Hopkins, especially effective and happy in its influence upon young men, was the hopefulness, the large expectancy with which he surveyed the future. "He taught us," said one of his pupils, "to shun the pitfalls of pessimism." That men of a morbid and despondent cast have influenced society powerfully, it would be impossible to deny. But the minor strain, so distinctly audible in the writings of

97

Goethe, especially in *Faust* and the *Sorrows of Werther;* the constant and profound melancholy, the ever present sense of mental unrest which pervade the political pamphlets, the histories and even some of the essays of Carlyle, are by no means their most effective qualities. The great success of these men must be attributed chiefly to the presence of other and less gloomy characteristics. In the long run, writers who work in the sunshine, who view men and things with eyes of hope rather than of foreboding and despair, will attract and hold the attention of the world.

Dr. Hopkins' cheerfulness was a natural result not only of his temperament but of his system of philosophy. This is not the place to enter upon any exposition of his theories. I am concerned here and now with the method rather than the substance of his teaching. It is necessary only to say that in his philosophy love is the paramount word. Love he believed to be the supreme power that lies behind the vast array of second causes — behind the confusions and disasters of human history — the power that will at length triumph over all opposition and dominate the total processes of the globe. "Rational love," he said, "is the central, plastic, unconsciously organizing and adjusting force of a rational society, as natural law and instinct are of the inanimate and animal creation . . . Abide steadfast in it, and . . . you shall work with the providence of God." This optimism antedated the construction of his philosophical system. As early as 1843 it was in full strength. "Rich as are the golden sands that have been brought down by the river of time," he then said, "there is every reason to believe that those will be richer yet which shall be borne still farther on." And, thirty years afterward, in the last baccalaureate sermon that he ever preached, in which, with a poetic fitness for time and occasion, he discussed the circular and onward movements of life, he caught up the same strain. "I do know that 'God is Love,' " he said. "Whatever else I hold on to or give up, I will hold on to that. That I will not give up." He did not give it up. The

98

last time he spoke in public he brought out this sentiment. One could not come into familiar converse with a man of such large discourse, looking before and after, yet sincerely, confidently expectant withal, and not be conscious that he himself grasped life more firmly, and hopefully.

Charles Edward Garman

➤➤ 1850 – 1907 ◄◄

THE NAME OF GARMAN has come to have for Amherst College the legendary meaning that Mark Hopkins has long had for nearby Williams. Both philosophers, both teachers in the fullest sense, they were as unlike as two men could be — the one a prolific inexhaustible public figure, the other a frail recluse moving between his home and his class room. We might better compare Garman with Emily Dickinson, that other elusive spirit of Amherst who evinced little interest in the public or in publication.

It was in reply to a letter of inquiry by G. Stanley Hall that Garman described fully the nature and purpose of his famous course after eighteen successive years of devoted experiment. In order to break down "an inevitable resistance to new ideas" on the part of his students, he used two devices: "First, the pamphlet system, which I think is as much of an invention as printing by movable type. These pamphlets I have printed at my own expense; they are very fragmentary, taking up a single topic or part of a topic and treating it as one would in a lecture; these I loan to the students, and they return them for the use of the next class. In this way I can state a question without answering it by having them turn over to the next chapter of the book and find the answer there. If I find the question is really appreciated, the effort is a success . . ."

"My second device is the order in which our subjects are taken up. . . . It makes the matter as serious and personal as possible, and as a result it has often cost the students a very great effort to satisfy themselves instead of simply meeting the requirements of the recitation room."

Then after further discussion of the need for freeing the students from imitation and obedience to authority, Garman went on to say: "It is my conviction that a young man can obtain inspiration, enthusiasm, and absence of self-consciousness only by the steady contemplation of great truths; that if he is wholly absorbed in imitation he is like a person whose work is that of a proofreader; if he is successful he is taken as a matter of course, and gets no credit; if he is unsuccessful and makes no mistakes, he is awkward; he is ridiculed beyond endurance; he soon realizes that the most promising rewards for the most careful efforts are negative, and he soon becomes indifferent, and is simply goaded on from fear of consequences of failure. But the young man who philosophizes, who really understands himself and appreciates the truth, is no longer a slave of form, but is filled with admiration that is true and lasting.

"This, I believe, is exactly the issue which is settled at this critical period of a young man's life. But the question arises, why should philosophy, psychology and ethics be the studies which most favor self-reliance, rather than mathematics or the sciences?

"It seems to me that mathematics fails to meet the demand for two reasons: there is no difference of opinion on all these subjects, and the student does not really have to stand on his own feet; thus it may become more a discipline in ingenuity than in decision and self-reliance. Secondly, he oftentimes knows pretty nearly what the answer will be, and therefore gets decided hints as to the means; that is, he really has some guidance either from textbooks or from experience; he is not a Columbus sailing over unknown seas with everything before him untried.

"With regard to the physical sciences, there is some difference of opinion here, but his main time is spent in undergraduate work on matters that are generally accepted; he has more or less assistance about the use of the apparatus, and his main consciousness of need is of ingenuity and of quickness; and then the enormous admiration which our age has for the discoveries of physical science gives him a superstitious reverence for anything that can be called scientific. I mean by this that he accepts a great many positions in science without really testing them, and thus he almost gets back into the imitative work again; but when he comes to philosophy it is a new world."

Thus Garman went on in that remarkable letter to Hall, to the length of a dozen pages, a brief apologia pro vita sua written without thought of publication. But subsequently it appeared, with his permission, in the American Journal of Psychology for 1898, in a volume of Studies in Philosophy and Psychology by his former students, and finally in a posthumous volume of his Letters, Lectures and Addresses.

"I have often raised the question," said Garman, "as to whether I would not let down my course and take a little rest and devote myself to publishing" — but he resisted the temptation to the end.

Garman of Amherst

WALTER A. DYER

-->>> ·<<<--

A MAN OF MYSTERY — I think I am not guilty of overstatment when I call Charles Edward Garman just that. He was mysterious to those of us who sat daily in his classroom, listening to his strangely resonant voice, watching his hypnotic eyes. His private life was largely a secret to us. There was something of the mystic about him, something of the prophet and seer.

And since his death in 1907, the years have only served to increase the mystery. The reactionary and the iconoclastic and the envious have questioned his power and a sort of controversy has arisen over him. Was he not overrated by the more impressionable of his students? What is the truth about him, anyway? And so stories have become current about him, some authentic, and some apocryphal, until he has become a sort of legendary figure, almost a myth, in Amherst College tradition.

One of these stories concerns a visit paid to Amherst by William James. One evening, at the home of President Seelye, after Garman and his wife had left, James is said to have settled back in his chair with an air of finality, saying, "That man is the greatest teacher in the United States today."

"The greatest teacher of philosophy?" he was asked.

"No, no," said James, "the greatest teacher."

Garman created no school of philosophic thought, contributed nothing to the literature of philosophy. He left virtually no published record of his work. He rarely spoke in public. His few sermons were conventional. His colleagues never heard him lecture on philosophical subjects. Educators of national repute knew him only by hearsay. He welcomed no visitors to his class-room. No one, except his own students, had any way of knowing what or how he taught, and he discouraged discussion outside of class. His only witnesses, indeed, were immature youths; it is only natural that their testimony, after all these years, should occasionally disagree.

And yet there are few, I believe, who will deny that Garman was the greatest teacher Amherst College ever had, and that he exerted an influence over his pupils that has had few parallels in the modern world. He was a sort of American Erasmus. At the time of his death it was said that "no educational force in his generation was more widely felt and less known to fame."

There is something unexplained and perhaps inexplicable about all that. There was mystery, too, about the living man, with his curious fear of microbes and draughts, his social shyness, his large but frail body, his intellectual and spiritual fire. One of his former students (I think it was the late Rev. Howard A. Bridgman) spoke of "that straight, tall figure clad in ministerial black, and that dark, smooth-shaven face whose lustrous eyes looked straight at men and sometimes straight through them." It almost seemed to the more devoted of his disciples as if the divine spark within him had been fanned to such a heat that, in his later years, it was burning him up. He lived and died, indeed, for a vision, and the ecstasy of it was in those eyes.

Garman's life was remarkable because of its effects, and perhaps because of a certain sense of continuity which it produces, rather than for any dramatic or colorful incidents. It was a life of productive devotion rather than of conflicts. The chronological details may be set forth in briefest outline. The important thing is appraisal and interpretation.

He came of a New England line. His grandfather, Joseph Garman, was a Revolutionary soldier. His father, John Harper

Garman, was a clergyman, born in 1811 in Laconia, New Hampshire, and graduated from Andover Theological Seminary in 1845. After holding several pastorates in Maine, he moved with his family in 1866 to North Orange, Massachusetts, where he preached until about the age of seventy and where he continued to live until his death at the age of ninety-three.

Charles was born December 18, 1850, in Limington, Maine, and grew up in a devoutly religious household. His remarkable knowledge of the Bible and his appreciation of its imagery and phraseology were due largely to this childhood environment. He prepared for college at the high school in Athol, Massachusetts, walking the three miles each way and doing the chores at home, night and morning. He entered Amherst College in 1868 and was graduated with the Class of 1872.

Like many of his fellow students, Garman was obliged to earn a part of his college expenses and he worked much more than he played. He lived, in fact, a somewhat isolated and solitary existence, engaging in no sports and in no social activities. He was a conscientious and industrious student, and during his course took prizes in natural philosophy, chemistry, and anatomy and physiology. But efforts which have been made to picture him as a brilliant scholar have not been very convincing. He was, as a matter of fact, a grind and a memorizer, learning by rote rather than by understanding. His powers of memory, to be sure, were remarkable. "It was a common remark," says one classmate, Professor John Bates Clark, "that if the editions of Hickok's works were totally destroyed, Garman could restore them without change of a word." In the early years of his college course, however, he showed small indication of those powers of ratiocination which later distinguished him. It was not until he began to study the sciences that he found himself intellectually, and not until his senior year, when he studied moral philosophy under Professor Julius Seelye, that he began to show signs of his genius for analysis and independent thinking.

In April, 1873, he accepted a position as principal of the high school in Ware, Massachusetts, and here he discovered his true vocation — teaching. It was a restricted field, but he was extraordinarily successful in it. He broadened the school's teaching in the natural sciences and introduced college preparation. Of the nine girls who made up the freshman class entering Smith College, in 1876, three were fitted by Garman.

In the fall of 1876 he entered the Yale Divinity School, but whether he at that time contemplated the career of a preacher, or whether he took his theological course as a preparation for the teaching of philosophy, is not clear. It is sufficient for present purposes to state that he distinguished himself at Yale as a scholar, a thinker, and a logician, standing head and shoulders, intellectually, above his fellows. His habit of memorizing stood him in good stead here, for he absorbed at this time a vast amount of formal learning, his familiarity with which appeared so astonishing in later years.

At the time of his graduation in 1879 he was awarded the coveted Hooker Fellowship and continued his studies for another year in New Haven. Though his major subject was theology, he was constantly delving into philosophy, and during this year conducted a patient, minute examination of Herbert Spencer's *First Principles*. He was formulating, too, his own system of reasoning, of seeking the ultimate truth through the impartial examination of all data.

Professor Seelye, who had now become President of Amherst College, had long had his eye on this young man, and in 1880 invited him to become Walker Instructor in Mathematics, with the understanding that a professorship in philosophy would follow. During the winter term of that year Garman offered an elective course in philosophy to Seniors, and at the end of the year he was appointed instructor in philosophy. Kant's *Critique of Pure Reason* supplied the material for this first essay in the teaching of philosophy. In 1882 he became Associate Professor and in 1889 Professor of Mental and Moral Philosophy.

In the summer of 1882 Garman married Eliza N. Miner, who had been a teacher with him in the Ware High School. The home they established in Amherst became less of a social center than an extension of Garman's classroom. All through his life he worked and seldom played. And in this work Mrs. Garman was always an invaluable helpmeet.

In a life so completely devoted to the one aim of teaching, there was little room for much else. Garman seldom lectured outside the college, seldom occupied a pulpit. Most remarkable of all, he published no books and left but the scantiest written record of his work. Nevertheless his fame as a teacher spread. He was offered the presidency of three different colleges and, in 1894, the chair of Philosophy at the University of Michigan. All of these offers he refused, feeling that he could best accomplish his purpose in his classroom at Amherst.

In the autumn of 1884 he taught the course in philosophy at Smith College, during a vacancy there, and it is a remarkable fact that in that short time he so impressed his students that at least two of them took up philosophy as a lifework and now fill the chairs of philosophy and psychology in two important women's colleges — Professor Mary Whiton Calkins, at Wellesley, and Professor Anna Cutler, at Smith. In later years Professor Cutler testified to "the torch of inspiration which he handed to us," and "that clear flame of enthusiastic devotion to truth and coherency of thought and statement."

As a boy and young man, Garman had a strong physique and vigorous health. Through his college course and during his years at Ware his endurance seemed equal to any strain which his insatiable passion for work placed upon it. But while in New Haven he became subject to an affection of the throat, and this organ was ever afterward sensitive to infection. Attacks of grippe in 1890 weakened his system and he fell a victim to chronic bronchial trouble. Students of the last decade of his career remember him as a semi-invalid, curiously weak physically and always cold, wearing an overcoat even in warm weather. At the beginning of the year 1907 he was laid low by an attack which proved to be a streptococcus infection of the pharynx. He died on February 9th, in his fifty-seventh year.

So much for the formal facts of Garman's life. In themselves they are not significant. But from that man has gone out a tremendous impulse and stimulus which has made itself felt in no unnoticed degree in many walks of life. To attempt to account for this, to arrive at some sort of evaluation and understanding of the man and his work, is the important thing.

It was my privilege to study under Garman during the college year 1899–1900. Even in those days there were cynics and scoffers, boys who refused to be impressed with Garman's personality, literal-minded students who rejected the magic of Garman's mind. Among them, indeed, were some of the keenest students in the class. There were those frivolous ones, too, who discovered something comic in Garman, in his mannerisms, in his overcoats, in his fear of night air and germs. It has been said that no student could speak lightly or disrespectfully of Garman, but I remember distinctly that he was not neglected by the undergraduate lampoons and that we often spoke of him by the incongruous name of Charlie. But I think I am safe in saying that no teacher I have ever known was held in greater reverence by the majority of the class or exerted a more profound and immediate influence on their processes of thought.

While the remarkable results obtained by Garman in his teaching were doubtless due to his whole-hearted devotion and zeal and to the subtle influence of an unusual personality, it is possible to examine to some extent his method, his materials, and his line of thought. Even in this former students will differ, their recollections being colored by their predilections. For one thing, I believe that too great an emphasis has been placed on the religious content of Garman's teaching. There is no denying that there was this element, but those who remember only that have, I fear, missed the point.

110

The tradition that Garman was primarily a religious teacher, however, is so persistent that the question requires examination. In these modern, free-thinking days there are those who would belittle Garman as a pedant and a dogmatist. Not long ago a student asked me if Garman was much more than an apologist for Christianity. I answered in the affirmative, and yet I was aware of the fact that there were grounds for believing that his course was in a measure a plea for religious faith. Garman was innately religious himself and possessed something of the evangelistic spirit. He could not have kept religion out of his teaching if he had tried. He himself believed implicitly in God and in an essential conception of immortality. Without this he saw no logic, no guiding force in the universe. But he required that belief should be grounded not on dogma but on reason. He was very earnest in his insistence on this. In no sense, however, did he teach a course in theology.

What he taught was far bigger and broader and more fundamental than that. It was not even the exposition of a philosophical theory or doctrine. Garman taught — and this is perhaps the most important thing I have to say about him — he taught primarily a process of thought. He taught a method of thinking things through to their ultimate conclusion after a thorough examination of all available data, conducted along lines of psychological, philosophical, and ethical research. He taught, through philosophy, a system of reasoning applicable to any sort of problem that might arise in scholarship or in life. His classroom was a laboratory of experimental thinking. He taught what has been called a course in tests and evaluations.

Another way of putting it is this: Garman taught a course in logic — not in the formal sense, not the technique of logic, but the practical application of logical methods. In outline his system was simple — the wiping out of preconceived ideas, the search for data, the weighing of evidence, and the groping for a conclusion if such were to be found. It is not the conclusions arrived at that remain in the memory, nor yet the material of the course, but the inductive method of reasoning. That and a peculiar inspiration that must have been largely personal and magnetic.

The materials of Garman's course were broad and varied. In the curriculum it was called Mental and Moral Philosophy. He himself said that he taught psychology, philosophy, and ethics. The students sometimes referred to the course as "Psych," for short, but more often as "Garman," and that was, I think, the best name for it. He considered philosophy a subject to be studied not for its own sake but as a means to an end.

He used textbooks and apparatus in experimental psychology. He assigned for study extracts in pamphlet form from the great philosophers from Aristotle and Plato down to William James, and outlines of famous philosophical controversies. He presented illuminating treatments of such philosophers as Spencer, Berkeley, Hume, and Kant. He had his students read books on economics and on political and social science. In his earlier years he delved into theology and later into sociology. In a single year he seemed to explore the whole realm of human thought and knowledge, so far as the student mind was capable of taking it in. And yet it was not so much the thing studied and learned that counted as the extraordinary use he made of it. He desired original thinking, but far from encouraging facile improvisation, he required thinking to be based on knowledge.

At the risk of becoming tedious, I am inclined to attempt a somewhat more specific outline of Garman's teaching method, for after all, his remarkable success depended in large measure on just that. Former pupils do not entirely agree as to this method, and it is altogether likely that he varied his procedure as time went on. Any memory may be faulty in such a matter, and I can only present my recollection of the one-year course as it was offered to seniors at the beginning of this century.

As I recall it, the fall term was devoted largely to what may be called physiological psychology, based on laboratory experiments and on the works of such writers as James, Carpenter and Royce. We discovered that nine-tenths of life is habit, heredity, brain paths, association of ideas, instinct (inherited habit), etc. This study appeared to prove that practically all thought is a function of a physical and wholly destructible brain. This, it will be noted, is more or less the doctrine of the materialists and mechanists, and also of the modern behaviorists, who have supplemented brain functions with nerve stimuli and the functions of the glands.

These tentative conclusions, it will readily be seen, could scarcely fail to produce an upsetting effect on the preconceived ideas of a boy brought up in a conservative and conventional religious atmosphere. It left his conception of his immortal soul tottering. It is interesting to recall that fundamentalists of that day were much concerned by what they heard of Garman's liberalism, his apparent teaching of agnostic ideas. On more than one occasion he is said to have been the subject of earnest prayer at the Union Theological Seminary. In some quarters he was considered a dangerous and anti-religious man. Nothing could have been farther from the truth.

For Garman did not leave the matter there; he had merely cleared the way for progressive thinking. We had not yet gathered all the evidence. During the winter term there was a further examination of data and the discovery of certain human attributes that could not be traced to any proved functions of the physical brain — the power to reason and to weigh evidence, the will, the power of choice, the creative imagination, the ideals, aesthetic appreciation, the moral and ethical sense, and the deeper sentiments such as loyalty, altruism, kindness, and love in its higher forms. This led us into metaphysics and transcendentalism, and we began to examine the works of the more profound and significant philosophers, like Kant. We discussed Carlyle's blessedness and Spencer's happiness as ends of life. There was, it appeared, a spiritual as well as a physical realm, but what was its nature? Whither were we bound? What guidance had we?

Spring term was largely devoted to a consideration of these questions and an attempt to apply and consolidate such conclusions as seemed to be indicated. We discussed from all angles such difficult subjects as abstract justice and righteousness, that is, conformity with the laws of the universe — divine law, if you will; traditional morality, altruism, and self-determination and self-realization through a recognition of fundamental truths. And these discussions were accompanied by a great wealth of illustration, in my day largely sociological in character.

If anything approaching a final conclusion was reached, it was that the end of living was self-realization, but with the attachment of Garman's famous formula of A and B, which brought up the whole subject of human and divine relationships and responsibilities. It is difficult to give this formula its full significance without the background of the entire course and the subsequent elucidatory discussions of business morality, punishment, charity, and atonement. The following form given to it by Professor James H. Tufts is probably as accurate as any:

It is a general law of all mental life that consciousness of self is possible only through consciousness of objects. A similar law holds in moral life and the social order. We may state this in the formula, A determines himself never directly, but always through B; i.e., a man determines his character and personality by the attitude and relations he assumes toward his world of nature and persons.

In other words, though self-realization is the ultimate end of living, it is conditioned by one's entire environment.

Thus the student was led through a fog of doubt and misunderstanding, through a confusion of theories and ideas, out at last upon a sort of plateau of clear thinking. What he decided about it all at the end mattered less than his acquired ability to think things through, to weigh evidence, to slough off prejudice.

114

Nevertheless Garman was undoubtedly concerned at times by a student's personal attitudes and beliefs. Particularly he did not wish him to be carried away by the materialistic logic of the first term.

In this connection a story is told which is very likely apocryphal, but which illustrates Garman's attitude toward his students and toward the thing he was trying to teach. One of his students whose religious ideas had been much upset by the studies of the fall term found himself unable to return to college. He wrote to Garman, explaining the situation and setting forth in some detail the troubled condition of his mind. Rather than leave the youth with this partial understanding of the course, to fight his mental and spiritual battle alone, Garman is said to have gone to him and to have spent the entire vacation period in an effort to explain the real significance of what he had learned and to straighten him out intellectually. If not precisely true, this anecdote is at least characteristic.

In his classroom Garman made use of books, apparatus, and the lecture system, but his methods were largely Socratic. He was a genius at propounding challenging questions and statements which never failed to arouse immediate objections and disagreements and to promote discussion. Garman could be dogmatic with this end in view. He was capable of making a false statement seem convincing, as a means to an end. This was extraordinarily stimulating; you never felt quite sure whether to accept what was said or not; you had to think. And Garman was forever watchful, forever guiding the class not to definite conclusions but to the extent of insisting on their discovering and weighing all the evidence.

Most memorable of all the materials of the course, perhaps, were the famous pamphlets which Garman prepared and supplied at his own expense, printing many of them himself on a hand press. These were carefully distributed and scrupulously returned; no former pupil possesses any of them, though many have since been found in Garman's house. There was something secret and mysterious about these pamphlets. Some were carefully chosen extracts from the philosophers; some were lecture syllabi; some were in the form of an outline presentation of questions for discussion, framed like problems in geometry. They made possible an introduction to many writers whose complete works it would have been impossible to study in the single year. Often they were fragmentary. They always had the effect of compelling the student to consider their significance, for he could not turn to the next chapter in a book to find the answer. By means of these pamphlets Garman was accustomed to hurl at his class some half truth, or one side of a famous controversy, or a partial statement, to see what the boys would do with it. And guessing and muddling through, they soon discovered, didn't go.

Garman's illustrations were famous and wide in scope. He drew from sociology, economics, business, politics, literature, domestic relations, and law, as well as from religion and philosophy. In making his academic points he dealt with living issues. He displayed a positive genius for apt illustration and example. And the illustrations themselves had a broadly educating effect. A large part of the value of the course was the imparting of general knowledge as well as the stimulation of thinking.

One of Garman's illustrative anecdotes was so characteristic and succinct that some of us learned it verbatim and were accustomed to recite it in unison on frivolous occasions. It was first presented, I believe, in connection with a discussion of the doctrine of the atonement or vicarious punishment. It ran as follows:

"In a shire town in England a man was sentenced for stealing sheep, and the judge said, 'I convict you not for stealing sheep, but that sheep may not be stolen in the future.' Then the culprit arose in open court and said, 'What is that to me?' And sure enough," concluded Garman, leaning over his desk and fixing us with his piercing gaze, "what was it to him?"

It is impossible to describe the impressive manner in which Garman presented his illustrations, or their effectiveness in driving home his point. It was largely in the way he did it. I shall never forget the day he recited Tennyson's *Flower in the Crannied Wall*. It was like listening to the voice of an oracle.

I have said that Garman left no written record of his work, and that is true so far as his intentions were concerned, but in 1911 a memorial volume was prepared and published by Mrs. Garman and a committee of the Class of 1884, in which appear a number of Garman's letters and pamphlets and addresses. To one who knew Garman, there is much in this volume that is vastly illuminating, but to others it must appear fragmentary, confusing, and even incoherent. Valuable as it is, it fails to do justice to the man and his work.

Garman's attitude toward his students was peculiar, as was their reaction to it. To many of them he remained ever remote, even mystical. He was not a mixer in any sense of the term; he was not companionable. And yet he unquestionably felt a deep and anxious interest in each student as an individual. He was working on each individual mind all the time. He was never too busy or tired to talk with one who was perplexed.

In various ways he impressed the intellectual, the religious, the shy, the skeptical, the frivolous. I believe his influence was always greater with the rank and file than with the few intellectuals. He was patient and sympathetic with the diffident, and he was willing to work with the light-minded until he had inculcated in them a sense of responsibility. He contrived to make philosophy a matter of vital importance to the average young man.

He was never fooled by flippant questions propounded by members of the class for the purpose of taking up time and covering unpreparedness. Sometimes he ignored them. Sometimes he reduced them quickly to absurdity. Sometimes he made use of them in a way that sobered and astonished his questioners. On one such occasion he sat silent for a moment, gazing with sorrowful eye at one of the class jokers. Then he said, very quietly,"This is a class in Moral Philosophy, Mr. Jones." The offense was not repeated.

I remember very well the day when one of my classmates, in waggish mood, raised the seemingly irrelevant question whether hat makers set the styles or whether they made hats to conform with the changing demands of fashion. There were other things on the docket for that hour, but Garman laid them all aside and plied this youth with questions about hats and fashions so searching that he was perforce obliged to think. The entire hour was given up to that discussion, and so far as that one young man was concerned, it was the most effective hour Garman ever put in.

In later years philosophers have arisen who have made a great point of liberalism and open-mindedness, and war has been waged on dogma, but I am inclined to think that the seemingly dogmatic Garman was not a step behind them. They have talked much of "questioning the verities," but that is only another expression for "weighing the evidence." They have counseled their students to "accept no dogma without examination, for it may be wrong." Garman, I think, would subscribe to that, but he would go farther and add, "Reject no dogma without examination, for it may be right." There is a world of steadying philosophy in that, if you stop to think of it.

Reading Garman's rescued pamphlets on such subjects as *Pleasure and Righteousness*, *Expediency as a Working Principle*, *Will and Sentiment*, and *The Twentieth Century*, in spite of their lack of continuity, one is impressed with Garman's devotion to that ideal of service which has influenced more Amherst graduates for good, I believe, than any other product of their education. It has become an ineradicable part of the Amherst tradition.

His ideal of the teacher's responsibility and opportunity was lofty and can perhaps best be expressed in his own words, "The moral excellence, the personal loveliness of the pupil is the true crown of glory to a teacher. As well instruct a brute as a child, if the beauty of manhood or womanhood does not unfold, if no ambition, no aspiration after a noble life is awakened, if there are no bright dreams of the future. It has long been known that certain plastic substances brought in contact with mother-of-pearl and allowed time to harden will take on its own variegated splendor. To impress oneself thus on an immortal being — an impression time can never efface — may well excite the envy of angels in Heaven. It is immortality."

I am convinced that Charles E. Garman was, in a curiously quiet and relatively obscure fashion, a truly great man and a genius. He possessed a passion for intellectual truth, combined with a rare talent for communicating a sense of its importance. He possessed dignity with the grace of humor and the salt of speech. He possessed a conception of philosophy as a spiritual force and a conviction that ultimate reality was spiritual. He was, withal, an adept practitioner with young minds. He could awaken and stir them. He was skillful in promoting the belief that a clear and satisfactory conclusion always waits on persist-ent thinking, leaving his students not with an airtight conclu-sion but with a certain conviction that they had acquired a method by which conclusions could always be found. In this, I think, lay the great secret of his teaching.

His aim, he said, was to develop not disciples but apostles.

It would be possible, doubtless, to analyze scientifically Garman's methods of teaching, to reduce them to a working formula, and to arrive at a more accurate appraisal of the work he did, but such analysis would surely fail to explain his extraor-dinary influence in many noteworthy individual cases. It was a matter of personality, and such a personality as his was and must always remain a mystery.

Francis Barton Gummere

⇨ 1855 – 1919 ⇦

To THE PRESENT GENERATION the odd name of Gummere may stand for monumental collections of old English ballads and learned controversies on the remote origins of English poetry without suggesting three decades of notable teaching at little Haverford College.

Descended from a long line of Quakers, the son of Samuel James Gummere, president of Haverford from 1862 to 1874, Francis Barton Gummere took his A.B. there at the age of seventeen, later studied for a year under Francis James Child at Harvard, and received his Ph.D. magna cum laude at Freiburg. "His facility in acquiring foreign languages was phenomenal, and his knowledge of both classical and modern literature was broad and accurate." Here was a man with the degrees, the erudition, and finally the professional reputation which would have made him an ornament on any university faculty. He was offered the headship of the Department of English at the University of Chicago, and an equally important post at Harvard — but he declined them both!

In explaining his decisions, Gummere told John Matthews Manly that "he believed the ideal life of the productive scholar was more nearly attainable in a small college with a well equipped library than in a great university, that he had at Haverford all the books he needed, that his college work was thoroughly familiar to him, and that he had greater leisure for research than he could ever hope for elsewhere." But what a loss Gummere would have been for Haverford! And how rare was his attitude!

This is a point worth dwelling on, for while we deplore the ruthless power of financial monopolies and cartels, we accept as a matter of course the way in which huge universities raid the faculties of small colleges. The universities have the prestige and they have the money and they can offer Professor X a higher salary with a lighter teaching load. But in building up a department at the university, does the president or dean seriously weigh the damage that he is doing to the smaller and poorer institutions which may largely revolve around Professor X? Unfortunately, that damage is scarcely debated — and often the result is a fatal loss to the college and no particular gain to the university.

This is a complicated problem, economic as well as psychological, and cannot be solved merely by asking powerful institutions to treat their smaller brethren more considerately. It also devolves on the small colleges to be less supine, and more generous with their key men in the matter of salary and teaching load. As for Professor X, it may be well for him to recall the case of Francis Barton Gummere before being lured away to another campus.

Quaker Scholar

CHRISTOPHER MORLEY

-»»·«<-

I OFTEN WONDER what inward pangs of laughter or despair he may have felt as he sat behind the old desk in Chase Hall and watched us file in, year after year! Callow, juvenile, ignorant, and cocksure — grotesquely confident of our own manly fulness of worldly *savoir* — an absurd rabble of youths, miserable flintheads indeed for such a steel! We were the most unpromising of all material for the scholar's eye; comfortable, untroubled middle-class lads most of us, to whom study was neither a privilege nor a passion, but only a sober and decent way of growing old enough to enter business.

We did not realize how accurately — and perhaps a trifle grimly — the strong, friendly face behind the desk was searching us and sizing us up. He knew us for what we were — a group of nice boys, too sleek, too cheerfully secure, to show the ambition of the true student. There was among us no specimen of the lean and dogged crusader of learning that kindles the eye of the master; no fanatical Scot, such as rejoices the Oxford or Cambridge don; no liquid-orbed and hawk-faced Hebrew with flushed cheek bones, such as sets the pace in the class-rooms of our large universities. No: We were a hopelessly mediocre, well fed, satisfied, and characteristically Quakerish lot. As far as the battle of learning goes, we were pacifists — conscientious objectors.

It is doubtful whether any really great scholar ever gave the best years of his life to so meagerly equipped a succession of

123

youngsters! I say this candidly, and it is well it should be said, for it makes apparent the true genius of Doctor Gummere's great gift. He turned this following of humble plodders into lovers and zealots of the great regions of English letters. There was something knightly about him — he, the great scholar, who would never stoop to scoff at the humblest of us. It might have been thought that his shining gifts were wasted in a small country college, where not one in fifty of his pupils could follow him into the enchanted lands of the imagination where he was fancy free. But it was not so. One may meet man after man, old pupils of his, who have gone on into the homely drudging rounds of business, the law, journalism — men whose faces will light up with affection and remembrance when Doctor Gummere's name is mentioned. We may have forgotten much of our Chaucer, our Milton, our Ballads — though I am sure we have none of us forgotten the deep and thrilling vivacity of his voice reciting:

> O where hae ye been, Lord Randal, my son?
> O where hae ye been, my handsome young man?
> I hae been to the wild wood; mither, make my bed soon,
> For I'm weary wi' hunting and fain wald lie doun.

But what we learned from him lay in the very charm of his personality. It was a spell that no one in his classroom could escape. It shone from his sparkling eye; it spoke in his irresistible humor; it moved in every line of that well-loved face, in his characteristic gesture of leaning forward and tilting his head a little to one side as he listened, patiently, to whatever juvenile surmises we stammered to express. It was the true learning of which his favorite Sir Philip Sidney said:

"This purifying of wit, this enriching of memory, enabling of judgment, and enlarging of conceit, which commonly we call learning, under what name soever it come forth or to what immediate end soever it be directed, the final end is to lead and draw us to as high a perfection as our degenerate souls, made worse by their clay lodgings, can be capable of."

Indeed, just to listen to him was a purifying of wit, an enriching of memory, an enabling of judgment, an enlarging of imagination. He gave us "so sweet a prospect into the way as will entice any man to enter into it."

He moved among all human contacts with unerring grace. He was never the teacher, always the comrade. It was his way to pretend that we knew far more than we did; so with perfect courtesy and gravity, he would ask our opinion on some matter of which we knew next to nothing; and we knew it was only his exquisiteness of good manners that impelled the habit; and we knew he knew the laughableness of it; yet we adored him for it. He always suited his strength to our weakness; would tell us things almost with an air of apology for seeming to know more than we; pretending that we doubtless had known it all along, but it had just slipped our memory. Marvellously he set us on our secret honor to do justice to this rare courtesy. To fail him in some task he had set became, in our boyish minds, the one thing most abhorrent in dealing with such a man — a discourtesy. He was a man of the rarest and most delicate breeding, the finest and truest gentleman we had known. Had he been nothing else, how much we would have learnt from that alone.

What a range, what a grasp, there was in his glowing, various mind! How open it was on all sides, how it teemed with interests, how different from the scholar of silly traditional belief! We used to believe that he could have taught us history, science, economics, philosophy — almost anything; and so indeed he did. He taught us to go adventuring among masterpieces on our own account, which is the most any teacher can do. Luckiest of all were those who, on one pretext or another, found their way to his fireside of an evening. To set entranced, smoking one of his cigars,[1] to hear him talk of Stevenson, Meredith, or Hardy — (his favorites among the moderns) to marvel anew at the infinite scope and vivacity of his learning — this was to live on the very doorsill of enchantment. Homeward we would go, crunching across the snow to where Barclay crowns the slope with her evening blaze of lights, one glimpse nearer some realization of the magical colors and tissues of the human mind, the rich perplexity and many-sided glamor of life.

It is strange (as one reviews all the memories of that good friend and master) to think that there is now a new generation beginning at Haverford that will never know his spell. There is a heavy debt on his old pupils. He made life so much richer and more interesting for us. Even if we never explored for ourselves the fields of literature toward which he pointed, his radiant individuality remains in our hearts as a true exemplar of what scholarship can mean. Gropingly we turn to little pictures in memory. We see him crossing Cope Field in the green and gold of spring mornings, on his way to class. We see him sitting on the verandah steps of his home on sunny afternoons, full of gay and eager talk on a thousand diverse topics. He little knew, I think, how we hung upon his words. I can think of no more genuine tribute than this: that in my own class — which was a notoriously cynical and scoffish band of young sophisters — when any question of religious doubt or dogma arose for discussion among some midnight group, someone was sure to say, "I wish I knew what Doctor Gummere thought about it!" We felt instinctively that what he thought would have been convincing enough for us.

He was truly a great man. A greater man than we deserved, and there is a heavy burden upon us to justify the life that he gave to our little college. He has passed into the quiet and lovely tradition that surrounds and nourishes that place we all

[1] It was characteristic of him that he usually smoked *Robin Hood*, that admirable five-cent cigar, because the name and the picture of an outlaw on the band, reminded him of the Fourteenth Century ballads he knew by heart.

126

FRANCIS BARTON GUMMERE

love so well. Little by little she grows, drawing strength and beauty from human lives around her, confirming herself in honor and remembrance. The teacher is justified by his scholars. Doctor Gummere might have gone elsewhere, surrounded by a greater and more ambitiously documented band of pupils. He whom we knew as the greatest man we had ever seen, moved little outside the world of learning. He gave himself to us, and we are the custodians of his memory.

Every man who loved our vanished friend must know with what realization of shamed incapacity one lays down the tributary pen. He was so strong, so full of laughter and grace, so truly a man, his long vacation still seems a dream, and we feel that somewhere on the well-beloved campus we shall meet him and feel that friendly hand. In thinking of him I am always reminded of that fine old poem of Sir Henry Wotton, a teacher himself, the provost of Eton, whose life has been so charmingly written by another Haverfordian — (Logan Pearsall Smith).

THE CHARACTER OF A HAPPY LIFE

How happy is he born and taught
　That serveth not another's will;
Whose armour is his honest thought,
　And simple thought his utmost skill!

Whose passions not his masters are;
　Whose soul is still prepared for death
Not tied into the world by care
　Of public fame or private breath;

Who envies none that chance doth raise,
　Nor vice; who never understood
How deepest wounds are given by praise;
　Nor rules of state, but rules of good;

Who hath his life from rumours freed;
　Whose conscience is his strong retreat;

Whose state can neither flatterers feed,
  Nor ruin make oppressors great;

Who God doth late and early pray
  More of His Grace than gifts to lend;
And entertains the harmless day
  With a well-chosen book or friend;

This man is freed from servile bands
  Of hope to rise or fear to fall:
Lord of himself, though not of lands,
  And having nothing, yet hath all.

Such was the Happy Man as Sir Henry Wotton described him. Such, I think, was the life of our friend. I think it must have been a happy life, for he gave so much happiness to others.

Woodrow Wilson

»»» 1856 – 1924 «««

AlthOUGH WOODROW WILSON *was the author of a highly publicized* History of the United States, *it is well to remember that he came to Princeton in 1890 as Professor of Jurisprudence and Political Economy, and his final posts as Governor of New Jersey and President were in direct line with the subjects of his earliest and most important books,* Congressional Government *and* The State. *He was always primarily interested in the problems of power, and, throughout his teaching career, he had the urge to put his ideas into practice.*

In the second volume of Ray Stannard Baker's monumental biography of Woodrow Wilson, there is a lengthy chapter on "The Princeton Professor: 1890–1902" with a section on "Methods as a Teacher — Hold upon Students" which is far more laudatory and far less graphic than the portrait we are about to see. The ever-admiring Baker made up his picture at second hand from a series of enthusiastic quotations whereas Alfred Pearce Dennis was actually there, in Wilson's classroom for four years, and he sees the teacher in the perspective of the later triumphs and final tragedy. However, they both present Wilson as one who spoke ex cathedra, with little interest in questions or comments from his listeners.

Yet there was an undeveloped Socratic side to his nature, if we may judge from a revealing passage in a campaign speech of 1911:"One of the valuable lessons of my life was due to the fact that at a comparatively early age in my experience as a public speaker I had the privilege of speaking at Cooper Union in New York. The audience in Cooper Union is made up of every kind of man and woman, from the poor devil who simply comes in to keep warm up to the man who has come in to take a serious part in the discussion of the evening. I want to tell you this, that in the questions that are asked after the speech is over, the most penetrating questions that I have ever had addressed to me came from some of the men who were the least well-dressed in the audience, came from the plain fellows, came from the fellows whose muscle was daily up against the whole struggle of life. They asked questions which went to the heart of the business and put me on my mettle to answer them. I felt as if those questions came as a voice out of life itself, not a voice out of any school less severe than the severe school of experience. And what I like about this social center idea of the schoolhouse is that there is the place where the ordinary fellow is going to get his innings, going to ask his questions, going to express his opinions, going to convince those who do not realize the vigor of America pulses in the blood of every true American, and that the only place he can find the true American is in this clearinghouse of absolutely democratic opinion."

Many more such experiences might have made Woodrow Wilson more flexible and conciliatory and therefore more effective at his supreme moment in history. There is always the danger that the professor, long isolated among naive or docile adolescents, will acquire a false sense of infallibility, a dogmatic tendency that impairs his usefulness in the outside world. Perhaps every undergraduate teacher should give part of his time to adult education.

Princeton Schoolmaster

ALFRED PEARCE DENNIS

>>>·<<<

LOOKING BACK through the thickening mists of thirty-five years, I see the vivid apparition of Professor Wilson in his Princeton classroom. Dickinson Hall, where he lectured, has been razed these many years to give ground for a splendid new academic building. The material self of Professor Wilson has also fallen, but no splendid successor has risen to occupy his vacant place.

I write of him out of my own vivid memories of his personality and of his teachings. As to his public career and the great transactions in which he bore a part, I can write no better, and probably no worse, than some millions of his contemporaries. I shall stick to what I know of him from personal contacts corresponding to a period of his life about which relatively little has been recorded. The record of his schoolmaster days is to be read in the intangible influence of his teachings upon the minds and hearts of his students.

What I am trying to present is a picturization of a tiny segment of the great sphere of a great man's life. I knew him well during the first four years of his teaching work at Princeton. Not being satisfied with two elective courses under him in my senior year, I returned for three years of postgraduate work, taking every course which Professor Wilson offered during his teaching days at Princeton.

Professor Wilson came to Princeton from Wesleyan University in the autumn of 1890 to fill the chair of jurisprudence and political economy. As a young Titan in the educational world, he made a great stir from the start. His political writings — notably *Congressional Government* and *The State*, the one a masterful dissection of our public-law system, the other a review of the morphology of our own state system and those of Europe — brought him wide public recognition. What was more important to the undergraduates was his fame as a patron of athletics. His title deeds to glory in this respect turned out to be defective. He was never on the personal side a devotee of athletics, and his interest in football, the major Princeton sport, was like the seed which sprang up apace on stony ground but withered quickly for lack of root. In the year preceding Mr. Wilson's avatar, Princeton's star team of veterans had overwhelmed both ancient rivals — Yale and Harvard. In the following season the situation was completely reversed. Most of the crack players had been lost through graduation, and the first and only Princeton team which Professor Wilson coached on the field was a lamentably weak one and was beaten by Yale at the close of the season by the heartbreaking score of 32 to 0. My classmate, Edgar Poe, of the famous Baltimore football family of Poes, captained the team in both years. He says of Professor Wilson's coaching that it was inspiring but not instructive.

But as I say, his fame as a patron of athletics at Wesleyan had preceded him. The tale ran that, smarting under the injustice of a rank decision against Wesleyan in a football game with Amherst, Professor Wilson had rushed on to the field demanding the immediate expulsion of an obviously incompetent referee — indeed, some had it that he cried out, "Kill the referee!" This, of course, is one of those myths that great enthusiasms weave about heroic personalities. It is enough to say that Professor Wilson came to us with the happiest credentials. We expected great things of him, and our hopes were not disappointed when we gathered in Dickinson Hall for the first lecture of his first course.

132

How Mr. Wilson came to consider himself unprepossessing in appearance, I can't imagine. His first appearance made quite the contrary impression on us. At the age of thirty-four, he was a man you would turn twice to look at in a crowd, and he became more distinguished and patrician-looking as he grew older. He knew the arts of pleasing — particularly mass pleasing. I should rather have looked like Wilson than any matinee idol of his generation. His lean spareness of figure conveyed the impression of dominating height as he stood on the lecture platform, an impression which was lost, of course, with later-day accretions of flesh. His prognathous Hapsburg jaw closed after a rounded period with the snap of finality. Every inch of the jaw — and there were three inches of it — was that of fighting man and oracle combined. Those windows of the soul, his luminous eyes, looking out of the body, commanded it, but these same eyes, reflected backward to the seat of intelligence, indeed conveyed the impression of pure intelligence itself. His mind worked as if he secreted thought easily, naturally, unaffectedly, as a cow secretes milk or the liver secretes bile.

His teeth were lamentably bad, ignobly patched and cobbled by sundry artificers in metals. The consummate arts of odontology in later years completely redressed to outward seeming these defects of Nature. His smile thus became more engaging with the years. His black stringy locks, which later became a beautiful silver, revealed his character — hair typical of the man, stark, straight and unsocial, rather than sleek, sinuous and gregarious. He waxed in personal pulchritude with the passing years. He was never so handsome as the day he was driven through the streets of Rome in a landau, seated beside the abbreviated King of Italy. It was the American rather than the Roman who looked the part of Imperial Caesar returning from successful wars.

He dressed, as some erroneously thought, after the fashion of a southern gentleman, appearing before us in a black cutaway coat, low turnover collar with black string tie, looking quite the part of a nonconformist Scotch parson or a meticulous undertaker's assistant officiating at an ambitious shabby-genteel funeral. His spike-tail coat served when he mounted a bicycle as well as on the lecture platform and as his home on Library Place was a goodish mile from his lecture room and he found a time conservator in his bicycle, which he bestrode with the stately dignity of the King of Siam making stately progress on the back of the royal white elephant. The low collar disclosed beneath an Adam's apple, which oscillated as he talked, a wisp of nethermost beard which through its strategic defensive situation remained unscathed by the ravages of an inimical razor.

Professor Wilson habitually stood during his lectures. Speaking from a mere skeleton of notes, he hammered in his teachings with an up-and-down, full-armed gesture. Thus he was a perpendicular lecturer, his talking nose and his oscillating Adam's apple moving up and down with speech, along with his pump-handle gestures. He gestured as if operating the handle of a spray pump. He was there to spray students with a shower of knowledge, his superior mind acting downward upon the mass — a Scotch Covenanter bent upon describing how man acts politically, hammering information into reluctant minds. He was essentially the lecturer rather than the teacher, nor were his lectures as helpful as the books, such as Bagehot and Dicey, from which his own inspirations were drawn. Having sprayed his audience, Professor Wilson little recked whether inoculations of knowledge took or not. In those days not a few indolent, good-natured students attended lectures as a matter of condescending concession to certain disagreeable academic formalities.

These lollers out front conveyed the tacit challenge: "Here we are. Teach us something if you can!" Unimpressionable Arctic puffin birds of the classroom! But as far as Professor Wilson was concerned, the loafers could either take it or leave it. He gaged his discourse to the requirements of the serious-

134

minded, taking no pains to conceal his contempt for inferior minds. Unlike the great Apostle who suffered fools gladly, Professor Wilson suffered them not at all.

Professor Wilson could not bear to be crossed and his dignity was quick to resent restlessness, inattention, or the least sign of disorder in his classroom. He conducted his classes with an air of imperiousness, suggesting the grand manner just as his writings carry the suggestion of the grand style. He clearly imitated Burke — a master in the use of the grand style. A whispered conversation in the back benches would instantly stiffen him into the grim, magisterial defender of his own dignity. His stock rebuke, uttered with Olympian superiority, was: "Gentlemen, try to remember that you are supposed to be gentlemen."

Professor Wilson's touchiness, his quick irritation over trifles, may be laid, I think, in some measure to the fact that he was unused to opposition at home. Mrs. Wilson was put into this world, it would seem, to make it an easy place to live in for those she loved. His three daughters also lived to please and to ease. Professor Wilson, habituated at home to ease, to softness, to amiable compliances, never got to understand how people can be rude, thoughtless, uncomprehending, non-co-operative. If he had been blessed with a headstrong if not troublesome son, he would have better known how to be patient under the irritations of jarring, difficult, cantankerous souls.

In his younger and obscure days, I am wondering if he ever consciously put before himself an exalted self which he intended to realize. He could say, "These are my books, this is my typewriter, this is my gifted brain — what are these things for?" And he could answer, "They are for me — for my help, my convenience, my security, my livelihood." But did he ever ask himself, "These things being for me, what am I for?" What was his *summum bonum*? Fame? Glory? Yes, he intensely craved honor, esteem, fame. These things he set about to attain, hitching together a powerful thinking machine with habits

135

of invincible industry. He was as industrious as Mr. Hoover, without possessing Mr. Hoover's genius for the concrete. He was as zealous in answering the great call as Peter the Hermit or Paul the Apostle, but they sought after an incorruptible crown.

He cared little for the affection or companionship of men. He never could have been a clubman or risen to phantom dignity as a Serene Potentate in a fraternal lodge. In the classroom he was theorist rather than idealist. He had no concrete plan to make for augmenting human happiness — indeed, he ignored the element of individual happiness — but he had principles to apply, and these principles, though agreeable to the auditory nerve, were on analysis difficult of practical application. Later the world came to know of him through the enunciation of felicitous phrases which were flattering to the human heart but contradictory to the human understanding: "Making the world safe for democracy"; "Open covenants openly arrived at"; "The heart of the world is awake and the heart of the world needs to be satisfied"; "Self-determination" for the divers swarming peoples that dwell upon the surface of this planet.

Professor Wilson could always find in convenient doctrines a refuge from inconvenient facts. He had a striking talent, too, for definitions which inadequately defined a subject by over-defining it. He stated on one occasion that his father had taught him the value of definitions. Here is how he defined the properties of political sovereignty: 1. Habit of obedience; 2. Sentiment of loyalty; 3. Reverence; 4. Sense of duty; 5. Fear or awe; 6. Race or national feeling. One might, of course, add a half-dozen more attributes, just as one might analyze Lincoln's Gettysburg Address by breaking it down into its attributes: 1. Simplicity; 2. Sincerity; 3. Earnestness; 4. Tenderness; 5. Clarity; 6. Restraint; 7. Propriety; 8. Precision; 9. Purity; 10. Solemnity; etc., but after all the attributes have been catalogued, the best estimate of the qualities of the address is the thing itself. He defines the Federal State as composed of "self-originated, self-constituted, self-competent, self-sustaining, veritable communities." Almost any intelligent man with a feeling for the concrete would find something lacking in this definition. The concept of sovereignty, by the way, was one of his pet topics of discussion. He would comment by the hour upon the conflicting notions of such publicists as John Austin and Sir Henry Maine and delighted to follow Dicey in the contrast he draws between the American types of nonsovereign law-making bodies and the legislative omnipotence of the British Parliament. So far so good; it was delightful; but the moment he began to turn aside to his own abstractions, as for example to the discovery of the locus of sovereignty in the United States, he would wind up with the academic conclusion that the locus of sovereign power in our governmental system is to be found in a duly organized, constitutional convention clothed with power to modify our existing organic law. The plain man with a feeling for the concrete would not have to go so far as a hypothetical constitutional convention. He would find the locus of sovereignty in the policemen's club, the tax collector's bill, the sheriff's writ. The practical man sees sovereignty diffused through a multitude of local, state, and federal organs of authority, with supreme power ultimately lodged in the living, breathing millions of persons who compose the citizenry of this Republic.

Professor Wilson was wont to insist that sovereignty was not susceptible of limitation. That is the judicial view. Blackstone undoubtedly would agree, but Blackstone was concerned with the letter, with the written word. *Littera scripta manet.* But the letter killeth. If you go by the written word, you have an entirely false idea of both the British Constitution and our own. Of course, to the practical man sovereignty is susceptible of limitation, if by nothing else by the community's habit of obedience, by revolution, by assassination. Walter Bagehot more than any other master was Professor Wilson's guide and pattern. The Wilsonian style as well as its content of doctrine

137

was formed by Bagehot, Burke, Maine, Dicey, but Bagehot is king of them all. Bagehot too was given to definition, though his definitions are not a string of attributes but epigrams as sound as they are colorful and clever. For example, Bagehot defines a constitutional statesman as a "man of common opinions and uncommon abilities." He distinguishes between a civilized man and a savage by pointing out that a savage is unable to postpone the present to the future. He describes the emptiness of the voluptuary's life as misery striving to be gay and gaiety feeling itself to be miserable. If for nothing else, I have to be thankful to Professor Wilson for introducing me to Bagehot and Burke, but particularly to Bagehot whose style and savor so got hold of me that to this day I risk unconscious plagiarism of Bagehot in everything I attempt to write.

Professor Wilson, like other scholars with a taste for history, was strong on the genetics of the state. He would theorize both backward and forward, taking us backward to the uttermost limbo of the known facts of human group life on this planet and beyond that into the fields of pure speculation or, again, on an ascending scale, he would carry his speculations about the state into the rarefied air of German metaphysics. He recoiled before the concrete. As far as I can recall, he made no mention in his course—Administration—of the Interstate Commerce Commission. For some years the writer has been a member of one of the federal administrative boards—the United States Tariff Commission—but Professor Wilson's course in Administration did not supply what the scientific man would call a chemical trace of practical preparation for his daily task as a petty government administrator. That might not have been Professor Wilson's fault, since a lecturer may give a dull student information without giving him understanding. So one might say that he had never been able to make the smallest practical use of higher mathematics studied in college. We received, however, from Professor Wilson things that are more valuable than practical profit. He had an affection for certain words, and one of his blessed and overworked words was "fountain." He himself was a fountain—a fountain of inspiration. The best thing which many of us received from Princeton was not information but inspiration.

So it was that Professor Wilson opened the doors of an ampler life to us. As for what he actually taught, it was the inspiration of his personality rather than what he actually taught that caused our hearts to burn within us while he talked with us by the way. His was precisely the type of scholarship which would have won me to the man. Forty years ago this country was swept by a craze for the German type of dry-as-dust scholarship. It was about the time that kiln-dried historical students were toppling Macaulay from his pedestal and enthroning the dreary and meticulous Stubbs in his stead. Let us be thankful that, according to the precepts of the day, Professor Wilson did not undertake an analysis of the functions of the Carlovingian Mayors of the Palace or delve into the genealogies of the Hittite kings.

An anatomist seeking to know the secrets of the human body dissects a cadaver with the breath barely out of its body; he is not asking to work with fossil bones unearthed in the Gobi Desert. *Non omnia possumus omnes.* We can't all be Leonardo da Vincis. Plodding scholars we must have, just as there must be cart horses as well as race horses. The most scholarly student I knew in Princeton was a man of the plodding type who led our class consistently for four years. His studies in English literature led him back to the old texts of Bede and Caedmon, and these in turn to the parent Germanic languages, and these again into the far hinterlands of Sanskrit and whatever might lie beyond. A revered scholar who could parse in Icelandic and pun in Coptic, for all I know. He came as near as any living man to settling the vexed question, raised in the Vedas, as to whether the implements used in braying shoots of the haoma in the pre-Indian ethnic period were press stones such as mortar and pestle or a press of the type described by Apastamba, representing a crude form of revolving millstones.

> He settled Hoti's business — let it be! —
> Properly based Oun —
> Gave us the doctrine of the enclitic De,
> Dead from the waist down.

The subject of his doctor's thesis was The Gruhasangraha — Parisishta of Gobilaputra. Such scholarship does great honor to a man, but it is not for the multitude.

The powerful mind of Professor Wilson transmuted baser elements into golden inspirations, and made his culture accessible to the multitude above whom he towered. There is nothing ignoble in knowledge, even though it be useless. Art is long and time is fleeting, with most of us under the necessity of sweating for our daily bread and butter. Culture is a long job.

Professor Wilson was not born to be a Gradgrind scholar; he was essentially a man of humane letters, and that was the self that he consciously set before himself to be realized. He spoke to be heard; he wrote to be read. He schooled himself in the arts of persuasion. His scholarly passion was not horizontal, pushing to the far periphery of the known in seeking to lift the veil which divides it from the infinite spaces of the unknown. His passion was vertical; he would tread the dominating heights. This passion for dominion goaded him to the end — hastened the end.

"You may write a chronicle," he tells us, "but you will not serve yourself thereby. You will only serve some fellow who will come after you, possessing what you did not have — an ear for the words you could not hit upon; an eye for the colors you could not see; a hand for the strokes you missed."

Let the pedant retailers of dullness attend to the coral-insect business, each man furnishing his mite to the great reef of human knowledge. Dull boys who know everything about literature except how to write it or how to enjoy it. Professor Wilson taught himself the artistry of writing. The cultivation of the language one speaks is the most important factor, I take it, in a liberal education.

Professor Wilson's genius for the spoken and written word was a genius that consisted in infinite capacity for taking pains. He labored for a distinguished literary style as a man labors to become an opera singer. That he might become a lord of language, he served, he slaved, he obeyed. Becoming an artist in the use of words, the more artistry he put into his craft, the more individual his style. His writings and public addresses are full of character. They grew more Wilsonian with the years. The more imitative and conventional the mental processes are, the more a man is of the sheep type. See one sheep and you see them all; know one savage and you know all savages. A Rembrandt or a Botticelli doesn't have to sign his pictures. The artist has his own mode. He is *sui generis*. In setting out to cultivate the graces of literary style, Professor Wilson chose the language of the quaint prose writers of the Seventeenth Century, — the language of John Bunyan and the King James version of the Scriptures. Speaking of Charles Lamb's literary style, Professor Wilson depicts his own. He has Lamb "taking care to perfume every sentence, if possible, with the fine savor of an old phrase." He was sparing with polysyllables and did not employ a word of Greek or Latin lineage if he could lay hold of a pure English synonym for it. His literary training is English, just as his training in jurisprudence is English. He rarely made a direct quotation, labeling it as such, but he continually used the language and pet ideas of admired authors. Like Burke, whom he intensely admired, he took his materials wherever he found them, transmuting grosser into finer elements. Professor Wilson's gift of expression in the formative period of his educational work was of the art that conceals art. He

141

came to possess words; later words came to possess him. Having mastered ideas, ideas came to master him.

Mimi says of Rodolphe, "I came to love him because he taught me how to feel." We came to admire Professor Wilson because he taught us how to feel the beauty and power of words. He had a knack of selecting plain, simple English words and tricking them out with an unwonted significance. His addiction to the word "quick" arrests the attention, because he employs "quick" not in its colloquial connotation of "swift" but in the old Biblical sense of the "quick" as opposed to the "dead." He describes a speech as "quick" with eloquence. Or an honor bestowed as "quick" with responsibility. Similarly he wrests "handsome" — another pet word — from its accepted significance and thus employs it: "When peace is as handsome as war, there will be no more war." But is war ever handsome? one may ask. "Process" is another proprietary word he used as if he had a patent on the peculiar significance or multiform significances which he attaches to this blessed vocable. He speaks of giving his whole mind and energy "to every process of difficult counsel." He contrasts "the hard processes of law with the more helpful processes of counsel." "Common counsel," he tells us, "is not jumbled counsel; nor is common counsel aggregate counsel." What then, one asks, is common counsel? Certain other honorific words are "polity," "heart," "vision."

All good words and true, but all twisted and turned until their accepted, clean-cut meaning becomes blurred and nebulous. "Now the heart of the world is awake, and the heart of the world must be satisfied." "America took its origins in visions of the human spirit." And so, according to the Lamb formula, taking care to perfume every sentence, if possible, with the fine savor of an old phrase, he went through life "at pains to do" something, or "fain to believe" something, or in need "to be quit" of something, or he sets somebody down at just "turned of twenty," or "giving leave" to a thought of which nothing else "is of the kin."

Billiard players understand the meaning of putting a reverse English on English. Similarly, Professor Wilson rode certain concepts, and these concepts rode him. Take such a concept as virtue of Nature. The stoic Brutus cries, "Alas, virtue, I have found thee only an empty name!" We personify such a concept as Nature, speaking of "Nature's largess," "Nature's injustice," "Nature's designs." The mind of Professor Wilson, infatuated with certain concepts, clothed them with talismanic virtues. Let one illustration suffice.

He talked endlessly of democracy, as one would talk of honesty or virtue in the abstract. Now democracy in the abstract, provided it has no partisan significance, is always a safe and popular principle to uphold. "All God's chillun got wings," and under the divine scepter all are commoners and all are equal. The practical vote-getter proceeds on the theory that the common people greatly outnumber the uncommon people, and he will no more go wrong defending the common people than he will go wrong defending the under dog or the Ten Commandments. From the social angle, Mr. Wilson was never a democrat at all. By birth, training, environment, personal preference, he was an aristocrat. He was of Scotch Covenanter lineage, and was prone, in his combative moods, to proclaim that he was of fighting stock. The whole strength of the position of warriors in human history finds its correlative in the timidity and credulousness of subservient masses. Some of us came to know that the price of Professor Wilson's friendship was subservience. To mix with underbred, sweaty, garlic-smelling inferiors was always unpleasant to him. The laborers about the university grounds instinctively disliked him. They resented, if they had been able to put their resentment in words, his superior bearing. But of democracy in the abstract Professor Wilson could not have enough.

143

Professor Wilson employs "democracy" as a word to conjure with. As Moses lifted up the serpent in the wilderness, so the standard of democracy was lifted up in every crisis as a talismanic symbol of salvation.

Yes, democracy was something to be cried up in every campaign. He waged his fight on the social clubs at Princeton in the name of democracy. It was a losing fight. Much could be said against the club system — the waste of time, the cliques, the expense. Making democracy the issue, his fight was foredoomed to failure. Except in a prison house, men can not be put on exact equality by fiat. You can't make a man fraternize with another man against his liking any more than you can make water run up-hill. The tiniest village has its social cliques. Then, too, there was no great call in Princeton for a return to democracy. You can't repossess yourself of something you already have.

Later Professor Wilson raised the standard of democracy in his fight on Professor West's project of a graduate school physically detached from the old Princeton campus. Graduate students are supposed to be scholars. The best scholarly work is done in quiet places. Graduate students are supposed to get down to the serious business of life, having satisfied their herd instincts in cheering and singing, frittering and dilettanting for four years as undergraduates. Pascal tells us that most of the troubles of life are caused by man's inability to sit still in a room, and certainly the great scientific achievements of the age have been the work of men who have been content to sit still in a laboratory and there challenge the secrets of the universe.

I quote from an address of Professor Wilson to the Pittsburgh alumni during the fight over the location of the graduate school:

"Will America tolerate the seclusion of graduate students? Will American tolerate the idea of having graduate students set apart? America will tolerate nothing except unpatronized endeavor. Seclude a man, separate him from the rough and tumble of college life, from all the contacts of every sort and condition of men, and you have done a thing which America will brand with its contemptuous disapproval."

Any one of twenty criticisms might have been made against Professor West's graduate school program. Professor Wilson chose to fight the project on the democratic issue.

Years after, Professor Wilson, as President of the United States, delivering a memorial address at the door of the lowly backwoods cabin where Abraham Lincoln was born, had this to say:

"How eloquent this little house. Within this shrine is of the vigor of democracy. There is nowhere in the land any home so remote, so humble, that it may not contain the power of mind and conscience to which nations yield and history submits to processes. Genius is no snob; it affects humble company as well as great; it serenely chooses its comrade. This little hut was the cradle of one of the great sons of men who presently emerged upon the great stage, himself the center of the great plot. It demonstrates the vigor of democracy. Such are the authentic proofs of the validity and vitality of democracy. Here no less hides the mystery of democracy. Who shall guess this secret of nature and providence and a free polity?"

Do we account for the great-souled Lincoln in these mystic phrases about democracy? What was the relation of causality between Lincoln's genius and democracy? Possibly Lincoln might have been a mute, inglorious, Milton but for the opportunities afforded by democracy. Certainly a man stands a better chance of making something of himself when born into the wide opportunities of America than into the narrow opportunities of China; yet democracy has little to do with the manifestations of human genius in the world. The great efflorescence of many-sided geniuses of the Italian Renaissance corresponded precisely with the age of despots in Italian history. Michael Angelo owed nothing to democracy but much to the patronage of the Papal Court. What is the connection

145

between Mussolini's powerful personality and democracy? Long before democracy was recognized as a workable theory of government for great nations, obscure and lowly men came to sit in the chair of Saint Peter, the highest position to which the sons of men might aspire. Jesus of Nazareth, the humble provincial, founder of a despised sect of an outcast race, was born in a stable.

Professor Wilson possessed a positive genius for covering an entire plexus of ideas with some suavely elegant moral doctrine. He believed in democracy in much the way the Russian leaders of today subscribe to the doctrines of Communism. We render lip service to some beautiful doctrine of non-resistance, but it's something to declaim by and not something to live by. Men with a gift of eloquence, speaking down to the masses from a platform, are under a constant temptation to tell the audience what the orator thinks it would like to hear rather than attempt to lift the audience to the level of his own sincerities. It is hard not to take shortcuts to appreciation, such as palpable hits, unqualified generalizations, crudifications rather than clarifications of the issue. When all else fails to stir a popular audience, let the band strike up *Dixie*.

Students are not the best judges or the most lenient critics of the young professor during the trying years he is organizing his material. After taking three courses under Professor Wilson, my interest began to wane. Even professors themselves tire of their own repetitions, and their task would become intolerable if they were not inspired by the eager interest of new classes, to whom the old story is a fresh revelation. And so it was that, after four years of Professor Wilson's lectures, I came to tire of definitions and repetitions, unrealities. One began to question his infallibility—particularly his judicial instinct. His temper was easily irritated by dissent, nor could he brook any rival in his field. Professor William M. Sloane, head of the history department, lectured to crowded classrooms. A latent antagonism developed between the two men, with bad feeling displayed on both sides in later years.

I had taken all of Professor Sloane's courses and had been awarded, on his recommendation, fellowships for two succeeding years. In the winter of 1893, Professor Sloane was granted leave of absence and sailed for Europe. He commissioned me to examine papers submitted in competition for two history prizes to be awarded the following commencement. In making the awards, I found difficulties in choice as between two papers of somewhat equal merit. I applied to Professor Wilson for help. He graciously received me in his home on Library Place, one May afternoon, and made no difficulty about complying with my request. Warmly suffused with pleasure over my charming reception, I made my adieus and had reached the front door when Professor Wilson called me sharply back; his voice was cold and incisive:

"I see these papers are submitted in competition for the Class of 1876 history prize. Why did you not tell me that you were asking me to do Sloane's work for him?"

"I was asking a favor myself and not for Professor Sloane, who knows nothing about it," I replied.

With his square jaw set high, he brushed aside the explanation.

"Professor Sloane is enjoying himself in Europe; I am swamped with work here. I am something of a logician — either Professor Sloane should remain at home and attend to his own business or else leave someone instead capable of doing so."

I started to speak and, indeed, did form sentences, but my words were as ineffectual as the buzz of a gnat above the roar of Niagara. Without another word, he handed me the two offending papers and dismissed me by turning to his typing machine.

Try as I might, I could never get back into his good graces.

147

I had done an unpardonable thing. Attempts to soften his heart had about the same effect as a lighted parlor match on the polar ice cap.

As Cibber is reported to have remarked of the great Doctor Johnson: "There is no use arguing with him, for when his pistol misses fire, he knocks you down with the butt of it."

In the case of Professor Wilson, the man who disagreed with him was often not worth taking a pistol to; instead he consigned you to an oubliette.

When Doctor Patton unexpectedly resigned the presidency of Princeton, he suggested Professor Wilson to the trustees as his successor. In his brilliant inaugural address, the new president had much to say about Princeton, past, present, and future, but not a word about his predecessor, Doctor Patton.

Later, when Doctor Patton was made president of Princeton Theological Seminary, President Wilson was asked to deliver an address. It was a finished effort in every respect except that it made no reference directly or indirectly to Doctor Patton. It was clear that Professor Wilson did not approve of Doctor Patton.

Early disciples, such as myself, followed Professor Wilson's rise to fame with pride and exultation, but of necessity we followed him afar off. What seemed at first but a frail and impalpable barrier — his displeasure over some small matter — really proved to be a wall of adamant against which one might beat one's life in vain.

> "We that had loved him so, followed him, honored him,
>   Lived in his mild and magnificent eye,
>   Learned his great language, caught his clear accents,
>   Made him our pattern to live and to die!"

Of all the duties, rights, proprieties and obligations of life, Professor Wilson had his unalterable code. He interpreted non-conformity as a species of treason. The essence of treason is giving aid and comfort to the enemy. His brain rather than his heart governed him in estimates of human conduct.

Deficient in sympathy himself, he was hurt and worn down in the end by the inevitable misunderstandings, frustrations and unfairness of minds that possessed the same unyielding, non-co-operative qualities as his own.

If he had possessed the heart of a Lincoln, history, with clear and luminous eyes, might have seen in him another Lincoln; but his speech proceeded from the head rather than the heart.

Will the suave and measured cadences of any speech of Mr. Wilson live with Lincoln's Gettysburg speech? Will any polished letter of Mr. Wilson survive Lincoln's note to Mrs. Bixby?

Here is the Lincoln letter written from the heart to Mrs. Bixby some sixty-six years ago:

(November 21, 1864)

"Dear Madam:

"I have been shown in the files of the War Department a statement of the Adjutant-General of Massachusetts that you are the mother of five sons who have died gloriously on the field of battle. I feel how weak and fruitless must be any word of mine which should attempt to beguile you from the grief of a loss so overwhelming. But I cannot refrain from tendering to you the consolation that may be found in the thanks of the republic they died to save. I pray that our Heavenly Father may assuage the anguish of your bereavement, and leave you only the cherished memory of the loved and lost, and the solemn pride that must be yours to have laid so costly a sacrifice upon the altar of freedom.

"Yours very sincerely and respectfully,
"Abraham Lincoln."

If President Wilson had been moved under similar circumstances to write to Mrs. Bixby, it is not improbable that the letter would have read somewhat as follows:

149

"Dear Madam:

"I have learned through the duly constituted military authorities that your five noble-hearted sons have given their lives to America. May I not embrace this opportunity to observe that America took its origins in visions of free and common counsel? Your valiant sons died to hold the counsels of America together. If I did not believe that, I would not believe that people are fit to govern themselves. If I know the temper of America to-day, — and I am fain to believe that I do know America's temper — America is quick with the purposes and processes of democracy. Your sons, if I do not mistake the breed, are of the stuff of that noble fighting stock who would be quit of tyranny and who with united counsel set up this government of America. Valor is no snob. It affects humble company as well as great. It serenely chooses its comrades. And here, if I see clear, lies the authentic proofs of the vigor and validity of democracy. Here no less lies the mystery of democracy. Who shall guess this secret of nature and providence and a free polity? It is our lofty privilege and our solemn duty to consecrate ourselves afresh to these high objects for which your sons nobly fought and died.

"Cordially yours,
"Woodrow Wilson."

After leaving Princeton, a great interval of time and space lay between the writer and President Wilson. Years later, he burst dazzlingly upon us in Italy, as the apparition of a superman. I was serving in the American Embassy in Rome as commercial attaché.

President Wilson's welcome surpassed in fervor and magnitude anything that might be imagined. Imperial Caesar returning in triumph from the wars never received a more delirious acclaim by Roman citizens. To the Italians, he was more than a personality — he was a symbol of deliverance.

Poverty-stricken and oppressed human beings viewed him through the haze of faith, yearning, ignorance. The old Italian characters of emancipation were palimpsests scrawled over with defeated hopes and unfulfilled desires. President Wilson, the savior, was a blank scroll upon which every man inscribed his dreams and his aspirations.

George Creel, able advertiser, had distributed poster pictures of the American President by the million. Candles burned in humble huts before the paper likeness of the American President, and simple-minded peasants knelt before these simulacra of the Great Deliverer, half in admiration, half in interrogation.

Then came the swift reverse! The hopes of the Italians were dashed in pieces; the nation was frustrated and confounded by a single will. President Wilson awarded the Adriatic port of Fiume, claimed by the Italians, to the Jugo-Slavs. Orlando returned from Paris as a protest against the Wilson verdict.

The tide of anger and bitterness rose to such a point that it became necessary for the American Embassy in Rome to be protected from mob violence by a platoon of Italian soldiers.

During the customary recriminations with an Italian hack driver over the amount of his tip, Italian words were spoken which can bear no repetition here. But the crowning imprecation and ultimate insult lay in the phrase:

"Sei figlio di Veelson!" Thou art a son of Wilson!

Yes, I was a son of Wilson, and proud of it. Wilson had helped to form me back in those university days in Princeton. In that narrow life of a small world, he had been an inspiring influence. Now, in the great life of the huge world, he had become a mighty influence. He who had taught the principles of political sovereignty in the fetid atmosphere of a Dickinson Hall classroom had now become sovereign lawgiver in his own right for the world.

Some years later, for the last time, I was brought within physical nearness to my old Princeton professor. Mr. Hoover had called me back to Washington to serve him, and I was living within a few blocks of Mr. Wilson's home on S Street. For days he lay dying, with weeping men and women on their knees, silently praying, in the hushed street.

"Alas, alas," cried the dying pagan warrior, "what is this thing stronger than the strength of kings that pulls down the mightiest of warriors!"

Is there a further chapter in the amazing career of the man? What lies behind the mysterious veil that shrouds the state of the dead from that of the living? What of permanency in this shadowy world stretching out into thousands of years will survive his transient earthly endeavors? What will ultimately be salvaged from the wreck that is the doom of all human deeds? One wonders.

"There are no fields of amaranth on this side of the grave; there are no voices, O Rhodope, that are not soon mute, however tuneful; there is no name, with whatever emphasis of passionate love repeated, of which the echo is not faint at last. . . ."

Simon Nelson Patten

≫ 1852 – 1922 ≪

FOR TWENTY-NINE YEARS at the University of Pennsylvania a gnarled, ungainly, Lincolnesque man from Illinois taught what Carlyle called "the dismal science" and made economics the most living subject on the campus. Although Simon Nelson Patten was the father if not the founder of the pioneer Wharton School of Commerce and Finance and the author of numerous books and articles in economics and social philosophy, he was above all a teacher who sent out from his classroom scores of vigorous and hopeful students who were proud to be known as "Patten men."

His long and continuous thesis was that we had passed from a pain (deficit) economy to a pleasure (surplus) economy, or rather, as he later contended, into a "creative economy," where the main problem is one of consumption. In contrast to William Graham Sumner who also branched out from economics into wider and wider social fields, Patten did not write essays on "The Absurd Attempt to Make the World Over," but saw the world as a place to be made over steadily and surely.

After a spotty education in the Middle West, Patten felt the lure of German scholarship with so many other young Americans and went to Halle in 1873, receiving his Ph.D. degree there three years later. Then for a full decade he seemed to mark time, plowing, studying law for a few months, teaching school; but he managed to complete The Premises of Political Economy which was "a correction of the work of John Stuart Mill in the light of American conditions." It was through that little book that he was made a professor at the University of Pennsylvania—his first and last position beginning at the ripe age of thirty-six.

153

Perhaps it was that decade of patient waiting, of lonely maturing, that helped to give him a depth rarely achieved by those who pass immediately from graduate study to college or university teaching.

When Patten reached the age for retirement in 1917, the United States was at war and his pacifism was hardly an inducement for the University to keep him on. He left the campus embittered, but active and eager. His final work was a touchingly awkward and groping college novel centered around a Professor of Greek, his untramelled pagan daughter and his favorite student. Mud Hollow: From Dust to Soul has little to recommend it as a novel but it heaps together much of its author's unsystematic learning and most of his dreams. One passage in particular is more than fiction: "Few realize how ardent is the attachment between gray-haired teachers and their promising pupils. The old feel their failures and wish to cast them on younger shoulders. To the young the confidence of their seniors is an inspiration which transforms vague dreams into pleasing realities."

Educational Frontiers, a Book about Simon Nelson Patten and Other Teachers by Scott Nearing, has on its title page a sentence from Patten: "The place of the teacher is on the firing line of civilization." Scott Nearing has never left that firing line.

A Prince Among Paupers

SCOTT NEARING

→»·««←

U P TO THE TIME when I entered the University of Pennsylvania, I had had but one teacher who used his mind easily. Most of them taught without thinking, quite as a matter of course, and those who did think were generally so clumsy that their heavy, jolting intellectual processes sent echoes through the classroom.

My first year in college was far from stimulating. The teachers were, on the whole, much less able than those in high school. One instructor, in a tinny voice that came from the top of his throat, read endlessly from notes that he had used in preparing the textbook that was supposed to be in the hands of every member of the class. Another, when interrupted by a question, looked about with the terror that one sees in a wild rabbit who has heard a twig snap in the thicket. The economics instructor was a type.

The class was using Seager's *Introduction to Economics* as a text. The book is simply written, and well divided into chapters and sections. The instructor was in the habit of reading the chapter assigned for the day, making notes on it, and then reading the notes in class.

"Gentlemen," he would begin, "with regard to the question of value, I wish to call your attention . . ."

There would follow, in his own words, a repetition of the points brought out in the text. As a rule the text was clearer than the explanation, and in any case, many of the students had read the chapter in advance, and were therefore in a position to anticipate everything that the instructor was saying. This experience was repeated, monotonously, day after day.

Occasionally, there was a diversion. "Professor," one of the students would ask, "what is marginal utility?"

Instead of replying to the question, the instructor would go through his notes, find Seager's definition of marginal utility, read it to the class, and then repeat it "in other words."

At another time the instructor was unable to find the required definition, so he said: "We will come to that a little later on." Then he continued to read his commentaries on Seager.

"Doctor," someone would insist, (the man was neither "doctor" nor "professor" and all of the students knew it), "I do not get that last point."

Whereupon the instructor would read the passage in his notes over again, pausing here and there for emphasis. He tried. He meant well. As the students put it: "He may know his subject all right, but he can't tell what he knows."

That was literally true. The man was a careful student of economics, with some teaching experience. If he had been asked to write answers to ten questions on economic theory, he could have spent six or eight hours to very good purpose, but his knowledge was so poorly organized that it was not readily available. It was like drygoods laid away in a storeroom instead of out on the counter. By the time the goods were located, the customer had grown tired and gone away.

Furthermore, and this was by far the most serious of his misfortunes, he did not trust himself to use the facts and theories that he knew. Textbooks and notes were the two intellectual crutches on which this word-bound pedant shuffled along the academic highroad.

One or two of the first year instructors knew their subject-matter thoroughly, and had it so effectively pigeonholed that they could turn to it without a moment of hesitation. One, in particular, a professor of English, had his facts at his finger-

156

tips, but they were so numerous, and they came tumbling, one after another, in such a literary avalanche, that he never had an opportunity to look them over critically. They were raw and undigested, just as he had culled them in the library and swallowed them piecemeal.

Imagine the contrast between such teaching and that which one encountered in the classroom of Professor Patten. He came like a cool September breeze after the sultriness of those stuffy, murky freshman experiences.

I shall never forget the first day that I heard a man ask him a question. I had come from classrooms where questions were considered impertinent; where they were looked upon as a bore; where they were resented, brushed aside, or even feared. As a freshman I had learned to regard economics as a rather stodgy subject, and I had no great hope for this sophomore course in John Stuart Mill's *Principles*. With such a background I sat listening to a talk on Adam Smith and his reasoning concerning capital.

"But Professor," one of the students interrupted, "what do you mean by capital?"

Dr Patten's face lighted up. His mouth relaxed. His eyes shone. He thrust his head eagerly forward. Then, without a pause, he gave his definition and his explanation.

The experience was a revelation. Here was a man who not only knew his subject (many men knew their subjects) but who was ready, nay, eager, to impart what he knew. Furthermore, and this was the important point, he welcomed a question as a thirsty traveler welcomes water. He had been working and waiting for this very result. It aroused and inspired him because it showed him that he was stirring thought, and it indicated the kind of thought that he had stimulated. It gave him his teaching opportunity. That question was an elixir which he seized and joyously quaffed.

Questions, in other classrooms, disturbed the sequence of ideas or the flow of words. Here, questions and answers — the

157

exchange of ideas — were woven into the fibre of the course. No questions annoyed him. None ever seemed to stump him.

It was not that he knew so many facts, although his range of reading and of observation was immense, — but that he knew what ideas were, knew where they belonged, and how to relate them to other ideas.

Professor Patten's attitude toward ideas may be well illustrated from baseball, which was his favorite sport. Some infielders, seeing a hot liner coming, get out of the way; others muff it; others, when they get the ball, do not know where to throw it. Whenever Dr. Patten saw a hard question coming, he stepped out to meet it, scooped it up, and dropped the answer, neatly, just where it belonged.

He lived on ideas. Discussion was his meat and drink. Intellectual activity pleased and thrilled him, and he went to his classroom with anticipation written all over his face.

Under such circumstances, it was little wonder that the students enjoyed the work. The anticipation was mutual, and the thought training received in his classes was regarded as one of the most valuable experiences of the entire four years' course.

One of the most delightful things about Professor Patten was that he never lectured. He did not know how. He never said anything to which he compelled his students to listen. His remarks were intended to evoke a reply. His aim was to arouse mental activity. At examination time, instead of asking his students to tell what they knew, he framed his questions in such a way as to discover what they thought.

Once the student's ideas were committed to paper, Patten lost all interest in them. But for the necessity of sending marks to the office at stated intervals, he would have deposited the examination papers in the waste basket the moment they were written. He aimed, not to give a mark, but to afford the student a chance to formulate a statement of his own mental progress.

Dr. Patten set out to break the ice of teaching from formulas and from textbooks which covered the whole academic world when he began his work in 1888, and throughout his long teaching career he treated books, not as a source of authority but as a point of departure. The book told what someone else had thought. It became the business of Patten's students to examine this thought, both as to its character and as to its origins; to criticise it, and to build upon it.

He was a quaint figure, tall, a little stooped at the shoulders, with long legs and an immense stride. He usually walked with his eyes on the ground, fingering his watch chain and sunk in thought.

One winter there was an ice storm that left the sidewalks glassy. During the evening, he had a bad fall. Talking about it afterward, he said:

"I was walking along, and not paying much attention to where I was going. I had a new formulation that I was trying to get straightened out and pieced together in my mind, and just as I got it in shape, my heels went up and my head down, and for the life of me I haven't been able to get it worked out since."

His clothes were usually old, and sometimes very shabby. One overcoat in particular, which had been cut from a piece of black cloth, had turned so green that it might have passed for a green garment had it not been for its mottled appearance. Over the shoulders, along the outside of the sleeves and down the front, the green was very pronounced. The back of the coat was darker, and under the arms it was still quite black.

This overcoat I remember as well as I remember Dr. Patten, and I always imagined that he parted with it only because one of his more diplomatic students persuaded him that it was time to buy a new coat and give the old one away.

He very frequently walked at night. On one occasion, when he was tramping through West Philadelphia after midnight, dressed in old clothes, a policeman stopped him and asked him where he was going and what he was about. Dr. Patten refused to answer so the policeman took him to the station house. Patten saw an opportunity for a little adventure and refused to give any information about himself. The sergeant put him through the third degree and kept him until well on toward morning. The next day he gleefully told us of his "prison" experiences.

Again and again freshmen took him for the janitor, when they met him, bareheaded, in the halls. But no one that had ever spent an hour in one of his classes made another such mistake. Once a student had seen his forehead wrinkle, his eyes shine, and his long, sinewy fingers pointed in the enthusiasm of exposition, he recognized Patten as the master.

"Uncle Si," he was familiarly called; never to his face, however, but in conversations among the students, graduates and undergraduates alike. There was no note of ribaldry in the appellation. He was respected, in many cases almost reverenced, by the men who came into contact with him.

How did this grotesquely appearing caricature of a man win his students? Only by understanding and loving his subject as he understood and loved his pupils.

During those early years of my acquaintance with him, Dr. Patten suffered greatly from insomnia and from indigestion. This made his teaching work difficult, and at times impossible. But despite physical suffering he struggled along, always gentle, patient, kindly, considerate.

He had almost no memory for names. In order to do his work as a teacher he felt that it was necessary to know the names of the students. After experimenting in many ways, he finally hit on the following plan: He started the term by giving a number of examinations very close together, and asked the students to write their names at the top of each sheet of their examination papers. Then he spent all of his time in the classroom walking around and reading over the shoulders of the students, memorizing their names and linking them up in his mind with their faces.

He was unusually diffident. As a young man he must have been painfully bashful, and through his life he never ceased to be shy. He did not like to speak to classes of more than twenty or thirty, and he really shone in groups of less than a dozen. Then, settling down into a big chair before a fire, he would talk by the hour, his eyes eager, his face glowing with the warmth of his irrepressible eloquence.

His uncanny power in the classroom lay in his ability to make men ask and answer questions. There was a tradition among Patten's students,—"When you go into Uncle Si's classes, you must sleep or think."

There was no escape. Mentally lazy, inert natures were stirred to opposition. Most of the students differed with Patten at one stage or another, a process that was rendered more inevitable because of the constant change in Patten's interests and activities.

On a certain famous occasion, Dr. Fugate, one of the graduate students, made a careful analysis of heredity and social progress which showed that the point of view expressed by Dr. Patten in this book was quite opposed to that which he was presenting to the class.

"What do you say to that?" demanded Dr. Fugate, with a mischievous satisfaction in the contradiction of which he had convicted Dr. Patten.

Without hesitation, Dr. Patten replied: "I should say that I had changed my mind since I wrote that book."

Through his whole career as a teacher he held to that attitude. When new experiences seemed to warrant it, he admitted that he had been wrong and changed his position.

Anyone who knows teachers (or other specialists for that matter) knows how difficult and rare a thing it is for a teacher to stand up before a class and admit that he has made a mistake. On the other hand, there is nothing that gives a student more confidence in a teacher's ability than the frank admission of ignorance, of error or of a change of view. An admission of ignorance or of error places the teacher in the same class with all other human beings — including the students. A frankly acknowledged change in point of view indicates that the teacher, as well as the students, is learning. Patten never knew too much more than his students. He learned with them and grew with them.

Dr. Patten did not make converts, but each man who came under his influence was forced to rush every available reserve to the defense of cherished ideas and prejudices. Even then, he frequently saw the flanks turned, and was forced to abandon the positions one by one.

Patience was one of Patten's greatest virtues. "Wait, wait!" he used to insist. "What we need above anything else in Philadelphia is a number of first class funerals, and in time they will come."

He was fond of quoting the deacons in his home town in Illinois, who had the church sewed up in their pockets. "One thing troubled them," said Patten. "They realized that sooner or later they must die, and they knew that when that time came the church that they controlled so completely would sweep clean away from its old moorings. That thought hurt them more than anything else." It was that same thought that helped Patten more than anything else. He was forever looking ahead, rejoicing in the changes that he saw coming.

Patten never tired of quoting the remark of Nicholas Murray Butler, when, as a young insurgent at Columbia he ran foul of the established order there. "Go out in the park, Nicholas," Butler said to himself. "Get plenty of sunshine and fresh air. Keep your health. They'll die." Patten ended the story with the words: "And they did."

Tolstoi and Karl Marx never believed more devoutly in a new social order than did Dr. Patten, and with this belief he combined the patience of the East — a kind of supreme faith in the ultimate working out of things that might be called chronic optimism. It was difficult for us young hotheads to get this point of view. We wanted action, but we never succeeded in stirring him up very much, even under the most trying circumstances. He usually went quietly into a corner, sat down, stroked his chin reflectively in a deliberate, quaint way he had, waited, and usually won.

During the period when Patten was at the Wharton School there was a bitter struggle going on between the Wharton School faculty and the Arts faculty. On two or three occasions there were rumors that different members of the Economics faculty were to be dismissed. On one of these occasions, Patten worked out the following formula: "No resignations. If they come after us, let them drag us out one at a time with hooks."

There was nothing pedantic about the man. He did not gloat over his victories, and desisted in his attacks before he had pushed the students too far. He knew the signs; knew how hard it was for untrained minds to wade out of the mire of irrational preconceptions; knew that it required time, patience, and repetition, hence he returned day after day to the attack.

"Let me put the thing this way," he would say, placing the tips of his long fingers together. Then would follow a careful exposition. The next day he would begin: "Now let's look at the matter from this side," and point by point he would build and elaborate another line of argument. Thus, with tireless insistence he would go around his subjects, approaching them from one angle after another until all of the possibilities had been exhausted.

Patten dealt with a subject as a botanist deals with a specimen. When he had finished with it, it was examined and described in minute detail.

Though Dr. Patten was the embodiment of modest simplicity, his thought was ironshod, and its thrust was irresistible. He never stopped trying until he had made his point.

He followed well-defined methods in the handling of his ideas, and used quaint, shrewd formulas in his argument. One of his commonest methods of procedure was:

163

1. First, use your opponent's facts to disprove his argument.
2. If this is impossible, disprove or deny the validity of his facts.
3. If both of these fail, shift the ground of the argument, and approach the issue from another point of view.

He had an unusually detached attitude toward facts. On one occasion, in a seminar, a graduate student of considerable ability had spent many hours in compiling a table to answer one of Dr. Patten's arguments.

"There," said the student decisively, after reading his table, "what do you say to those facts?"

Dr. Patten smiled. "I should say," he answered, "that they are bad facts."

When there was a University debate that dealt with some aspect of economics, the team always consulted Dr. Patten. His slant on the question was invariably original, and usually he was able to suggest winning arguments. One of his students expressed the point thus: "Did you ever know a man whose mind took such an extraordinary path in going from one point to another?"

One of the great charms in Simon Patten's teaching was that he said what he thought. No question was ever raised in class but that he had a frank analysis and a clean-cut answer. He was not a babbler. He never talked for the sake of hearing his own voice. He did not seek to air his views unnecessarily, but once a matter was presented, the issues that it raised were threshed out whether it required minutes or weeks, and throughout the discussion the members of the class felt that their leader was speaking his mind. They might, and often did, differ with him. That point was never at issue. Patten's classes were vantage grounds for the exchange of ideas, and the members of the class as well as the teacher were expected to have ideas which they were prepared to justify.

Perhaps there was no characteristic of Patten's teaching that was so refreshing as his willingness to state his side and then to give a full hearing to the opinions of those who differed with him in all of the essential details of the argument. There are many classes where students who differ with the instructor are graded down. With Dr. Patten, to differ meant to establish and to maintain mental contacts. Under him, mind met mind in the stimulus of frank discussion. Students went from his classes as from a refreshing bath. By opening the pores of the mind and increasing the disposal of waste, they had made room for the tissue of new ideas.

It was this very freedom that made Professor Patten so unpopular with the vested interests controlling the city of Philadelphia. If there were traction franchises up for discussion, they were handled on their merits; the Pennsylvania Railroad was spoken of without mental genuflection; coal, oil, and steel were considered like any of the other economic issues. There was no protection for the privileged few in the classroom where Patten presided. And more to the point, his students left the classroom to investigate the doings of the United Gas Improvement Company, the Philadelphia Electric Company, the Hard Coal Combine, and the other aggregations of capital that held the city and state in the hollow of their hands. One standard was set up in these classes — the public welfare, and it was in the light of these class discussions that Patten's men attacked the problems that lay all around them in the economic and social world.

Patten was one of the teachers who thought and who uttered his thought. He spoke and wrote fully and frankly on the questions that he believed to be uppermost in the field to which he had devoted his life.

Is there any wonder that a graduate student who had done work in several of the leading universities of the United States and of Europe should have said of him: "He is the Prince of Teachers. His ability to evoke thought is without parallel."

The statement was exaggerated, of course, but the title "Prince of Teachers" applies more nearly to Dr. Patten than to any other teacher I have ever known.

He was more than a teacher, however. He followed his students closely after they left the University, and with them took part in varied activities. He lived alone, for many years, in a big, sparsely furnished apartment on Thirty-ninth Street within five minutes' walk of the University. Few were intimate with him. He seldom talked of himself, but his vast store of emotional energy found its outlet in the varied contacts that he had with his students and with the members of the faculty.

Then, too, he followed baseball diligently. He was an ardent bridge player. He loved the woods and the hills, and spent his summers tramping. When the development of the movie business began, he became a movie fan, and took a keen interest in the types of pictures that were presented. He tried to keep in touch with all phases of life. Anything that was new interested him immediately, and he was fond of estimating the social possibilities of each discovery or invention or social experiment. He was in touch with many angles of life, and always believed that whatever was alive was significant.

One of Dr. Patten's habitual methods of making contacts with people was to eat breakfast with them. When a student or a friend came to him for advice, he would say:

"Let me see; suppose we take breakfast together tomorrow morning."

The meeting was arranged for perhaps eight o'clock, and implied a session that lasted until eleven or even till noon.

These breakfast conferences took place at the University Club, at 1510 Walnut Street. Dr. Patten walked each morning from his Thirty-ninth Street apartment, across the Walnut Street Bridge, to the Club. There, day after day, he talked with those who came to him for advice and counsel.

And such advice!

166

"Sell all your clothes and get a new outfit," he told a former student who was taking a post in New York. "Borrow the money if necessary, but go over there to capture the town."

"Never stay too long in one place," he told another. "Men grow stale. Get out into the world. You are needed there. Always you will find plenty to do."

Many men came to him. He listened to all of them, gave them the best that he had to give, and then sent them out to live their lives.

The characteristic that distinguished Professor Patten from most of the other teachers at the University of Pennsylvania was that while he always had one eye on the classroom, the other eye was forever on the community. Day after day, his glance swept the social horizon, and whenever he spied a task that seemed to need doing, he would call it to the attention of one of his students. Thus he was eternally multiplying himself by picking men and women to follow the trails that he indicated.

"Why doesn't Williams stay here in the University and mind his own business?" asked one of the professors who was reputed to be liberal. "He can always command a good salary and can pick up enough on the side to give him a very comfortable position."

But the man in question was one of Patten's students, and to him Patten had said: "Go!"

"Never hold a man here if he can grow by going somewhere else," was one of the formulas that Patten followed religiously. "We can make shift to get another man who will fill his place," he used to say. "He may not have another equally good opportunity!"

Thus he sent them out, one by one, to do the work which he felt the world needed. They did not proclaim a dogma. They carried the will to service. He was always sorry to see them go, because he held his students very dear, but he rejoiced to see them enter the struggle for social welfare.

Patten was always insistent that the young men who worked with him should use modern efficiency methods. In 1908 he had three of us with him in a small office where we were much hampered by the lack of space and of clerical assistance. As the University refused to provide a stenographer Patten solved the problem by finding some editorial work in which we all took a share, and for which we received enough to pay a stenographer.

Then Patten's troubles began. There were four of us in a tiny office. The stenographer made five. Patten was quite unaccustomed to the rattle of a machine (he always wrote by hand) and whenever he entered the office he was compelled to face a barrage of people and clatter. At about the same time we added to his troubles by installing a buzzer in the office so that we might be called quickly to the telephone, located on the floor below. Although he was a great advocate of efficiency, Patten never grew really accustomed to the noise of the new devices. Whenever the buzzer sounded, Patten jumped.

One of his favorite doctrines was that the big things of life lie in the future, and consequently he was always looking ahead. He once said to a group of us: "I am a great deal more interested in what will happen five hundred years from now than I am in what will happen tomorrow."

"But five hundred years is so long ahead," we protested. "Why not be interested in tomorrow?"

He answered: "Because the things that will happen tomorrow have already been settled. They were decided by the people and by the forces of yesterday. They are fixed — inevitable. But we can take a hand in deciding the events of the coming centuries.

"Look at this pencil," he continued. "I raise its point only a fraction of an inch from the table, but continue that line for a few miles, and it will pass over the top of the highest mountain. So it is with the events that take place in a society. We can modify them only a little at best. If we exert our energies on tomorrow, we are working against the full force of tradition and social inertia. But here among you, in these classes, there are the men and women of the future. If we influence them—deflect them—only slightly, the work that they do through all the coming years will be deflected, just as the line of the pencil is deflected by raising its point only a little, and the net result, in twenty generations, will be immense."

No one can ask more than that of life—a chance to play a part in painting the dawn for the coming generations. Such was the role that Patten always played. He worked untiringly with the young, assisting them and directing them toward their future. He believed that "death is not death, but new life. We go that it may come. We die that others may live. Beyond the mountains and the snow is a land that we may see from afar, even if we cannot enter. Better be a Moses seeing what others can enjoy than a worshipper of idols that once were gods, but now are merely crumbling clay. Any fool is better than the pickled remnants of ancient creeds."

Patten lived a part of his life in the lives of his students. That is one reason why he never grew old. He had discovered the fountain of perpetual youth. His thoughts were ever on the morrow. His eyes were turned continually toward the East, where he knew the sun would rise, and until he drew his last breath he never stopped telling his students about it.

"The ideals and programs of an age are no more eternal than its industrial machinery. Let us lay flowers on their biers. Honor is due all past effort at attainment, even if deeds were few and results meagre. But if we want to see the seed we planted blossom and bear fruit, we must not patch and revise. Our acts, as seed, die and live again in their own way. If we have no faith in the ground, sun, and rain, it is better to keep the seed in closed jars so that it may remain intact. Death precedes life, and the life of the next generation comes more from the warmth and glow of the new environment than from inherited ideals. What we have done for the soil in which new life grows counts for more than the poles put up to aid the new life to climb. Will not plants grow up into the sun even if no ancestral stalks remain to point the way of the past?"

Simon Patten attracted young people because he was always looking beyond his day into their day. With his imagination he built the structure of the future. With his mind he investigated its recesses. He spoke to his students constantly, not of the things that had passed, but of the things that were to be. He possessed that faculty of immortal youth — the power to project himself beyond the confines of the immediate, and across the boundary of the now.

George Lincoln Burr

⋙ 1857 – 1938 ⋘

I<small>N HURRYING</small> to his office a professor noticed a long line of students waiting to consult him — so he quietly took his place at the end of the line. On another occasion, after a class, he was heard muttering to himself, "Anyway, I can always earn an honest living as a printer." Both of these stories are told on George Lincoln Burr, Cornell's beloved teacher of history for more than three decades. But they are more than anecdotes on the absent-minded professor; they are curiously symbolic of a gentle, modest, selfless man who was always too busy helping others to further his own career in the obvious academic fashion.

After graduating from Cornell in 1881 he spent some of his best years in Europe collecting books for the Cornell library and doing research for President Andrew D. White's monumental polemic, **The Warfare of Science and Theology.** Later energies were put into editing bibliographies and manuscripts on witchcraft, including Henry Charles Lea's huge unfinished history which he completed with a colleague shortly before his death. On Burr's lectures on the Middle Ages and the Renaissance two excellent textbooks were frankly based. "Hundreds of other scholars have been indebted to Burr for suggestions and criticisms." In consequence, he failed to carry out his own larger plans, most regrettably a history of the rise of religious liberty.

Fortunately we outsiders can catch some of the spirit of "Poppy" Burr from a recent volume, with his biography by Roland H. Bainton and selections from his writings, edited by his last Ph.D., Lois Oliphant Gibbons. Professor Bainton, who now teaches history at Yale, ends with this salute to his old master: "His students and friends have long lamented that the treasures of his mind so richly stored passed largely with him. How tragic, say they, that he never wrote a book! He wrote hundreds of them. His books are to be found wherever the sons and daughters of Cornell have gone to the ends of the earth, for he wrote, 'not on tables of stone but on tables of flesh—your hearts.' "

In building up the faculty of Leland Stanford Jr. University, President David Starr Jordan reached out boldly and shrewdly to all parts of the country—with more than climate as inducements. There were many reasons why Burr might have accepted Jordan's flattering offer. His long letter weighing the proposition reveals a sense of scholarly responsibility, a reverence for the tools of his trade, that is not so common as it should be.

Years ago in the Cornell Library a young woman heard a familiar voice saying: "Why, hello, little friend, I didn't know you were here." She turned around to see "Poppy" Burr, addressing not a person but a book!

"Poppy" Burr

ROLAND H. BAINTON

>>>·<<<

BOOKHUNTING, research, publication were always subordinate in Burr's mind to teaching. As a librarian he deprecated the acquisition of costly museum pieces if it were at the expense of the ordinary tools of instruction.

He was himself a teacher and one of the greatest of our time. His courses for undergraduates in European history were conducted chiefly on the basis of three sessions a week, of which two were lectures and the third an examination. Burr would come cantering into class with his head tilted on one side to balance an armful of books on the other. With the treasures of the White Library before him on the desk, sometimes he would appear to be carrying on his studies in front of the class. Occasionally he would examine the books and bog down in bibliographical details. One can understand the mistake of a student who on examination gave back Burr's statement that the besetting sin of the Age of Faith was bibliolatry, by substituting for the latter word bibliography. But at other times, and they were vastly more frequent, he would be wrapped in the subject, oblivious of the books which were never once opened, to the chagrin of the student who helped him to carry them over and back. He discouraged all note taking and made it practically impossible. On the bookish days his comments would be too unsystematic to take down, and in the inspired hours the listener was too enthralled to write, even were he able to keep up with two hundred words a minute. Those

173

lectures were works of art, symmetrical in structure, rich in diction, rhythmic in their periodic cadences. The notes which were occasionally gleaned by students give the impression of someone plucking a few gorgeous feathers from the plumage of a bird on the wing.

Burr was seldom on the course schedule; that did not matter. He might skip one hundred years or fail to reach the end of the course. His object was not to cover precisely so much ground nor to impart an exact quantity of information, but to recreate an atmosphere, to serve as a stereoscope for the class through which they could see the figures of the past taking on three dimensions.

What then of examinations? He would say that the textbook was the library. Yet he did not turn his students quite adrift. They were provided with outlines giving the main points and a page of annotated bibliography for each week. Most of the titles were in foreign languages. That did not matter either. The student should realize at once the necessity of mastering the tools of scholarship. He equipped them also with excerpts from the sources. There were, of course, the printed collections published by the University of Pennsylvania for which he did the one on witchcraft. Besides these he prepared a number of his own and had them multiplied in the old days by the gelatin process, later by the mimeograph or the press. The selections ranged all the way from the inscription of Sennacherib to Voltaire. *The Edda of Saemund* and *The Ship of Fools*, *Praise of Folly* and *The Rights of Man*, Savonarola and Montesquieu, with many another, were represented.

The weekly examinations were searching. Take this for example:

"By what stages did the monk, whose name denotes a solitary, find organization in communities and change from a layman to a cleric? What were the aims of Benedict of Nursia as a monastic reformer, and what seem to you the secrets of the wide acceptance of his rule? Tell something of the place in monastic history of Bruno, of Bernard, of Norbert. How did a friar differ in religious aim from a monk, and how a Franciscan from a Dominican? An old Latin verse tells us that 'Benedict loved the mountains, Bernard the valleys, Francis the towns.' Explain this; and, if you were to add what Dominic loved, what would it be?''

There might be a dozen questions for an hour, but Burr meant them more as an exercise than as an inquisition. Dorsey W. Hyde, Jr., now director of archival service for the National Archives at Washington, tells what happened to him on an examination. Confronted with twelve questions, all save one on factual detail, he found that on this one alone was he able to say a thing. It called for an appraisal of Erasmus, to whom he had devoted special study. Passing up all the rest, he wrote an essay on this theme. When called to the front at the next class, he fully expected a public reprimand. Instead, Burr, with a captivating smile, announced that this was one of the finest papers he had ever received. In that hour an undergraduate was transformed into a graduate student.

Undoubtedly Burr's lectures went over the heads of the undergraduates. Some were at times bored and some were a trifle amused when he stopped to reflect in class, or when his voice, in a moment of excitement, became high pitched. Yet even the most frivolous recognized quality when they saw the reverence with which he fondled a book, and many a boy or girl was stirred to crave the secret of his loves. Those who did not always understand, vaguely sensed exposure to greatness and in after years testified to having received much more than at the time they ever suspected.

But there were those examinations. Save for the first few, Burr stacked the papers until, with about a dozen in hand for each person, he could arrange them chronologically and read them in sequence for indications of progress. If there were occasion for consultation the student was invited in for an hour, when Burr passed on what he had learned from Tracy Peck as to foretastes of the Judgment Day. Professor Arthur L. Andrews of the University of Hawaii describes one such interview. He was a Woodford orator, and Burr, who had judged the orations, knew that he could write. His examination was so slipshod as to suggest that the other effort might have been plagiarized. Satisfied on that point, Burr said, "Well, Andrews, any one that *can* write as well as you should be *ashamed* to write as poorly as you did in answering that examination question. You should develop a *literary* conscience. You should be ashamed to do inferior work. . . ." "That talk has made me lots of work," said Andrews, "and I am duly grateful. . . . For the first time in nearly four years in Cornell, a professor had shown some *personal* interest in me. I had been only one of hundreds. Now I was *one* among hundreds. Some one really cared whether I did well or ill." (*To Simon Henry Gage, July 19, 1938.*)

The ultimate fate of the papers was a little suggestive of the sequel to the Judgment Day. Toward the end of the academic year they were stacked tightly in the fireplace. On the first cool day of the ensuing fall a match was struck. They would then smolder for weeks.

The graduate courses were numerous and unusual. He gave at times seminars on the Renaissance and Reformation, on historical method, paleography and diplomatics, and on historical geography. The one on the rise of tolerance was particularly renowned. In making the assignments the professor must have consulted in advance the records of the Registrar. How else would he have known to allocate Calvin to a Methodist, Luther to a Jew, and Sebastian Franck to a daughter of a Russian revolutionist?

A very unusual course was devoted to the sciences auxiliary to history, such as sphragistics, numismatics, heraldry, genealogy, chronology, and geography. He was particularly insistent on the indispensability of geography, and sometimes in undergraduate course would ask on the examination for a tracing of the routes of the barbarian invasions. He would come in, the next hour, chuckling because many had taken the invaders over the Danube in the spots hardest to ford and over the Alps and Pyrenees by way of the highest peaks and down Italy along the crest of the Apennines.

Burr himself was a past master in utilizing details for vitalizing the past. In his seminar on the Basel humanists he would take you to the creek where Felix Platter nearly drowned, to the house of Erasmus and the press of Froben, to the cathedral where Curio looked on the slab erected to those gifted children snatched from him by the plague. One would see David Joris, arch-heretic from the Netherlands, living ostensibly as an orthodox nobleman, sumptuously clad, riding up the hill to the *Spiesshof*, or one would hear Sebastian Castellio declaim that magnificent plea for religious liberty which Burr knew by heart. And how he loved to peep in on the romance of Felix Platter.

The secret of this power to reconstruct the past lay only in part, however, in a gift for detail. The deeper reason is well described by Charles Beard. "I do remember one thing," he writes, "that I heard him say in his seminar during the fall term of 1899, when I was a student at Cornell . . . The saying was: 'It is only through sympathy, never through hatred, that we can understand an age or a people.' . . . It struck fire in my mind then, and has burned there for more than forty years." (*To R. H. Bainton, June* 20, 1941.)

The professor had an even greater hold on many a student outside the classroom than in. There were numerous occasions for contacts. Meals are very convenient in that regard. During some of his bachelor days Burr elected to eat with the girls at Sage Hall, doubtless to give his support to coeducation, which was still regarded somewhat askance. He sat at the table of the Thetas, with whom his relations were plainly hilarious. They sent him a solemn document enjoining upon George Lincoln Burr that seven days in the week should he labor and do all his work, but on the eighth day of each week he should rest from all his labors, and on the said eighth day he should take two naps of eleven hours each and likewise on that day he should eat three meals. How the meals were to be geared into the naps they do not explain.

For a year he deserted the Thetas for another table. Word reached him that a colored girl was coming the following year. Some of the Thetas were from the South and he feared embarrassment. For that reason he went to Winifred Sprague (Mrs. George Sabine) and asked whether she could get up a congenial table with which he promised to eat. It was done. Jessie Fauset was cordially received. She distinguished herself as a novelist after graduation.

Burr's aversion to special privilege was well known to the girls, and they endeavored to favor him unbeknownst. Cream was served for coffee only at his table in a little blue pitcher popularly denominated the "Purple Cow." The facetious references to this little beastie were so frequent that Burr twigged the truth and thereafter would never touch a drop.

Another form of fellowship was the picnic and hike. Burr often organized tramping parties. If many a lifelong romance flowered on such occasions he was gleefully unperturbed. When someone once remarked to him that western universities were regular match factories, he retorted: "All the world's a match factory. The question is where the best matches are made."

The summer offered still further opportunities for camping parties, whether of students or of alumni. Burr's expansive nature would invite an unwieldy crowd and his zeal once betrayed him into picking up two suit cases which did not belong to the party and could be returned only a fortnight later. This was on the trip in 1899 to the Cornell Forest Preserve by way of steamer down Saranac Lake. John Burroughs was a member of the party and another was Winifred Ball (Humphrey). She tells of the spelling bees staged by "Herr" Burr in which he proposed words which all protested were of his own making. He had not discomfited all the spellers of Newark Valley for nothing. Usually the party did its own cooking, but the year that Mrs. Coville came with her daughter Katharine he hired a cook to give the mother a complete relief.

Yet the qualities which endeared him to his students do not make for advancement in the academic world. Books are demanded and Burr had written none. The prophet who is without honor in his own country, however, sometimes comes into his own after being recognized abroad. David Starr Jordan knew his man and invited Burr first to Indiana, and afterward to Stanford. Every inducement was dangled before him: the sunny skies, the purple mountains of the enchanted land of Aladdin. Burr, after months of pressure and pondering, replied:

"Dear Dr. Jordan:

"I am ready to make you a proposition. I do not think you will accept it. I do not know that you can do so. But I shall be glad to have made it.

"As I reflect on your offer I am sure that the only thing which seems to stand insuperably in the way of my acceptance is the loss of my books. With them all my plans for teaching, all my plans for writing are wrapt up. It is not a few books I want — it is many. Even here we are barely equipped for work in history; yet our collection in European history alone must have cost fully a hundred thousand dollars. And here we are in comparatively easy reach of the rich collections at Boston, at New York, and at Philadelphia. What would one do at Palo Alto?

"But I have long maintained — and I know that President White, at least, has largely agreed with me — that our only hope of building up permanently a great university at a place so remote from the great centres as is Ithaca lies in the building up of our collections and our libraries. Is it not doubly true for California?

"You know what is my notion of teaching history. I can no more teach it from a mere textbook than you can teach zoology so. My men must study history for themselves and at first hand. They must see and handle it for themselves, as your men do fishes, or Comstock's men bugs. Now, my fishes, my bugs, are almost all in books. Great things, indeed, your noble archae-ological collections will do for us; but they are the merest beginning. As you know, my conception of history is not a narrow one. It is not of wars or of governments alone that it treats. It is of the whole life of men from the beginning: their institutions, their ideas, their lives, their hopes and fears and loves and aspirations. My boys and girls must be brought into the full current of this pulsing stream of human history by breathing the very breath and thinking the very thoughts of the past. Not else can they face fairly into that nobler future whither its tide is bearing us. There is no science, no art, no phase of experience, nothing which has helped to shape human civilization or human character, whose story is not an essential part of the literature of history. But this means books, books, books.

"It does not mean *all* books. For books whose value is that of an accident — a fashion, a chance rarity, a printer's blunder — for such and their collectors I have little love. Even for books which have in themselves great intrinsic value, for the part they have played in history or for their worth as illustration of a time, I should claim, if they are rare and costly, no place in a university library. These may well be left to private col-lectors, whose generosity will some day endow us with them. But the great collections of the sources of history, the master-pieces of narrative, the ripest products of modern historical criticism, these are what a university library must have and must have in fullness. Most essential of all are the collections of sources. They are costly and are rapidly multiplying in num-ber. Yet they will not multiply long, and they will not be always procurable. Already many periods of history are covered with virtual completeness. Today, with these collections there is no reason why one may not study the ancient civilizations, the greater part of the Middle Ages, and many modern epochs as fruitfully and almost as exhaustively at Palo Alto as beyond the Atlantic. There is no reason why that may not be made the one place in America for such study. . . .

"Forgive my prolixity. I ought to know that you need none of this argument. You are yourself a man of science and of the present. Let me come at once to my proposition. I cannot so much as begin my work without a costly equipment of books — I cannot keep it up without constant and costly additions. But *how* costly? I need not less than ten thousand dollars for a foundation; not less than five thousand dollars a year for the ten years that follow. Or, what is the same thing, five thousand a year for each of the first eleven years of the university, including this year of my absence. After that time I am willing to trust it to its share of what will be then the generous income of your library. Is this preposterous, this demand? I cannot help it. To me it is almost inadequate. If you can pledge me this amount for expenditure in the field of General History, I will gladly accept your professorship. You may associate with me in its use whomsoever you please. You may ask what guarantees you will. I only ask that the sum may be set aside for this use. I make no other condition. What do you say to it?

"It is nearly a month since I wrote you the foregoing pages. I have held them because I wanted to think them over. I find they represent my deepest conviction, and I shall send them to you. Whatever comes of it, I am glad to have written you frankly.

"They are not an ultimatum. I am not afraid of pioneer work. I am glad to rough it, if my colleagues must. What there is in *me* to teach I can teach, and teach with delight, anywhere under the blue sky and without a printed line. But I am not history, any more than *you* are nature; and without books history cannot in any true sense be studied at all. They are my laboratory, my museum, my world. I turn to them for facts in time as you turn to nature for facts in space; and my students must turn to them, for I am but their guide, and my mission is but to train them to search and to interpret. A few books are almost worse than none at all: a *university* must have the whole truth. But I can wait. I know how to be patient and to do with little. Only there must be a sure hope, or I must stay where hope is. Will the Leland Stanford Junior University *ever* have, in History, the noble library its noble plan demands? Have you assurance of it?

"If so, I want to work with you. If not, I cannot.

"Yours most truly,
"Geo. L. Burr."

Jordan could not quite meet these terms, but he was able to point out that the Sutro Library near by had 200,000 volumes and multitudes of pamphlets, seven or eight cords of books from Mexico, all the tracts issued under the Commonwealth in Cromwell's time, and moldering mounds of musty incunabula from the secularized monasteries of Bavaria (since, alas, partly destroyed in the San Francisco fire). The library of Stanford itself was growing at the rate of a thousand volumes a month. Then, too, there were those who were uncharitable enough to suggest that if Burr would leave that unhealthy Ithaca and come to the summer clime he would be able to write his life of Charlemagne on the basis of what he already knew.

But after all it was not just books that Burr wanted but *his* books, the ones he had collected and knew, and which were to serve for the works which he had elected to write. When the question was definitely settled that Burr should remain at Cornell, Jordan remarked to a friend that he had used the wrong bait by offering a soft berth with only one seminar to teach and the task of building up the library. If he had suggested lecturing eight hours a day plus a multitude of other duties Burr would have regarded such a challenge as irresistible. At any rate, Jordan opened the eyes of Cornell with regard to the quality of this teacher of history, and in 1892 he was advanced to a full professorship.

John Dewey and Others

⇒⇒ 1859– ⇐⇐

LOOKING BACK on his college years, particularly in a small college, one may recall a single teacher standing out above all the rest. Others may remember with almost equal gratitude a veritable galaxy of unusual men. Such was the experience of Irwin Edman at Columbia College during the first World War. Those were the great days before Beard and Robinson resigned, before Dewey made his long trip to the Far East and John Erskine wrote The Private Life of Helen of Troy.

Irwin Edman has written limericks and lyrics, familiar essays and technical philosophical articles but his most charming and perhaps his most enduring book to date is his semi-autobiographical Philosopher's Holiday in which he devotes a chapter to six Columbia professors. Four of them are still alive, and all of them are widely known through their numerous books, except the late Dean Woodbridge who remains the teacher par excellence for Edman and for so many others. There is beauty, power and depth in his writings but they do not quite reveal the mind that we felt in those eloquent lectures, those groping seminars. As Woodbridge always liked to think of Plato as "the son of Apollo," so his students like to remember him as the son of Plato.

Although Professor Edman is now nearly fifty and has been teaching philosophy at Columbia University for nearly thirty years, he may still be taken at a distance for a slightly dishevelled, absent-minded freshman looking for a nonexistent class room. But there is nothing absent-minded about this little man with the incredible memory and strange voice when he lectures to large classes on the philosophy of art or conducts seminars on Idealism, Mysticism, or Contemporary Thought. He has the kindling

185

touch that can hold an audience of a thousand or even a dozen with his anecdotes, his erudition, and his clarity.

In Professor Edman's little gallery there is no portrait of his elder colleague, William Pepperell Montague, who has been a genial presence on Morningside Heights since 1903. A twentieth century Epicurus, with a religious delight in thought and friendship, Montague found his Garden at Barnard College, but he has long given graduate courses on the other side of Broadway. In his autobiographical essay he pictures the great Harvard galaxy under whom he studied — George Herbert Palmer, William James, Josiah Royce, Hugo Munsterberg, and George Santayana; but he pays special tribute to Charles Sanders Peirce, that brilliant and eccentric genius who never held a regular academic post. "While his intellect was cold and clear, his metaphysical imagination was capricious, scintillating and unbridled": in characterizing Peirce in those words Montague unconsciously helps us to describe his own unforgettable lectures on "the ways of knowing" and "the ways of being." From the most abstruse problems of time and space, he could move easily to the most concrete problems of pleasure and pain, often leading up to a philosophic heresy as if he were shyly confessing a crime.

On his book-plate there are three figures — Dionysus, Prometheus, and Saint Francis.

Columbia Galaxy

IRWIN EDMAN

—»»·«««

W HEN ONE SPEAKS of one's old teachers, it is generally
to one's college teachers that one refers. For it is
then, if one is lucky, that one comes in contact with
men who communicate and articulate the things and ideas
which become the seeds of one's later intellectual and imaginative life. Every college has five or six men who in essence
are its educational system. I was very lucky. For during my
undergraduate days at Columbia, there was a galaxy of teachers
available to the student who in their respective ways and as a
group would be hard to duplicate at any college in any period.
As a freshman straight from high school, I heard Charles A.
Beard lecture on American Government; as a sophomore — and
in 1914 — I heard Carlton Hayes lecture on European History;
as a junior I heard John Erskine talk on Shakespeare, and was
in a small class where he taught us, really taught us, writing;
and in my senior year I had the unique and irrecoverable experience of traversing the history of philosophy with Frederick
J. E. Woodbridge. It was not until my graduate study that
I came to know John Dewey.

Charles A. Beard illustrates something very remarkable about
the art of teaching. Today everybody, even the literary youngsters, are interested in government. For even literature seems
less in the Ivory Tower than it did in 1913. But the study of
government, then officially known at Columbia as "Politics,"
did not, to most of us addicted to poetry and music, seem to

187

be our meat, and there was nothing in the big dark blue tome, Beard's *American Government and Politics*, that seemed arresting. There were endless details about the mechanisms and structure of State and Federal government. It was not the Beard of the *Economic Interpretation of the Constitution*.

But his lectures were another matter. The lanky figure leaning against the wall, drawling wittily with half-closed eyes, made the questions of government seem the most vital that anyone could broach, and touched matters that lay far deeper than the mere forms of constitutional government.

Every good teacher has his own special art; with some, it is a genius for a clarity that sometimes is more lucid than the complexities of the subject justify. Sometimes it is a talent for apophthegm or leading suggestion, a word that evokes a vista or an idea that opens a world. I cannot now quite remember what Professor Beard's special technique was. He was clear, he was suggestive, he was witty. But none of these things could quite account for the hold he had on the smug and the rebels alike, on both the pre-lawyers and the pre-poets. I suspect it was a certain combination of poetry, philosophy, and honesty in the man himself, a sense he communicated that politics mattered far beyond the realm commonly called political, and an insight he conveyed into the life that forms of government furthered or betrayed. One morning he came into class as usual, stood against the wall, and, half-closing his eyes, said:

"Gentlemen, today we are to discuss the budget system in State government. I am sure that must seem to you a dull subject. But if you will tell me, gentlemen, how much per capita a nation spends on its Army, on its Navy, on education, on public works, I shall be able to tell you, I think, as much about that nation as if you gave me the works of its poets and philosophers."

We listened with revised and revived attention to an exposition, full of figures and detail, of the State budget system. Charles A. Beard showed us what politics had to do with the

188

life beyond it and which it made possible. And he taught us, too, the difference between the forms of government and the living substance of its operations. Under his easy, drawling manner, we sensed a passionate concern for an understanding of the realities of government, the economic forces and the interested persons involved in it, and the ideal of government: the liberation of the energies of men. Nobody who has ever listened to Beard can disdain the study of politics in favor of the study of "higher things." He has been too well taught, as tragic world events have since shown, how government may nourish or destroy "higher things."

Up to the autumn of 1914 Europe seemed to most American college students a solar system away. In the autumn of 1914, when the war had been going on two months, Europe came for the first time in the imagination of many Americans to be vivid and near. European history ceased to be the anthropology and archaeology of distant peoples who spoke remote languages. It became as alive as yesterday's events: it was what explained today's news. It was, therefore, no wonder that at the beginning of the college year Carlton Hayes's course in "Europe since 1815" had become the most popular course in Columbia College. But it was not only the war that accounted for that. Carlton Hayes had for some time been one of the most popular professors in the college. His lectures were the most famous dramatic spectacle on the campus. Nor was it as a performance alone that they were famous. Everyone had heard that Hayes could actually make clear French political parties; I have never met anybody since who could or can. . . . The complicated history of Germany in the second half of the Nineteenth Century took shape as well as drama under his presentation of it. And in the midst of being taught and taught clearly, one had the incidental and additional pleasure of hearing a man to whom the great catastrophe of war had its roots in a past he knew, in the traditions of nations among whom he had lived familiarly, and in the desperate mythologies of nationalism, to which he had given special study and concern. One was treated, besides, to unforgettable vignettes of Disraeli dropping his morning walking stick as the cannons boomed noon at Gibraltar; of the Manchester school of economists, the "spiritual advisers" to the robber barons of early Nineteenth Century industrial England; of the black walnut furniture of the Victorian period; of the times and the manners of Louis Napoleon; of the studious German Jew in the British Museum whose studies produced the Communist Manifesto. One was shaken out of the smugness of the middle-class world in which most students were brought up and out of the provincial Americanism in which most of us had lived.

It did not matter, it served only as spice, that some of the barbs delivered in a dry voice by this baldish, sharp-featured man in his thirties were directed at us, at our very smugness, at our laziness, or at our fathers: when he was explaining the attitude of the manufacturers of the early Industrial Revolution, he reminded us that we all knew manufacturers; "some of your fathers," he drawled, "are manufacturers." It did matter a little to some of us that he mocked poetry and philosophy (this in re Shelley and Godwin) . . . "philosophy is what is taught in Philosophy Hall . . ." But it did not matter much. For during a whole year, we sat through a whole century of European history, and Bismarck, Garibaldi, Social Legislation in England. Benevolent Tories like Shaftesbury, and reformers like Cobden and Bright, "nationalism"—what devastating force Carlton Hayes put and can still put into the word—democracy, the Third Republic, became familiar parts of our imagination. In the midst of cries of "pro-German" and "pro-Ally," "preparedness," and "pacifism," during the three years before America went into the war, we knew somewhat better than many of our older compatriots what had brought the tornado about. Carlton Hayes had brought European history, as Charles Beard had brought American government, from the abstraction of a textbook to an experience lived and a problem to be faced.

And it always surprised some of us that, in the midst of the lectures — first-rate theatrical performances, words shot out for emphasis, silences sustained for a moment, gestures and movements deployed like those of a good actor — when we looked down at our notes, they were as ordered and clear as if we had listened to a scholastic metronome . . . I confess with shame that I achieved only a B.

You were allowed, if you had a fairly good academic record, to take in the senior year a graduate course that was at the time one of the famous academic enterprises of the period. It was James Harvey Robinson's course in the History of the Intellectual Classes in Western Europe. Everyone who had gone to high school knew the two volumes of Robinson and Beard's *Development of Modern Europe*. But the Robinson we came to know as a legend and a rumor by the time we were sophomores was the Robinson who had invented the "new history" — the history of causes and consequences, the history that treated politics as the surface of more fundamental matters, economic and social and cultural, and that regarded the date of the invention of the steam engine as more important than the dates of a king, and the industrial use of steam as more significant than monarchies and dynasties. We had also heard of Robinson, along with Dewey and Beard, as among the intellectual-liberal forces that were making our university famous in some quarters, notorious in others. And, finally, we had heard of the remarkable brilliance of the lectures in History 72.

The latter was a graduate course to which undergraduates, a handful of us, were admitted on sufferance. The majority of the class of over two hundred were graduate students of history, many of them women high school teachers from all over the country, particularly the West and South. Professor Robinson was a short man, with thin, greying hair and a deprecating, half-tired, half-amused, drawling voice. He seemed to be having a half-weary good time examining the origins of human stu-

191

pidity, and those vestigial remains of our culture that blocked the free and hopeful functioning of human intelligence. It took us a few weeks in the course to get to the beginnings of intellectual history. For Robinson, with saturnine delight, liked to show us the mind of the child, the slave, and the animal still functioning in us. Once he brought in a leading editorial from *The New York Times* to illustrate the theme, and another time quoted from a batch of Sunday sermons reported in that journal the next day. The course was not a course in intellectual heroes, but a course in the changing fashions of adult follies taken seriously in various ages. It only gradually became clear what intellectual heroes were presiding over the whole story as he gave it. They were Freud and Marx and Dewey and the anthropologists, and H. G. Wells, the prophet, then, of intelligence reshaping the world. There were only two or three gods of the past left unbesmirched, or whose clay feet were not recognized. They were Lucretius, who saw the diabolism of religion; Francis Bacon, who saw the human possibilities of science; Voltaire, who exhibited the foolishness of superstition. Plato was a man who believed in Truth, Goodness, and Beauty because he saw the actual world as a chaos which, Robinson loved to remind us, he compared to "a man with a running nose. . . ." Aristotle's science was childish (Robinson did not know how soon again it was to be fashionable and how more fundamental than fashion it is); St. Augustine was a most amusingly and scandalously human saint. It was not until the enlightenment of the Eighteenth Century that anybody, so most of us gathered from the course, was very enlightened.

Many of the graduate students were shocked, especially by the treatment of religion. The undergraduates from Columbia College had heard much of this before and had no faith (as did some of the graduate students) to have taken away. One of the young women complained to Professor Robinson: "You are taking away my faith." He looked at her oddly. "But if I took away a headache," he said simply, "you would not complain."

We undergraduates enjoyed the sallies, the freshness, the ir-reverence, and enjoyed, too, the fundamental feeling that lay at the basis of it all—that man, if he took his own intelligence into his hands—could make the world less a shambles and an idiocy than it had so often been. It was in the great days of the liberal faith when trust in intelligence was in the ascendant. If Robinson made the world appear a satire to intelligent ob-servation, he made it seem a lyric hope to generosity and under-standing. Dixon Ryan Fox, now President of Union College, was the young instructor who took the third quiz hour with the undergraduates. He felt it his special obligation to let us see the other side. And after a week, when he knew Robinson had been "exposing" modern Protestantism, he called in the chap-lain as a counterweight. He need not have bothered; we had our own grains of salt. One of the reasons we had grains of salt was that some of us had been studying with a man who will go down, I am quite certain, as one of the great philosophical teachers of our generation. His slender published writings will live, but they will live for a small circle of students. But Frederick J. E. Woodbridge has educated a whole generation of students in philosophy; and a whole circle of them scattered over the country, including Morris Cohen and Sidney Hook and J. H. Randall, Jr., and Herbert Schneider (to mention only a few), are living testimonies to his influence and his power. In my college days, the great thing was to have taken his course in the History of Philosophy. Some of us were taking it at the same time that we took Robinson's History of the Intellectual Classes in Western Europe. It was rather a different story we were told. It was not a story, but a succession of experiences of philosophers whose importance lay "not in their truth but in their power." It was a shock that turned into a liberation for those of us who had come to philosophy looking for the Truth with a dogmatic capital letter. There were other shocks, too. Much that was said in the textbooks we never heard in class, or we heard the contrary. Professor Woodbridge, who looked like a bishop and would have made a very eloquent one, talked like a poet whose theme happened to be the human mind. He talked most like a poet on the days when he was most interested; one remembers what days those were: the early Greeks, Plato, Aristotle, Marcus Aurelius, Lucretius, Spinoza with his sovereign detachment, and Locke with his sovereign common sense. He was not an unprejudiced observer and we rather liked the frankness and the brevity with which he dismissed the Germans and Rousseau. But what one was most moved by was the things by which he himself was most moved: the Plato who was the son of Apollo, the poet and the dramatist of ideas; Marcus Aurelius, the disillusioned statesman whistling to keep up his cosmical courage; Lucretius looking out with dramatic sympathy and equable understanding on the eternal nature of things. We were impressed by a mind whose maturity had not dulled its enthusiasms, and an understanding uncorrupted by the technical controversies of the academy, by the routine of the classroom, by the burden of administration of an elder statesman, for Woodbridge was graduate dean of the University. He taught a whole generation of students of philosophy to keep their eye on the object, to see a thinker in his own terms, to cease to raise foolish and irrelevant questions, and, above all, to raise the central and relevant ones about a man's teaching. On Aristotle's metaphysics, he began by reminding us that Aristotle was asking the simple and the ultimate question: "What does it mean to be? . . ." We found ourselves astonished to be reminded that the Middle Ages were in their own time not the Middle Ages at all. We were made aware of Locke's simple English attempt to be sensible, tolerant, and direct, and learned to understand what Spinoza meant and why he saw it as a liberation to see all things under the form of eternity. For in that wonderful class, as Will Durant (sitting next to me in alphabetical order) remarked, we were listening not to a professor of philosophy but to philosophy itself. It was impossible to feel you were listening to a doctrine; Professor Woodbridge

194

has never founded a school. You were hearing philosophy itself and came to understand it as an attempt to speak in the categories of mind of the categories of things.

I did not—I think not many of us did—understand it all. But we began to understand what understanding meant, in words that had eloquence without rhetoric. We heard great things nobly uttered. We learnt no doctrine but we grasped the significance of intellectual procedure; and to a whole generation of philosophers, though Professor Woodbridge has long since ceased to be their teacher, he remains their teacher still. He made us understand as none else had done, to use one of his own phrases, "the enterprise of learning."

A figure more widely known outside purely academic circles was and is John Dewey. In 1915, his name was already, if not a household, certainly a schoolroom word. His *How We Think* was used in all the normal schools of the country, and even fashionable ladies dipped into his far from easy books. I had read almost all of Dewey I could get hold of by the time I was a senior, but it was not until my first year as a graduate student that I heard, or, I believe, saw him. His familiar figure and speech, seeming at first that of a Vermont farmer, the casual gait, the keen but often absent eyes, seem so familiar now that I can scarcely believe I did not know them before.

I admit the first lecture was quite a shock, a shock of dullness and confusion, if that can be said. It was at any rate a disappointment. I had not found Dewey's prose easy, but I had learned that its difficulty lay for the most part in its intellectual honesty, which led him to qualify an idea in one sentence half a page long. In part also it lay in the fact that this profoundly original philosopher was struggling to find a vocabulary to say what had never been said in philosophy before, to find a diction that would express with exactness the reality of change and novelty, philosophical words having been used for centuries to express the absolute and the fixed. Once one had got used to the long sentences, with their string of qualifying clauses, to the sobriety, to the lack of image and of color, one sensed the liberating force of this philosophy. Here was not an answer but a quest for light in the living movement of human experience; in the very precariousness of experience there lay open to the perplexed human creature the possibilities that peril itself provocatively suggested. I had found here, as have so many of my generation, a philosophy that, instead of laying down a dia-gram of an ideal universe that had nothing to do with the one of actual human doings and sufferings, opened a vision of conscious control of life, of a democracy operating through creative intelligence in the liberation of human capacities and natural goods. In *How We Think* I had learned that thinking itself was simply a discipline of the animal habit of trial and error, and of the possible human habit of imagination and fore-sight. In *Democracy and Education* I had gathered that it was not in the forms of democratic government that true democracy lay, but in the substance of intelligent co-operation, largely de-pendent on education. Dewey was not easy, but once one had mastered his syntax, a vision of a liberal and liberated common-wealth was one's reward, and a philosophy that was not only a vision but a challenge.

I was naturally prepared, therefore, to expect something of intellectual excitement from the lectures in "Psychological Ethics." Intellectual excitement was the last term to describe what I experienced that September afternoon. The course came, in the first place, directly after lunch. It was well attended; there were even some fashionably dressed society ladies, for Dewey had become a vogue. But this famous philosopher who had written so much on "Interest in Education," as the essence of the educational process, could not, save by a radical distor-tion of the term, be said at first hearing to sound interesting. He had none of the usual tricks or gifts of the effective lecturer. He sat at his desk, fumbling with a few crumpled yellow sheets and looking abstractedly out of the window. He spoke very slowly in a Vermont drawl. He looked both very kindly and very abstracted. He hardly seemed aware of the presence of a class. He took little pains to underline a phrase, or emphasize a point, or, so at first it seemed to me, to make any. Occasionally he would apparently realize that people in the back of the room might not hear his quiet voice; he would then accent the next word, as likely as not a preposition or a conjunction. He seemed to be saying whatever came into his head next, and at one o'clock on an autumn afternoon to at least one undergraduate what came next did not always have or seem to have a very clear connection with what had just gone before. The end of the hour finally came and he simply stopped; it seemed to me he might have stopped anywhere. But I soon found that it was my mind that had wandered, not John Dewey's. I began very soon to do what I had seldom done in college courses — to take notes. It was then a remarkable discovery to make on looking over my notes to find that what had seemed so casual, so rambling, so unexciting, was of an extraordinary coherence, texture, and brilliance. I had been listening not to the semi-theatrical repetition of a discourse many times made — a fairly accurate description of many academic lectures — I had been listening to a man actually *thinking* in the presence of a class. As one became accustomed to Dewey's technique, it was this last aspect of his teaching that was most impressive — and educative. To attend a lecture of John Dewey was to participate in the actual business of thought. Those pauses were delays in creative thinking, when the next step was really being considered, and for the glib dramatics of the teacher-actor was substituted the enterprise, careful and candid, of the genuine thinker. Those hours came to seem the most arresting educational experiences, almost, I have ever had. One had to be scrupulously attentive and one learned to be so. Not every day or in every teacher does one overhear the palpable processes of thought. One came to enjoy and appreciate the homely metaphor, "the fork in the road," the child and his first attempts to speak, the New England town meeting, instead of the classical images one had been accustomed to from more obviously eloquent lips. Moreover, if one listened attentively one discovered apophthegm and epigram delivered as casually and sleepily as if they were clichés. I remember one instance. It had been rather a long lecture designed to show that the crucial tests of the morals of a group came in what that group regarded as violations of its conventions. The bell rang. Professor Dewey began to crumple up his notes. "And so," he said, "I think sometimes one can tell more about the morals of our society from the inmates of its jails than from the inmates of its universities." The student next to me who had been semidozing stirred in half alarmed surprise.

I learned later in a seminar to see Dewey's greatest gifts as a teacher, that of initiating inquiry rather than that of disseminating a doctrine. The subject matter of the seminar was innocent enough and removed from the immediacies of current controversy. It was a year's course, meeting every Tuesday afternoon, on "The Logic of John Stuart Mill." The seminar remains in my memory, it must be added, not simply for John Dewey or John Stuart Mill. It consisted, looking back on it and indeed as it appeared then, of a very remarkable group. It included two now well known professors of philosophy, Brand Blanshard of Swarthmore College and Sterling Lamprecht of Amherst, Paul Blanshard, later to become Commissioner of Accounts under Mayor La Guardia, and Albert C. Barnes, the inventor and manufacturer of Argyrol and collector of French paintings, even then a grey-haired man who used to come up from Philadelphia every week with his secretary expressly to study philosophy with his friend John Dewey.

I don't suppose Professor Dewey said more than five percent of the words actually uttered in that seminar. For the latter consisted largely of papers presented by various members of the group. But one remembered what he said. The subject matter was obviously close to him, for had not Mill been one of the great Nineteenth Century leaders of the empirical school of thought; — had he not been, in his way, a pragmatist and, like Dewey himself, a liberal? But one notices particularly Dewey's gift for pointing to the exact difficulty or the exact limitations of a man or a paper; his capacity for sympathetically seeing what a student was driving at, even when he did not quite succeed in saying it, and Dewey's candid expression of his own position or his own prejudices.

One instance of Dewey's frankness comes to my mind. There was among the group a young lady who had come from England where she had studied philosophy with Bertrand Russell at Cambridge. She listened patiently for weeks to Dewey's varied insistence that the truth of an idea was tested by its use. One day she burst out toward the close of the seminar in the sharp, clipped speech of the educated Englishwoman: "But, professor, I have been taught to believe that true means true; that false means false, that good means good and bad means bad; I don't understand all this talk about more or less true, more or less good. Could you explain more exactly?"

Professor Dewey looked at her mildly for a moment and said: "Let me tell you a parable. Once upon a time in Philadelphia there was a paranoiac. He thought he was dead. Nobody could convince him he was alive. Finally, one of the doctors thought of an ingenious idea. He pricked the patient's finger. 'Now,' he said, 'are you dead?' 'Sure,' said the paranoiac, 'that proves that dead men bleed. . . .' Now I'll say true or false if you want me to, but I'll mean better or worse."

There are all kinds of talents that go to make up a great teacher. Among those not commonly noted in the textbooks are simplicity and candor. These qualities in Dewey even an undergraduate could recognize and understand.

I cannot say that John Erskine seemed to me a great man in the sense that Woodbridge and Dewey did and do, nor did *The Private Life of Helen of Troy*, for all its bright entertainment, lead me to think I had been obtuse on this point as an undergraduate. But I am convinced he was a very remarkable teacher and it has always seemed to me a pity that he gave up the profession of distinguished teaching for that of the popular novelist. Erskine's quality as a teacher was that of communication by contagion; you felt the quality of the authors he talked about and books seemed to have something to do with life rather than libraries.

Literature was an exercise in imagination, not in archaeology and there must be thousands of students besides myself who learned to read authors in their own terms, to enjoy them for their own sakes, from John Erskine's famous course in Elizabethan Literature. It is true that one enjoyed Professor Erskine for other reasons. He had wit — often malicious — in his own right, and, when he was in the vein, poetry and philosophy, too. He obviously loved poetry and it seemed to him both to matter and a matter of course that we should love it, too. One felt about him something of the prima donna lecturer; it was evidenced by the pointed silence that would occur while some unfortunate latecomer found his way to his seat. It was clear, too, from the way in which, not infrequently, Shakespeare or Marlowe or Castiglione would be the springboards for little bravura lectures by our teacher on the importance of love or of being a cultivated gentleman, the latter one of his favourite themes. But if he was sometimes the prima donna, he always respected the materials he taught, and for many years no one at Columbia was a more devoted servant to the art and to the love of literature than he. And not the least of his services to that art were, first, the noble and musical way in which he read poetry itself; and, secondly, the pains he took to encourage signs of that art among undergraduates. Other teachers might make literature seem a set of documents to be investigated; no one quite knew why. Erskine made it an art to be lived and loved.

It is occasionally said that a good student needs no teachers and that all that he does need is a library and leisure. Neither the poor nor the good student needs bad teachers or bored ones;

he is better off without them. But he is very fortunate indeed if he can look back on his college days and enumerate half a dozen men who, by their passion for ideas, their clarity about them, their love for the communication of them, their exemplification in their own being of intellectual discipline and candor, have given a meaning to facts that, even with leisure and libraries, he would not have been as likely to find by himself.

I feel my college generation at Columbia was very fortunate. Half a dozen good teachers in a college are enough to make it distinguished. We had more than half a dozen very exceptional ones. But then I think current undergraduates at Columbia, if they are discerning, will, looking back, be able to say the same.

Louis Agassiz

1807 – 1873

THE FIFTH OF OCTOBER, 1946, *will be a date to celebrate,
for on that day, one hundred years before, the great Swiss
naturalist, Louis Agassiz, landed in Boston. He had come to give a
series of Lowell lectures and to investigate the zoology of the United
States but he remained for the rest of his life, to revolutionize biology
teaching throughout our educational system.*

*Not yet forty, Agassiz already had a fabulous reputation from his work
on living and fossil fish, the study of glaciers and fourteen years of brilliant teaching at Neuchatel. Here, he rushed on at the same pace, with
stirring lectures, travels inland, trips on Coast Survey vessels and the
duties of Professor of Natural History at the newly organized Lawrence
Scientific School at Harvard. Add to all this the four monumental
volumes of* Contributions to the Natural History of the United
States, *the world-famous Zoological Museum at Cambridge, the Brazil
Expedition of 1865, and the opening of the pioneer summer school of
science at Penikese, on Buzzard's Bay, six months before his death in
December, 1873, and one has a rough idea of that epic career. All the
great teachers have had the gift of contagious enthusiasm, but he possessed it in a supreme degree.*

*At the age of twenty-three William James was an assistant on that
Brazil expedition and years later gave one of his most eloquent addresses
in commemorating the fiftieth anniversary of Agassiz's arrival in this
country. " 'Go to Nature; take the facts into your own hands; look,
and see for yourself!' — these were the maxims which Agassiz preached
wherever he went, and their effect on pedagogy was electric. The extreme*

203

rigor of his devotion to this concrete method of learning was the natural consequence of his own peculiar type of intellect, in which the capacity for abstraction and causal reasoning and tracing chains of consequences from hypotheses was so much less developed than the genius for acquaintance with vast volumes of detail, and for seizing upon analogies and relations of the more proximate and concrete kind." . . . "We cannot all escape from being abstractionists. I, myself, for instance, have never been able to escape; but the hours I spent with Agassiz so taught me the difference between all possible abstractionists and all livers in the light of the world's concrete fullness, that I have never been able to forget it. Both kinds of mind have their place in the infinite design, but there can be no question as to which kind lies nearer to the divine type of thinking."

We may delight in this brilliant characterization of Agassiz without accepting the wider generalization, for as Whitehead says, "the paradox is now fully established that the utmost abstractions are the true weapon with which to control our thought of concrete fact."

Of Agassiz's many students who afterwards distinguished themselves as investigators and teachers, Nathaniel Southgate Shaler was certainly one of the most outstanding. Yet he might never have entered Agassiz's laboratory if he had not rebelled in disgust against "the succession of irrelevances" with which he was required to fill his mind in preparation for an entrance examination in Latin grammar! But he went on to become an important geologist, a wide ranging author and one of Harvard's most influential professors through nearly four decades.

Geology is not considered a "liberal" subject, but thousands of Shaler's students found it so. W. B. Donham, formerly Dean of the Harvard Business School, points the moral: "In the sciences, laboratory work designed for the future specialist displaces an imaginative presentation to the layman of the beauties, the importance, and the significance of science as it affects life. Science is rarely taught as a liberal arts subject. Yet men seeking general training can acquire a grasp of things needed to understand the place and importance of science without laboratory work, and laboratory work per se will never give it. Shaler's Geology 4 was a magnificent illustration. By making me an avid reader of science it inspired one great segment of my thinking for forty-five years."

"I Become Agassiz's Pupil"

NATHANIEL SOUTHGATE SHALER

→»·«←

IN 1858, when I was seventeen years old, it was determined
that I should have a good education. My parents could well
afford this, for my grandfather had left considerable property
and besides that there were other means. The plan was that I
should have a liberal training, and then make up my mind as to
what profession I would adopt. It was at first proposed that I
should go to West Point, but my fancy for war had passed, and
not even the argument that there was war to come, and that
soon, affected me. My desire, moved by my teacher Escher,
was to go to Heidelberg; fortunately it was determined that I
should begin my exploration of the realm of higher learning at
Harvard College. We supposed that I was far enough along to
enter the sophomore class in 1859, and after graduating that I
would go to Germany for further study. For my own part, I
cared little where I went or what I did. There was need of enlargement, the resources about me were used up, and I was so
shaped that if a change had not been made, I should have
wandered away in search of adventures.

My father went with me to Cambridge, and as it was well on
in the first term, I was placed under a tutor recommended by his
classmate, Dixwell. I was then a lank fellow, six feet high, very
slender, nimble from a good though limited physical training,
still rather feeble from attacks of malaria and megrims. As for
my training, what has been said before shows that it was from
the schoolmaster's point of view a jumble of unrelated matters

205

—a very poor basis for collegiate study, which took no account
of a training in arms and equitation, and as little of philosophy
and geology or a knowledge of human nature. Still, on going me
over, my tutor thought I could be put in the sophomore class in
the autumn of 1859.

Although my studies interested me—anything did, for I had
then and ever since a capacity to be interested in anything put
before me—my tutor most commanded my attention. He was a
senior in Harvard College, and had a well deserved name for
scholarship in the classics as well as for a miscellaneous assort-
ment of talents and knowledge. He was reputed to be the best
player of the game of checkers in the country; he knew the
political history of the United States amazingly well; was
learned in pugilism, having at his tongue's end the story of all
the prize fights of recent times; withal he was the merriest
little man I have ever seen. His curly head and radiant visage
charmed me at first, and remain as treasured recollections in a
whole gallery of such memories. I well recall my first morning
with him, when, after going over the best of what I could and
could not do, he asked me if I could box. I pleaded guilty to
some knowledge of that ignoble art. At that time I had not
learned of his interest in it, and thought that I would be
lowered in his eyes by the confession. To my surprise, indeed
to my horror, for I had a swordsman's contempt for the business,
he insisted on my having a bout with him at once. I had learned
boxing in Scherer's school of arms, where it was taught by a
competent man, but classed as a very degraded form of fighting,
ranking below quarterstaff. It was regarded as an ignoble if
sometimes necessary means of defence, only to be resorted to in
extremity when you were contending with common people and
had no blessed steel at hand. The eager little man proved very
unskilful. At the very first tap he tipped over, his head going
against a window-pane, smashing the glass but happily not
harming him. I shall never forget my mingled wonder and
exasperation at this incident. My training with the reverend

philosopher Escher had set up in my mind a category of the tutor into which this new-found specimen by no means fitted.

My work with my mentor went in a fair way for some months during the winter and spring in Cambridge, and during the summer in Keene, New Hampshire. In Cambridge, I found myself in an unhappy social position, for the reason that my station as a sub-freshman, as an inferior to the men of my own age already in college, was humiliating to my sense of self-importance, and in marked contrast to that I had won at home. In Keene, I found myself in a charming New England community, where the life resembled that to which I was native. There the fact that I could ride, shoot, act in theatricals, spout poetry, and descant on philosophy put me back into the class of men, so that I was myself again. While in Keene, there came an odd interest in my education which, though but a trifle, proved most telling. My tutor, with whom I had read much Latin verse in a manner which he approved, for my scanning was uncommonly good—I had a natural ear for it—one day asked me the rule for the quantity of a syllable, only to find that I was absolutely ignorant of such written prescriptions. The long list of these rules was then produced—they were to be learned at once. Now I cannot by any contrivance manage to fix in my mind a succession of irrelevances. If he had commanded me to commit all of Ovid, I should willingly have set about the task; as it was, I asked him if in his opinion Horace had learned these precious rules. He was sure that he had not, and equally certain that I must learn them if I had any expectation of getting into Harvard College. On that issue we parted. I refused to spend time on an unnecessary bit of purely formal work.

I was the more content to give up a training in Harvard College, for the reason that my stay in Keene had convinced me that I was more naturalist than humanist, in that I could not content myself with the book side of culture. The life of the fields, the brooks and rocks, was nearer to me than that of the men and thoughts of long ago. Moreover, in some way I had come across Agassiz's essay on classification, then just published, and in it I found something at once of science and philosophy. As I recall it, this essay was the introduction to Agassiz's series, never completed, of contributions to the natural history of North America, the volume concerning the *Testudinata*. These creatures had interested me in my childhood; I had one of them among my first "pets" when I was about ten years old, and fancied, I think with good reason, that he learned to know me and to come to my call. While at Keene, I became much interested in several aquatic species which were new to me. The essay and the descriptions in the memoir, along with the other contacts of nature in that lovely district, reawakened my enthusiasm for the world below man, so that the demand of my tutor that I should set me to learning rules for scanning Latin verse came most inopportunely for my college education.

At the time of my secession from the humanities, Agassiz was in Europe: he did not return, I think, until the autumn of 1859. I had, however, picked up several acquaintances among his pupils, learned what they were about, and gained some notion of his methods. After about a month he returned, and I had my first contact with the man who was to have the most influence on my life of any of the teachers to whom I am indebted. I shall never forget even the lesser incidents of this meeting, for this great master by his presence gave an importance to his surroundings, so that the room where you met him and the furniture stayed with the memory of him.

When I first met Louis Agassiz, he was still in the prime of his admirable manhood; though he was then fifty-two years old, and had passed his constructive period, he still had the look of a young man. His face was the most genial and engaging that I had ever seen and his manner captivated me altogether. But as I had been among men who had a free swing, and for a year among people who seemed to me to be cold and super-rational, hungry as I doubtless was for human sympathy, Agassiz's welcome went to my heart—I was at once his captive. It has been my good chance to see many men of engaging presence and ways, but I have never known his equal.

As the personal quality of Agassiz was the greatest of his powers, and as my life was greatly influenced by my immediate and enduring affection for him, I am tempted to set forth some incidents which show that my swift devotion to my new-found master was not due to the accidents of the situation or to any boyish fancy. I will content myself with one of those stories, which will of itself show how easily he captivated men, even those of the ruder sort. Some years after we came together, when indeed I was formally his assistant — I believe it was in 1866 — he became much interested in the task of comparing the skeletons of thoroughbred horses with those of common stock. I had at his request tried, but without success, to obtain the bones of certain famous stallions from my acquaintances among the racing men in Kentucky. Early one morning there was a fire, supposed to be incendiary, in the stables in the Beacon Park track, a mile from the College, in which a number of horses had been killed and many badly scorched. I had just returned from the place, where I had left a mob of irate owners and jockeys in a violent state of mind, intent on finding some one to hang. I had seen the chance of getting a valuable lot of stallions for the museum, but it was evident that the time was most inopportune for suggesting such a disposition of the remains. Had I done so, the results would have been, to say the least, unpleasant.

As I came away from the profane lot of horse-men gathered about the ruins of their fortunes or their hopes, I met Agassiz almost running to seize the chance of specimens. I told him to come back with me, that we must wait until the mob had spent its rage; but he kept on. I told him further that he risked spoiling his good chance, and finally that he would have his head punched; but he trotted on. I went with him, in the hope that I might protect him from the consequences of his curiosity. When we reached the spot, there came about a marvel; in a moment he had all those raging men at his command. He went at once to work with the horses that had been hurt, but were savable. His intense sympathy with the creatures, his knowledge of the remedies to be applied, his immediate appropriation of the whole situation, of which he was at once the master, made those rude folk at once his friends. Nobody asked who he was, for the good reason that he was heart and soul of them. When the task of helping was done, then Agassiz skilfully came to the point of his business — the skeletons — and this so dextrously and sympathetically, that the men were, it seemed, ready to turn over the living as well as the dead beasts for his service. I have seen a lot of human doing, much of it critically as actor or near observor, but this was in many ways the greatest. The supreme art of it was in the use of a perfectly spontaneous and most actually sympathetic motive to gain an end. With others, this state of mind would lead to affectation; with him, it in no wise diminished the quality of the emotion. He could measure the value of the motive, but do it without lessening its moral import.

As my account of Agassiz's quality should rest upon my experiences with him, I shall now go on to tell how and to what effect he trained me. In that day there were no written examinations on any subjects to which candidates for the Lawrence Scientific School had to pass. The professors in charge of the several departments questioned the candidates and determined their fitness to pursue the course of study they desired to undertake. Few or none who had any semblance of an education were denied admission to Agassiz's laboratory. At that time, the instructors had, in addition to their meager salaries, — his was then $2,500 per annum — the regular fees paid in by the students under his charge. So I was promptly assured that I was admitted. Be it said, however, that he did give me an effective oral examination, which, as he told me, was intended to show whether I could expect to go forward to a degree at the end of four years of study. On this matter of the degree he

was obdurate, refusing to recommend some who had been with
him for many years and had succeeded in their special work,
giving as reason for his denial that they were "too ignorant."

The examination that Agassiz gave me was directed first to
find that I knew enough Latin and Greek to make use of those
languages; that I could patter a little of them evidently pleased
him. He didn't care for those detestable rules for scanning. Then
came German and French, which were also approved: I could
read both, and spoke the former fairly well. He did not probe
me in my weakest place, mathematics, for the good reason that,
badly as I was off in that subject, he was in a worse plight.
Then, asking me concerning my reading, he found that I had
read the essay on classification and had noted in it the influence
of Schelling's views. Most of his questioning related to this
field, and the more than fair beginning of our relations then
made was due to the fact that I had some enlargement on that
side. So, too, he was pleased to find that I had managed a lot of
Latin, Greek, and German poetry, and had been trained with
the sword. He completed this inquiry by requiring that I bring
my foils and masks for a bout. In this test he did not fare well,
for, though not untrained, he evidently knew more of the
Schläger than of the rapier. He was heavy-handed and lacked
finesse. This, with my previous experience, led me to the conclusion that I had struck upon a kind of tutor in Cambridge
not known in Kentucky.

While Agassiz questioned me carefully as to what I had read
and what I had seen, he seemed in this preliminary going-over
in no wise concerned to find what I knew about fossils, rocks,
animals, and plants; he put aside the offerings of my scanty lore.
This offended me a bit, as I recall, for the reason that I thought
I knew, and for a self-taught lad really did know, a good deal
about such matters, especially as to the habits of insects, particularly spiders. It seemed hard to be denied the chance to
make my parade; but I afterward saw what this meant, that he
did not intend to let me begin my tasks by posing as a naturalist.

The beginning was indeed quite different, and, as will be seen, in a manner that quickly evaporated my conceit. It was made and continued in a way I will not recount.

Agassiz's laboratory was then in a rather small two-storied building, looking much like a square dwelling house, which stood where the College Gymnasium now stands. The structure is still extant, though in forty-six years it has three times changed its site and uses, having been first a clubhouse for his students on Divinity Avenue, where the Peabody Museum has been built; it went thence to a site on Jarvis Street, where it served as the clubhouse and theatre for the Hasty Pudding Club; from there a little further west to its present location, where, after being long the habitation for the department of French, it came to be a part of the little establishment for teaching students astronomy. Agassiz had recently moved into it from a shed on the marsh near Brighton bridge, the original tenants, the engineers, having come to riches in the shape of the brick structure now known as the Lawrence Building. In this primitive establishment Agassiz's laboratory, as distinguished from the storerooms where the collections were crammed, occupied one room about thirty feet long and fifteen feet wide — what is now the west room on the lower floor of the edifice. In this place, already packed, I had assigned to me a small pine table with a rusty tin pan upon it. Of other students, all somewhat older than myself, there were: Alpheus Hyatt, F. W. Putnam, A. E. Verrill, E. S. Morse, Richard Wheatland, Caleb Cook, and a person by the name of Lamb. Hereto also came from time to time but not regularly Theodore Lyman and Stimpson. There was also in some narrow quarters a translator, a Swede, whose name is gone from me, and a sterling old person, Gugenheimer, who served as a preparator. Agassiz's artists generally worked at his near-by dwelling or at his place at Nahant. One of the small rooms upstairs was a sleeping-place for Putnam, who served as keeper of the establishment. I have given what may seem unnecessary details concerning this primitive laboratory and museum, in part for the reason that there is, so far as I know, no record of it, and also that it may be set over against the existing conditions of what used to be called Natural History in the University.

When I sat me down before my tin pan, Agassiz brought me a small fish, placing it before me with the rather stern require-ment that I should study it, but should on no account talk to any one concerning it, nor read anything relating to fishes, until I had his permission so to do. To my inquiry "What shall I do?" he said in effect: "Find out what you can without damaging the specimen; when I think that you have done the work I will question you." In the course of an hour I thought I had com-passed the fish; it was rather an unsavory object, giving forth the stench of old alcohol, then loathsome to me, though in time I came to like it. Many of the scales were loosened so that they fell off. It appeared to me to be a case of a summary report, which I was anxious to make and get on to the next stage of the business. But Agassiz, though always within call, concerned himself no further with me that day, nor the next, nor for a week. At first, this neglect was distressing; but I saw that it was a game, for he was, as I discerned rather than saw, covertly watching me. So I set my wits to work upon the thing, and in the course of a hundred hours or so thought I had done much — a hundred times as much as seemed possible at the start. I got interested in finding out how the scales went in series, their shape, the form and placement of the teeth, etc. Finally, I felt full of the subject and probably expressed it in my bearing; as for words about it then, there were none from my master except his cheery "Good morning." At length on the seventh day, came the question "Well?" and my disgorge of learning to him as he sat on the edge of my table puffing his cigar. At the end of the hour's telling, he swung off and away, saying, "That is not right." Here I began to think that after all perhaps the rules for scanning Latin verse were not the worst infliction in the world. Moreover, it was clear that he was playing a game with me to find if I were capable of doing hard, continuous work without the support of a teacher, and this stimulated me to labor. I went at the task anew, discarded my first notes, and in another week of ten hours a day labor I had results which astonished myself and satisfied him. Still there was no trace of praise in words or manner. He signified that it would do by placing before me about a half a peck of bones, telling me to see what I could make of them, with no further directions to guide me. I soon found that they were the skeletons of half a dozen fishes of different species; the jaws told me that much at a first inspection. The task evidently was to fit the separate bones together in their proper order. Two months or more went to this task with no other help than an occasional looking over my grouping with the stereotyped remark: "That is not right." Finally, the task was done and I was again set upon alcoholic specimens — this time a remarkable lot of specimens representing, perhaps, twenty species of the side-swimmers or *Pleuronectidae*.

I shall never forget the sense of power in dealing with things which I felt in beginning the more extended work on a group of animals. I had learned the art of comparing objects, which is the basis of the naturalist's work. At this stage I was allowed to read and to discuss my work with others about me. I did both eagerly, and acquired a considerable knowledge of the literature of ichthyology, becoming especially interested in the system of classification, then most imperfect. I tried to follow Agassiz's scheme of division into the order of ctenoids and ganoids, with the result that I found one of my species of side-swimmers had cycloid scales on one side and ctenoid on the other. This not only shocked my sense of the value of classification in a way that permitted for no full recovery of my original respect for the process, but for a time shook my confidence in my master's knowledge. At the same time I had a malicious pleasure in exhibiting my *find* to him, expecting to repay in part the humiliation which he had evidently tried to inflict on my con-

ceit. To my question as to how the nondescript should be classi-
fied he said: "My boy, there are now two of us who know
that."

This incident of the fish made an end of my novitiate. After
that, with a suddenness of transition which puzzled me, Agassiz
became very communicative; we passed indeed into the relation
of friends of like age and purpose, and he actually consulted me
as to what I should like to take up as field of study. Finding
that I wished to devote myself to geology, he set me to work
on the Brachiopoda as the best group of fossils to serve as data
in determining the Paleozoic horizons. So far as his rather
limited knowledge of the matter went, he guided me in the
field about Cambridge, in my reading, and to acquaintances of
his who were concerned with earth structures. I came thus to
know Charles T. Jackson, Jules Marcou, and later, the brothers
Rogers, Henry and James. At the same time I kept up the
zoölogy, undertaking to make myself acquainted with living
organic forms as a basis for a knowledge of fossils.

.   .   .   .

Just after I entered with Agassiz, the construction of his
museum was begun with the small part of the now great edifice
which constitutes the end of the northern wing. There were
four rooms on the ground floor, each with galleries, and a like
number, similarly galleried, on the second floor. Early in 1860
the building was ready for use. Then came the work of transpor-
tation of the collections stored in the laboratory and elsewhere
to their new domicile, and the effort to arrange them in some
kind of order. . . . Into this work the students were in a way
impressed; so for a year I was with others occupied in sorting
and arranging a jumble of materials, odds and ends from all over
the earth. In the old storage place there was no chance to exhibit
any of the show specimens. So far as I can remember, the only
thing that people came to see was a large glass jar containing
several heads of Chinamen, which some one had brought from a

place of execution. The sight of this was much sought after, especially by women in search of a sensation. In the course of a year a collection was installed which in certain ways was then the best in this country.

My share in the work of bringing a preliminary order into the new museum was considerable, and while for some months it broke all systematic study it was largely profitable. It gave me a chance to gain hard contact with a great range of animal forms, both recent and fossil, and to it I owe a general knowledge of organic forms which I could not have otherwise acquired. There was at that time no other means of finding one's way to such information. Agassiz's lectures gave us little. Though very interesting from their personal quality, the field they covered was curiously limited. In the first term he gave about twenty-five lectures on zoölogy and in the second about the same number in geology. The first series began with a very interesting sketch of the general principles of the science, which quickly passed to problems of classification and thence to questions of comparative anatomy, practically limited to the polyps, acalephs, and echinoderms. In the years from 1859 to his death in 1873, when-ever he gave these lectures, perhaps six or eight years, their form and contents remained unchanged. The geological series was practically altogether devoted to the simpler problems of stratigraphy or the succession of geological periods; about one third of the course was given to the glacial period. Except for the noble and marvellously contagious enthusiasm with which he approached the subject and the admirable pictures of the masters he had known, the lectures were not profitable to his students; in those regards — the weightiest possible — they were most valuable.

By far the greater part of the instruction I had from my master was in divers bits of talk concerning certain species, and the arrangement of the specimens. He would often work with me for hours unrolling fossils, all the while keeping up a running commentary which would range this way and that, of men, of places, of Aristotle, of Oken. He was a perfect nar- rator, and on any peg of fact would quickly hand a fascinating discourse. Often when he was at work on wet specimens while I was dealing with fossils, he would come to me with, say, a fish in each hand, that I might search in his pockets for a cigar, cut the tip, put it between his teeth, and light it for him. That would remind him of something, and he would puff and talk until the cigar was burned out, and he would have to be pro- vided with another.

As soon as Agassiz's collections were removed to the new museum, the old building (now to be known as Zoölogical Hall) was put on rollers and taken across lots to its second station on Divinity Avenue. It was then given over to what was called the Zoölogical Club, an association of about a dozen students who were working with him. It was so arranged as to provide bedrooms, a dining room, and a room in the centre of the upper story with which the bedrooms connected, to serve as the meeting place of the Zoölogical Club, which was organ- ized at this time and became the centre of our life. I had the good fortune to receive in the allotment a sleeping place and a study connected therewith. These, as I did not lack money, were well furnished. As my quarters lay on the path from his house to the Museum, my master got into the habit of coming for a bit of talk, not always on science, perhaps oftenest about people he had known, about politics, in which he was keenly interested, or about his plans and perplexities. It seemed to me, as it did to some of my mates, somewhat curious, for I was the youngest of the lot and a newcomer. I now see that it was probably owing to the fact that in some ways I was then a good deal more of a man in my knowledge of the world than my elders and betters of the association. Something was due to the fact that I had been trained by Escher, an educated fellow countryman of his, and had known some of the "forty-eighters," and profited by the enlargement that acquaintance offered; still more, perhaps, to the fact that I had become in a way intimate in the houses of some of his friends in Boston.

In my room my master became divinely young again. He would lie on the sofa, drink what I had to offer—I brought with me the then Southern habit of offering wine to guests—take a pipe and return in mind to his student days, or to his plans for work, or to his scheme of a museum which should present the animal and vegetable kingdoms so plainly that he who ran would perforce read—and deeply. I have never known a mind of such exuberance, of such eager contact with large desires. I was in thorough sympathy with this museum and with his projects, so that I had large profit from these interesting meetings, for they awakened an enthusiasm for constructive work which I doubt if any other accident of life would have aroused.

The meetings of the Zoölogical Club, at which all sorts of problems were discussed, were never attended by Agassiz. To our request that he would join us his answer was that we had better work alone, though he advised us to gather about us all who were interested in our problems, and to give our joint studies a wide range. I see now that, while much concerned for our advancement, his aim was to have us stand alone, or at least to lean only on our mates. Although he could not help shaping those about him to his mode of thought and was often indignant with them when they departed from his path, he had a sound practical sense of the danger of founding a school of followers; more than once he commented on this error of other masters.

It was Agassiz's habit to use his students to explore fields for him. This was an inevitable element in his method of teaching, and has been inevitably followed by all inquirers who have taught. In this process of exploration it was his custom to set one of us to work on a group of animals concerning which he had some knowledge, so that he could guide his inquirer, at least at

the outset of his investigation. I recall that in this way I began
a study of the family of the conchifers known as the *Arcidae,*
including the fossil and recent trigonias. For a while I felt that
I was following on the trail which he had broken, and then, as
in the matter of the geographical and geological distribution of
the genera and families, etc., I began to teach him a bit that he
did not know. He was as eager to receive as to give, and what I
supplied went into his memory as his own discoveries, which
in a way they were, for the direction of the work came from his
mind. In time, as will be noted hereafter, this plan of collabora-
tive work gave him trouble, as it has given trouble to others
who taught in the same way — in that good old way that makes
the pupil feel that he is the master and thereby wins to his
powers.

William James

≫≫ 1842 – 1910 ≪≪

IN SENDING A FRIEND *a copy of* Talks to Teachers on Psychology: and to Students on Some of Life's Ideals (1899), *James wrote: "Pray don't wade through the Teacher part, which is incarnate boredom. I sent it to you merely that you might read the essay 'On a Certain Blindness,' which is really the perception on which my whole individualistic philosophy is based." It is the tragic preception of "the blindness with which we are all afflicted in regard to the feelings of creatures and people different from ourselves." That familiar yet ever heartening little essay, glowing with apt quotations, is indeed the key to James's philosophy and to James the man and teacher, who was amazingly hospitable to genius and crank alike.*

However we cannot agree with James that the Teacher part of his 1899 volume is "incarnate boredom." It is extremely readable and on the whole up to date, still valuable for those preparing to teach, as Professors Dewey and Kilpatrick have insisted in the introduction to a recent edition. True, James did not break up his text with minute divisions, sub-divisions and definitions, for he wanted teachers to "conceive, and, if possible, reproduce sympathetically in their imagination, the mental life of their pupil as the sort of active unity which he himself feels it to be."

James's tributes to two great teachers, Louis Agassiz and Thomas Davidson, "a Knight-errant of the Intellectual Life," and such essays as "The Social Value of the College-bred" and "The Ph.D. Octopus," along with Talks to Teachers, *make an unpretentious but rich contribution to the whole field of education.*

His own teaching career began more or less by chance in 1872 when

President Eliot offered him an Instructionship in Anatomy and Physiology in Harvard College. His dominant interest emerged in a few years with courses in psychology which in turn were entirely supplanted by courses in philosophy, long before he retired in 1907. But the central work of his life, indeed the central work of modern psychology, was The Principles of Psychology, published in 1890. It contained practically all of the themes of his later philosophical writing as it also contained many a phrase and thought on habit, self, emotion, will, "the stream of consciousness," that color our stream of consciousness today.

In his last year James was posing psychological questions that for us today have a much more terrible immediacy. Will constructive battle ever replace organized bloodshed? Will men ever march against nonhuman foes with the zest with which they march against one another? Can peace, for the mass of mankind, ever have the tingling excitement that war has — or is supposed to have? "Man wants to be stretched to his utmost, if not in one way, then in another." The problem is to find full scope for courage, self-sacrifice, duty, and endurance without widespread carnage. James thought that this could be done in the collective enterprises of the future and his classic answer in "The Moral Equivalent of War" should be a textbook everywhere.

Of James's many students who became distinguished philosophers, Dickinson S. Miller, "illustrious friend and joy of my liver," seems to have been the most beloved, but uncertain health and long absence in Europe prevented him from becoming a force in American life that might have been predicted. He has written several articles on James and a contribution to the Letters in which "the human quality of James's teaching has been admirably portrayed," according to Ralph Barton Perry.

It was to Professor Perry that another student wrote: "Sometimes Dr. James would put his hands to his head and say, 'I can't think today. We had better not go on with the class,' and he would dismiss us." But is not that the strangest reason for dismissing a class ever recorded?

Beloved Psychologist

DICKINSON S. MILLER

->>>·<<<-

I HAVE A VIVID RECOLLECTION of James's lectures, classes, conferences, seminars, laboratory interests, and the side that students saw of him generally. Fellow-manliness seemed to me a good name for his quality. The one thing apparently impossible to him was to speak *ex cathedra* from heights of scientific erudition and attainment. There were not a few 'if's' and 'maybe's' in his remarks. Moreover he seldom followed for long an orderly system of argument or unfolding of a theory, but was always apt to puncture such systematic pretensions when in the midst of them with some entirely unaffected doubt or question that put the matter upon a basis of common sense at once. He had drawn from his laboratory experience in chemistry and his study of medicine a keen sense that the imposing formulas of science that impress laymen are not so 'exact' as they sound. He was not, in my time at least, much of a believer in lecturing in the sense of continuous exposition.

"I can well remember the first meeting of the course in psychology in 1890, in a ground-floor room of the old Lawrence Scientific School. He took a considerable part of the hour by reading extracts from Henry Sidgwick's Lecture against Lecturing, proceeding to explain that we should use as a textbook his own 'Principles of Psychology,' appearing for the first time that very week from the press, and should spend the hours in conference, in which we should discuss and ask questions, on both sides. So during the year's course we read the two volumes

223

through, with some amount of running commentary and controversy. There were four or five men of previous psychological
training in a class of (I think) between twenty and thirty, two
of whom were disposed to take up cudgels for the British as-
sociational doctrine of the 'Principles' that a state of consciousness had no part or elements, but was one indivisible fact. He
bore questions that really were criticisms with inexhaustible
patience and what I may call (the subject invites the word
often) *human* attention; invited written questions as well, and
would often return them with a reply penciled on the back
when he thought the discussion too special in interest to be
pursued before the class. Moreover, he bore with us with never
a sign of impatience if we lingered after class, and even walked
up Kirkland Street with him on his way home. Yet he was really
not argumentative, not inclined to dialectic or pertinacious
debate of any sort. It must always have required an effort of
self-control to put up with it. He almost never, even in private
conversation, contended for his own opinion. He had a way of
often falling back on the language of perception, insight, sensibility, vision of possibilities. I recall how on one occasion after
class, as I parted with him at the gate of the Memorial Hall tri-
angle, his last words were something like these: 'Well, Miller,
that theory's not a warm reality to me yet — still a cold conception'; and the charm of the comradely smile with which he
said it! The disinclination to formal logical system and the more
prolonged purely intellectual analyses was felt by some men as a
lack in his classroom work, though they recognized that these
analyses were present in the 'Psychology.' On the other hand,
the very tendency to *feel* ideas lent a kind of emotional or
aesthetic color which deepened the interest.

"In the course of the year he asked the men each to write some
word of suggestion, if he were so inclined, for improvement in
the method with which the course was conducted; and, if I
remember rightly, there were not a few respectful suggestions
that too much time was allowed to the few wrangling dis-

putants. In a pretty full and varied experience of lecture-rooms at home and abroad I cannot recall another where the class was asked to criticize the methods of the lecturer.

"Another class of twelve or fourteen, in the same year, on Descartes, Spinoza, and Leibnitz, met in one of the 'tower rooms' of Sever Hall, sitting around a table. Here we had to do mostly with pure metaphysics. And more striking still was the prominence of humanity and sensibility in his way of taking philosophic problems. I can see him now, sitting at the head of that heavy table of light-colored oak near the bow-window that formed the end of the room. My brother, a visitor at Cambridge, dropping in for an hour and seeing him with his vigorous air, bronzed and sanguine complexion, and brown tweeds, said, 'He looks more like a sportsman than a professor.' I think that the sporting men in college always felt a certain affinity to themselves on one side in the freshness and manhood that distinguished him in mind, appearance, and diction. It was, by the way, in this latter course that I first heard some of the philosophic phrases now identified with him. There was a great deal about the monist and pluralist views of the universe. The world of the monist was described as a 'block-universe' and the monist himself as 'wallowing in a sense of unbridled unity,' or something of the sort. He always wanted the men to write one or two 'theses' in the course of the year and to get to work early on them. He made a great deal of bibliography. He would say, 'I am no man for editions and references, no exact bibliographer.' But none the less he would put upon the blackboard full lists of books, English, French, German, and Italian, on our subject. His own reading was immense and systematic. No one has ever done justice to it, partly because he spoke with unaffected modesty of that side of his equipment.

"Of course this knowledge came to the foreground in his 'seminar.' In my second year I was with him in one of these for both terms, the first half-year studying the psychology of pleasure and pain, and the second, mental pathology. Here each of us undertook a special topic, the reading for which was sug-gested by him. The students were an interesting group, includ-ing Professor Santayana, then an instructor, Dr. Herbert Nichols, Messrs. Mezes (now President of the City College, New York), Pierce (late Professor at Smith College), Angell (Professor of Psychology at Chicago, and now President of the Carnegie Corporation), Bakewell (Professor at Yale), and Alfred Hodder (who became instructor at Bryn Mawr College, then abandoned academic life for literature and politics). In this seminar I was deeply impressed by his judicious and often judicial quality. His range of intellectual experience, his pro-found cultivation in literature, in science and in art (has there been in our generation a more cultivated man?), his absolutely unfettered and untrammeled mind, ready to do sympathetic justice to the most unaccredited, audacious, or despised hy-potheses, yet always keeping his own sense of proportion and the balance of evidence — merely to know these qualities, as we sat about that council-board, was to receive, so far as we were capable of absorbing it, in a heightened sense of the good old adjective, 'liberal' education. Of all the services he did us in this seminar perhaps the greatest was his running commentary on the students' reports on such authors as Lombroso and Nordau, and all theories of degeneracy and morbid human types. His thought was that there is no sharp line to be drawn between 'healthy' and 'unhealthy' minds, that all have something of both. Once when we were returning from two insane asylums which he had arranged for the class to visit, and at one of which we had seen a dangerous, almost naked maniac, I remember his say-ing, 'President Eliot might not like to admit that there is no sharp line between himself and the men we have just seen, but it is true.' He would emphasize that people who had great nervous burdens to carry, hereditary perhaps, could order their lives fruitfully and perhaps derive some gain from their 'de-generate' sensitiveness, whatever it might be. The doctrine is set forth with regard to religion in an early chapter of his

'Varieties of Religious Experience,' but for us it was applied to life at large.

"In private conversation he had a mastery of words, a voice, a vigor, a freedom, a dignity, and therefore what one might call an authority, in which he stood quite alone. Yet brilliant man as he was, he never quite outgrew a perceptible shyness or diffidence in the lecture-room, which showed sometimes in a heightened color. Going to lecture in one of the last courses he ever gave at Harvard, he said to a colleague whom he met on the way, 'I have lectured so and so many years, and yet here I am on the way to my class in trepidation!'

"Professor Royce's style of exposition was continuous, even, unfailing, composed. Professor James was more conversational, varied, broken, at times struggling for expression — in spite of what has been mentioned as his mastery of words. This was natural, for the one was deeply and comfortably installed in a theory (to be sure a great theory), and the other was peering out in quest of something greater which he did not distinctly see. James's method gave us in the classroom more of his own exploration and *apercu*. We felt his mind at work.

"Royce in lecturing sat immovable. James would rise with a peculiar suddenness and make bold and rapid strokes for a diagram on the blackboard — I can remember his abstracted air as he wrestled with some idea, standing by his chair with one foot upon it, elbow on knee, hand to chin. A friend has described a scene at a little class that, in a still earlier year, met in James's own study. In the effort to illustrate he brought out a black-board. He stood it on a chair and in various other positions, but could not at once write upon it, hold it steady, and keep it in the class's vision. Entirely bent on what he was doing, his efforts resulted at last in his standing it on the floor while he lay down at full length, holding it with one hand, drawing with the other, and continuing the flow of his commentary. I can myself remember how, after one of his lectures on Pragmatism in the Horace Mann Auditorium in New York, being assailed with questions by people who came up to the edge of the platform, he ended by sitting on that edge himself, all in his frock-coat as he was, his feet hanging down, with his usual complete absorption in the subject, and the look of human and mellow consideration which distinguished him at such moments, meeting the thoughts of the inquirers, whose attention also was entirely riveted. If this suggests a lack of dignity, it misleads, for dignity never forsook him, such was the inherent strength of tone and bearing. In one respect these particular lectures (afterwards published as his book on Pragmatism) stand alone in my recollection. An audience may easily be large the first time, but if there is a change it usually falls away more or less on the subsequent occasions. These lectures were announced for one of the larger lecture-halls. This was so crowded before the lecture began, some not being able to gain admittance, that the audience had to be asked to move to the large 'auditorium' I have mentioned. But in it also the numbers grew, till on the last day it presented much the same appearance as the other hall on the first."

Frederick Jackson Turner

≫ 1861 – 1932 ≪

IN A RECENT BULLETIN *of the Superintendent of the Census for 1890 appear these significant words: 'Up to and including 1880 the country had a frontier settlement, but at present the unsettled area has been so broken into by isolated bodies of settlement that there can hardly be said to be a frontier line. In the discussion of its extent, its westward movement, etc., it can not, therefore, any longer have a place in the census reports.' This brief official statement marks the closing of a great historic movement. Up to our own day American history has been in a large degree the history of the colonization of the Great West. The existence of an area of free land, its continuous recession, and the advance of American settlement westward, explains American development."*

Thus began a paper read on July 12, 1893, at a special meeting of the American Historical Association during the World's Fair at Chicago, by Frederick Jackson Turner, a thirty-two year old professor from the University of Wisconsin. That paper, The Significance of the Frontier in American History, *was at once recognized as a contribution of paramount importance and its young author a leader in his profession. "The frontier hypothesis" provided themes for two generations of American historians who often overworked and oversimplified it, but no idea of equal power has taken its place.*

Born and brought up in Portage, Wisconsin, Turner knew the frontier at first hand as a geographical, economic and psychological fact — an end and a beginning of civilization. He studied at the University of Wisconsin, completed his work for the Ph.D. in history at Johns Hopkins with a dissertation on "The Character and Influence of the Indian Trade in Wisconsin" and returned to his state university for two decades of memorable teaching, finally accepting a call to Harvard in 1910.

In the matter of sheer quantity, Turner was not at all prolific. Besides some forty articles, he saw through the press only two volumes, The Rise of the New West and The Frontier in American History, a collection of essays. After his death appeared The Significance of Sections in American History, another collection of brilliant essays shaped by his second seminal hypothesis, and The United States, 1830–1850. This lack of mere quantity was due to Turner's overwhelming concern with ideas, with explanation, rather than with the easy accumulation of unassimilated details. It has been said that there are not five pages of straight narrative in all his published work.

It was in the fall, following that 1893 meeting of the American Historical Association at Chicago, that a young man from a village in Iowa arrived in Madison, partly lured by the name of Turner. Carl Lotus Becker found even more than he could have hoped for both as an undergraduate and graduate student; and his expression of gratitude many years later became the perfect portrait of the great teacher in action — perhaps unequalled by any other chapter in this book.

After serving at several institutions, Becker became Professor of History at Cornell in 1917, where he remained until his retirement in 1941. He was not very effective as an undergraduate teacher, but his wide, unobtrusive scholarship, his quiet wit, his polished phrases, were the joy and inspiration of many generations of graduate students. Like his master, he was a man of searching ideas who wrote short books, but what books by contemporary American historians can rival in sweep or wisdom Becker's study of The Declaration of Independence or The Heavenly City of the Eighteenth Century or How New Will the Better World Be?

Wisconsin Historian

CARL LOTUS BECKER

→≫·≪←

I WENT TO THE UNIVERSITY OF WISCONSIN (in 1893 it was) for the same reason that many boys go to one college rather than another — because a high school friend of mine, whose cousin or something had "been at Madison," was going there. As youth will, I at once endowed the place, which I had never seen and had only recently heard of, with a romantic glamor. Was not Madison a distant and large city? (I am speaking now of a prairie country boy who had never ventured from his small town into the world so wide). And was it not located on a great body of water, a lake eight miles in diameter, no less? One other bit of knowledge contributed to the splendor that was Wisconsin. On the faculty of that University there was a man whom a young lawyer in my town had belauded and bragged about, and familiarly referred to as "old Freddie Turner."

"Is he old?" I asked, picturing the long gray locks of a Faust before the devil comes in the spotlight.

"Oh no, not old. We just called him that, I don't know why — just a rough way of showing boyish admiration without being sentimental about it, I suppose."

"What does he teach?"

"Well, he teaches American history. But it's not what he teaches, the subject I mean. The subject doesn't matter. It's what he is, the personality and all that sort of thing. It's something he gives you, inspiration, new ideas, a fresh light on things in general. It's something he makes you want to do or be.

I don't remember much American history, but I'll never forget that man Turner, old Freddie Turner."

So I went to the University of Wisconsin clear about one thing—I would take a course with old Freddie Turner. Unfortunately he taught history. The word held no blandishments for me. In high school I had studied (that isn't the word, but what word is there for it?) history, general history, Barnes' *General History*, or some such misdemeanor against youth; of which I remembered only one sentence: "*Egypt has been called the gift of the Nile.*" That alone of all the history of the world I remembered; and even that I hadn't learned the meaning of, hadn't indeed supposed or ever been told that it was expected to have a meaning. A dull subject, history. And yet there I was at the University of Wisconsin determined to take a course in history because, unfortunately, that was the only "subject offered" by old Freddie Turner.

I was not many days in Madison before the man was pointed out to me, on the campus, going somewhere in a hurry, loaded down with an immense leather portfolio bulging with books and notes; belatedly hurrying up the hill to class I dare say, probably perspiring but certainly unbowed. Of course he wasn't old—thirty-three or thereabouts at that time. To a youth of eighteen, men of thirty-three, professors at all events, might more often than not *seem* old; were at least likely to convey the impression of having settled all disturbing questions, of having as it were astutely encased themselves in a neat armor of fixed defensive habit warranted proof against the slings and arrows of whatever unusual experience or risky adventure the mischances of life, within cloistered academic walls, were likely to threaten them with. No such impression was conveyed by "that man Turner" beating it up the hill at 10:02 A.M. Even to a boy of eighteen there was something essentially youthful in the rounded lines of the short compact figure, in the free and unstudied swing of arms and legs; something gay and larky about the head ever so gallantly held, with ever so slight and so engaging a lifted backward tilt of valiant defiance to all the associated fates; something mischievously boyish even about the ruddy complexion, above all about the eyes and lips—eyes and lips that seemed always smiling even in repose, or always ready to smile, as if the world were so full of a number of things that odd chances and interesting episodes were to be momentarily expected. Expected and welcomed. Such was the impression. Serious indeed the man was, you never doubted that, but not solemn, above all not old, not professionally finished; just beginning rather, zestfully and buoyantly beginning, out for adventure, up to something, in the most casual friendly way inviting you to join in.

Inviting you to join in, yes. I don't mean (God forbid!) soliciting students to take his courses. Heaven knows he didn't need to make sly maneuvers to get you. Well I remember the opening day of the second year when I stood in line by his desk, waiting to ask him a question (totally unnecessary question, invented for the precise purpose of standing there and being spoken to). There I stood, and presently he turned to me with the quick upward flash of blue eyes that seemed to lift and throw over and through me a shaft of live light. I seemed, dumb shy youth that I was, to stand fully revealed in the light of those extraordinary eyes—cool, steady, challenging, yet friendly too, and hoping for the best. Haltingly I asked my foolish question, and was answered. The answer was nothing, the words were nothing, but the voice—the voice was everything: a voice not deep but full, rich, vibrant, and musically cadenced; such a voice as you would never grow weary of, so warm and intimate and human it was. I cannot describe the voice. I know only that it laid on me a kind of magic spell which I could never break, and have never wanted to. Well, there it was, the indefinable charm. An upward lift of the eyes, a few friendly words, and I, like I know not how many other lads of nineteen, was straightway a devoted disciple and questionless admirer of "old Freddie Turner." I didn't care what he offered. For him I would even study history.

Even then I didn't study history. I took courses in history, and in due time I took Turner's "junior course" in American history. But I didn't study history, not really; because I didn't know how to study it. Remembering what things happened at what times — that was what studying history meant to me then. Learning these things out of a book. Well, we had a book. To begin with Turner asked us to buy Thwaites' *Colonies*, and I bought it. I have it yet, with certain dates set down opposite the successive chapters in the table of contents; all these "assignments" having been given us once for all at the beginning of the term. Simple enough, I thought — each week I will learn a chapter. But after the second week we were behind the schedule, and after the fourth week we didn't know where we were, and never found out. Of course I read the book — I think I did; was expected to and, being an obedient boy, must have done so. But the book was like all history books, dull, filled with uninteresting facts which I couldn't remember; and so it happened that when Turner sometimes for ten minutes asked us questions, — "Mr. Becker, what were the provisions of the Tariff Bill of 1816?" — I never could answer, or almost never. During the second term I did answer one question, a question which had just gone its weary round without eliciting any response. I forget what the question was. The answer was "1811." "Precisely," said Turner, in a tone implying that he now recognized me as of that select company of scholars who would see at once the peculiar significance of 1811.

But if I didn't study history that year, I was infected with the desire to do so. This of course was Turner's fault, not mine (Haskins' fault too, by the way; and if I were writing chiefly about myself instead of Turner, which it may be thought I am doing if I don't watch out, there would be much to be said about Haskins). For it was true, as my lawyer friend said, that Turner had a singular capacity for making you want to do and be something—to do, in short, what he was doing, and to be, if possible, what he was. And what was he? And what was he doing? Fascinated by the man, I attended to his every gesture and expression, listened to everything he said, less at first for the content than for the voice, the intention, the implication. The implication of the whole performance was of something vital being under consideration, something that had in itself only incidentally to do with students "taking a course." The implication was that we (all of us together, if *we* chose — that was our affair) were searching for something, ferreting out hidden secrets. Facts there were, plenty of them, and as a matter of course to be known; but that wasn't the end. There was something concealed there, in and behind the facts, some problem that concerned humanity at large waiting to be solved. The implication was that we might, on our own account, turn over the dead facts once more, on the chance of finding something, something the others had missed.

Inconceivable that Thwaites had missed anything, I couldn't suppose it! Yet so it appeared. For here was a "teacher," who at one moment confessed his ignorance and the next modestly questioned the textbook. Inviting us one day to consider the problem of sovereignty, he quoted Austin's definition; said he couldn't understand it; admitted he wasn't blessed with the logical mind; and drew two (or was it three?) overlapping circles on the blackboard illustrating the theory of "divided sovereignty," which he said seemed to fit the facts of American history better, but even of that he wasn't certain either. Well, a "teacher" was supposed to know everything, yet there was Turner not able to explain sovereignty. Supposed to know everything, a teacher was, but of course not more than the textbook. Yet there another day stood Turner saying, as casually as ever you please, "I do not agree with Thwaites on this point." What to make of a teacher who knew more than the textbook, but was still ignorant of something? After I know not how long it dawned on me, and with what a joyous sense of emancipation, that Turner wasn't, that no university professor need be, merely a teacher. Turner obviously hadn't just learned his history out of a book. The rash skeptic had gone out of his way to get the "facts" somewhere else, had "investigated" — that was the word — the documents on his own account, had taken his own notes from the "sources," was in short an "authority" in his own right, and might if he wished write his own book of American history.

From the moment Turner ceased to figure in my mind as a teacher, I began to learn something from him. Not "teacher" but "historian" he was, better still "author," whose main occupation it was, not to teach us, but to be deeply engaged in researches preliminary to the writing of notable books. Obvious enough, once you got the idea. For surely no professor, coming somewhat distraitly into class at the last moment, ever spread about such a cheerful happy air of having been interrupted in preparatory studies, or ever more successfully conveyed the impression of going cheerfully on, during the brief hour, for our benefit, with the morning's labors. Material evidence of those labors there was a plenty, in the stacks of notes deposited on the desk, notes on slips of paper 6 x 8, or some such size, filed in labeled manilla envelopes; more enveloped notes every day brought to class than could by any chance be looked into; as if the preoccupied scholar, leaving his study on the run, had hastily gathered together whatever he could conveniently lay his hands on, hoping to be prepared with illustrative material relevant to any one of a number of interesting topics which might, happily, turn up during the lecture.

The lecture itself, if that is the word for it, seemed never "prepared," never studiously "got up" under the lamp. It seemed rather the spontaneous result of preparations always going on and never finished. The lecture was just informal, intimately conversational talk, beginning as might happen with this interesting matter, and ending as might happen with that; always serious without ever being solemn; enlivened with

236

humor and wholesome infectious laughter, yet never falling to
the level of the sad professorial joke; running off into revelant
digressions occasioned by some student query; coming back
again to the main point; coming now and again to the full stop
while "notes" were eagerly searched for and found (oh, well,
usually found), if not in one manilla envelope, perhaps in another; notes containing some desired quotation from the documents, with exact reference given, illustrating a point, clinch-
ing an argument. No, lecture isn't the word. Nothing *ex cathedra*
here, no musty air of academic infallibility clouding the room,
no laying down of the law and gospel according to Turner; but
all compact of inquiry and novel ideas carelessly thrown out
with more questions asked than were answered, more problems
posed than solved. The professor seemed not at all concerned to
ladle out the minimum dose of American history suitable to our
complaint. He was just talking to us as a man might talk to men,
about the problems that interested him, problems which he had
apparently been thinking about after breakfast, and might very
likely, one felt, think some more about after luncheon.

Such was the impression. But where then did we, poor dazed
novices astray in the bright intellectual world, come in on this
business? No doubt the method, or lack of it, was not well
calculated to send the shining morning-faced student away rejoicing with neatly wrapped and labeled packets of "knowledge," to be held until called for, at examination time, and
then duly returned, unopened. No doubt the student often felt
like asking, as students will, what precisely the "required
work" was — "Professor, what are we expected to know for
examination?" Well, one could trust to luck, would have to
apparently. I at least knew that something (something about the
bank was it?) happened in 1811. Curiously enough I didn't
worry, timid and cautious youth that I was, I didn't worry much
about the packets of useful information; for you see I was getting, as failing students say, "a great deal out of the course." I
was getting a great deal out of Turner. I was daily enjoying the

inestimable privilege of watching an original and penetrating intelligence at work, playing freely with facts and ideas, handling with discrimination the problems of history, problems which so often turned out to be the problems of life itself. Unorganized the course was, certainly; but the resulting impression was nevertheless not one of confusion. The impression always was that of a brilliant light being thrown on dark places. For the talk, however desultory it may have been, was never merely rambling, but went always winding in and through and round about the matter in hand at the behest of some fresh idea, suggestion, or tentative hypothesis. Something vital and significant in the facts, these flashed ideas and hypotheses seemed always revealing. An ordered body of information I could get, and did afterwards get, for myself; but from no other man did I ever get in quite the same measure that sense of watching a first-class mind at work on its own account, and not merely rehearsing for the benefit of others; the most delightful sense in the world of sitting there waiting for ideas to be born; expectantly waiting for secret meanings, convenient explanatory hypotheses to be discovered, lurking as like as not under the dullest mass of drab facts ever seen.

In this happy way I got a new idea of history. It was after all no convention agreed upon to be learned by rote, but just the infinitely varied action and thought of men who in past times had lived and struggled and died for means or great objects. It was in short an aspect of life itself, and as such something to be probed into, thought about, written about. Who would not like to study history as Turner studied it? And write about it as he would write about it? Not possible of course to do it with his brilliant competence, not a chance; but still there was something to try for, a standard set, an ideal. And so in this eventful junior year I brought out my tiny little wagon and fumblingly hitched it to that bright particular star. Procuring quantities of paper and manilla envelopes, I began, "pen in hand," to study history; with patient, plodding abandon poring over such fascinating works as *Niles Register* and the *New York Colonial Documents*, or any other mouldy, crumbling, old tome, provided only it contained those "original sources" which Turner, by some species of white magic, had invested with color and charm. What a joy it was in those days merely to turn the yellow pages of old books! With what a sense of solid work accomplished one extracted the substance of no matter what official document, always, with reverent piety, noting the "exact reference" — *Niles*, XII, 749. Still preserved they are, those stacks of notes in manilla envelopes, aging now undisturbed on upper shelves, long since covered with dust!

With the novitiate ended, one took the full vows. For three years I pursued my researches in Turner's seminary, a group of twelve or fifteen men, with a stray woman or two, meeting in the Law Building, or, better still, in the state Historical Society Library, then housed in the Capitol. Here we did our work, each man having a table, or part of one, in an alcove; and all of us assembling, on Mondays, Wednesdays, and Fridays, round one of the larger tables, with Turner in our midst. To be so commoded was to be in the very center of the temple of learning; for we were here, all of us, professor and pupils, daily boxed about with walls of books, the books we needed and were currently using, those very collections of "documents" which exhaled the mothy odors of scholarship; so that just to sit motionless in the blest place breathing in the incensed atmosphere of research at its thickest enabled one to anticipate the illusions of the fully erudite.

Informal to a degree this seminary was, more informal even than the "junior course." Lectures there were none, or almost none, unless one prefers to say there were always lectures, or nearly always. For the engaging theory was that we were all scholars together, surveying broadly the field of American history, each man having his particular subject — the colonization of Virginia, Internal Improvements, or whatever — subjects large and unconfined, opening a career to talent. Each man was expected to master his subject as well as might be; to be responsible for it; to be ready like a cabinet minister to answer such questions, bearing upon it, as might be asked by the opposition; above all from time to time to make reports giving the matured results of his investigation. In this way each of us, including the professor, would lecture in turn, and all of the others, including the professor, would take notes. The professor, such was the theory, was just one of us, the principal one no doubt, organizing and directing the whole performance, but still not professing to know too much, modestly deferring to any one of us where our particular topics were concerned, and himself taking notes, when we lectured, with an alert and convincing air of being instructed, of having old matter freshly examined and interpreted for him. I swear he did take notes, and he has since assured me, with just a trace of asperity I thought, that it was no frame-up, but that he did actually obtain from us valuable ideas and information which afterward he sometimes made good use of. Well, I believe him. I do believe he did sometimes get from us some or other odd fact, such was his inordinate thirst for facts and his uncanny instinct for finding them in the most unlikely places, such his skill in disengaging what was significant from even the most confused jumble of the incompetent, the irrelevant, and the immaterial.

I took notes too, of course I did. It was part of the ritual; and I was nothing if not strong in the faith—in those old days. The notes I took are not such, I do confess, that one could reconstruct from them an adequate account of American history, but they had, and have had, for me at least, a high value nevertheless. Here before me, for example, are the notes, easily contained on one sheet of paper 6 x 8, of a two-days' report on the Mexican War.

Rogers' report—Mexican War. Polk. Taylor. Senate Bill. Biglow Papers frequently referred to. Turner asks: "By the

way, Mr. Rogers, what exactly are the Biglow Papers?"
Rogers says: "The Biglow Papers—" (Hesitates, seems a
little dazed, has at last a happy inspiration) "Why, the
Biglow Papers are—a well known work by—a famous
author." Hilarious laughter, led by Turner, who then explains Biglow Papers. Don't myself know B. P. Remember
look up and read B. P. Lowell, J. R.

Thus to my great regret I missed the significant points of the
Mexican War, but at least I read the Biglow Papers, and have
always remembered that the work is well known and by a
famous author. Another sheet lies before me.

Turner asks, why the unusual literary activity in generation
following 1815? Various suggestions. Becker says perhaps
on account of feeling of relief and freedom after War of
1812 and Napoleonic wars. Turner says, perhaps. Is that a
fact or only a plausible inference? What is an historical
fact? Can you prove an inference? May historian be satisfied
with inference? Have all great wars been followed by intellectual and literary activity? What in general is cause of
changes in character of thought? Fifteen minute talk, mostly
questions, a cascade of questions. No one answers these
questions. Why doesn't Turner tell us the answers? Something to think about.

Something to think about, sure enough! Well, I have thought
about it, off and on, for twenty-five years; but I don't now
wonder why Turner didn't tell us the answers.

As time passed I was made aware indeed that Turner very
often didn't answer questions. Heaven knows he asked enough,
was always handing out some riddle to be solved, always giving
us something to think about and then serenely leaving us to
think about it. But there were questions he neglected either to
ask or to answer. For example, did the colonies or the British

241

government have the right of it in the War of Independence? Should one properly sympathize with Jefferson or Marshall? Was the tariff a wise policy? Was Jacksonian democracy a good or a bad thing? Were the slave states justified in seceding from the Union? Important questions these were surely; questions which a teacher who had given his life to the study of American history might be supposed to answer for students who came to college expecting to be furnished with right opinions and convictions. But I don't recall that Turner ever answered these questions, or the like of them; so that to this day I don't know what his convictions are on the great issues. Is he protectionist or free trader? Democrat or republican? Baptist or infidel, or member of that great church which Lord Melbourne commended for never meddling with either politics or religion? Above all is he a conservative, satisfied with the evils we have? Or a liberal, willing to substitute for them others which formerly existed? Or a radical, eager for the shock of new ones never yet tried? I don't know. Turner never gave us answers to these questions. He never told us what to think.

I hope I am not conveying the impression that Turner appeared to his students in the somber light of a "strong silent man." Somber is the last word in the world to describe him, and silent isn't the word either. He talked freely enough, and he answered questions freely enough, questions of a certain sort. After I don't know how many months or years I learned that the answers he commonly neglected to give were answers which would have enabled me to borrow his opinions and judgments, and to save myself the trouble of thinking. He would do what he could to help me think, but he wouldn't if he knew it would tell me what to think. He was not much given to handing down final judgments.

This is important, and I wish to emphasize it a little. Turner didn't pronounce final judgments. In those days it sometimes troubled me that he didn't. But I have long since forgiven him, blessed him indeed, for it, having seen quite enough of those complacent people who go about recreating the world in their own image and expecting others to see that it is good. Turner might have said, with Mr. Justice Holmes, that one important article of his creed as a scholar was that he was not God. Like Margaret Fuller, he "accepted the universe," although, unlike that voluble lady, he did it silently. I am speaking now of Turner the scholar, not of Turner the man and citizen. As man and citizen he had, and always has had, convictions, knows what he thinks right and wise, and never leaves you in any doubt about it. As man and citizen he doesn't, I am sure, think this the best of conceivable worlds, or always find it a comfortable place to be in, as what intelligent or sensitive person does? He has indeed always met the reverses of life with serenity and high courage, no man I think ever more so; but I know not how many times he may in his heart have refreshingly damned the universe to extinction, as, on occasion, all good men do I hope. But I am now concerned with the scholar. As scholar, so it seems to me, Turner accepts men and things as given, the business of the scholar being not to judge but only to understand them.

To me at least it is a matter of no slight importance that he accepted us, graduate students, in that spirit. We, too, were apparently parts of the universe, to be accepted as given. He never made me feel that I was before the Judgment Seat. He was never the schoolmaster, standing behind me prodding, with sharp exclamation points pitchforking me up the steep path of learning. He criticized my work to be sure, but it was the work he criticized, and in the most honest friendly way, without leaving any aftertaste of personal depravity in the mouth. He appeared to take me as the associated fates had made me, more or less intelligent, and to assume that I would willingly do the best I could. Amazing, to me at least, was the casual friendly way he had of treating us as equals, as serious scholars with whom it was a pleasure to be associated in common tasks. Even our work he didn't criticize much, condemning it by silence mainly, commending it on rare occasions by a few hearty words of approval. How the rash man gambled on us to be sure, professing to see in us qualities and virtues marking us out for future savants. Perhaps there was some method in this madness. To get the best out of graduate students, or any students, it is perhaps just as well not to assume to begin with that there isn't any best there to be got out. Often enough there isn't, but then it doesn't greatly matter. If there was any best in me, I at least needed, in order to get it out, just the freedom and friendly confidence which Turner gave me, having until then been for the most part "criticized" and "trained" quite sufficiently; oh quite sufficiently told, by parents and uncles and aunts and teachers and pastors, what to do and what not to do; told in such an interesting variety of ways, and with such an implication of futility in the telling, as to leave me clutching the miserable little suspicion that I would probably never, all things considered, be much good at doing anything. Never having talked with my pastor, Turner didn't know this. He blandly assumed that I might amount to something, and at last one day told me that he thought I "had it in me" to become a scholar and a writer—seemed really to believe it. To be told by this admired master that I could probably do the very thing I most wanted to do released what little ability I had to do it. Released the ability, and intensified the desire to do it, because I then, and ever after, worked all the harder in order to justify Turner's faith in me.

This friendly method of dealing with graduate students (the honest ones, I mean; the occasional faker got the full blaze of his hot scorn) might not have been the best method for another, but I am sure it was the best method for Turner. It was the best method precisely because there wasn't any method in it. When Turner came into class he didn't put on the teacher's manner because he didn't think of himself as a teacher. He thought of himself—or no, he didn't think of himself, that's just the point. He was just Turner, man and scholar, absorbed in his work,

244

who met us because we were interested in the same thing he was; and who met us in the most casual democratic way in the world because it was perfectly natural for him to meet us in that way. The easy aristocratic grace and charm of this friendly democrat from Portage, Wisconsin, had about it neither a shade more nor less of any manner for his high placed colleagues than for the obscurest graduate student. It didn't, this unstudied friendly manner which at once put us at ease, seem to be even second nature. It seemed to be the instinctive expression of a lively and supple intelligence restrained and directed by some inexhaustible native fund of sincerity, integrity, and good will. This is after all one of the reasons, perhaps the chief reason, for his success with graduate students.

It is also, I think, one principal secret of his success as a scholar. For the scholar, the historian at all events, has to meet humanity in some fashion or other; and humanity will commonly reveal little to those who meet it with reticences and reservations and didactic motives. Even in those student days it seemed to me that Turner met humanity very much as he met us, graduate students; he didn't put on anything special for the occasion. Humanity, like graduate students, doubtless had virtues and qualities concealed somewhere about it, and might very well, such was the implication, stumble on, if you gave it rope enough, to some or other place worth going to. Best at all events to assume as much; for humanity is like graduate students in this, too, that it will be more likely to do well if you trust it a little, if you have faith to gamble on its hidden capacities.

But who could tell us where poor old humanity is headed for, rope or no rope? I would not willingly charge a reputable historian with harboring a Philosophy of History. Yet I recall that one day Turner quoted Droysen, apparently with approval, to the effect that "history is the self-consciousness of humanity." And another day he said: "The question is not whether you have a Philosophy of History, but whether the philosophy you have is good for anything." In extenuation I feel moved to say

245

that if Turner does indeed have a Philosophy of History, I can't imagine it taking the form of an answer. Much more likely to take the form of a question, thus: "If mankind could once really understand what it has done and thought in the past, is it not possible that it would stumble along now, and in the future, with more intelligence and a more conscious purpose?" I don't know whether this is a Philosophy of History or not. Whether, if it is, it is a good one, I know still less. But of one thing I feel quite sure: if Turner subscribes to it, whatever it is, it doesn't cost him much. It doesn't cost him anything in fact, for it doesn't burden him with any noticeable preoccupations or fixed ideas. He pursues his proper task, which is to find out what certain groups of men did and thought in past times, and to furnish the proximate explanation of their so acting and thinking; and this task he pursues as if he had no philosophy, as if it made no difference at all to him what they did and thought, or what the explanation might turn out to be. He pursues his task in short with detachment, with objectivity.

So at last we come to it, the inevitable word, objectivity. The word has many meanings. In those days I had myself got, or at least got up, chiefly out of books, a notion of objectivity scarcely distinguishable from complete indifference, a sort of stiff solemnity or *rigor mortis* of the spirit; so that I sometimes wondered if Turner really was "objective and disinterested," so lively and interested he always seemed. Certainly indifference, such as Renan's *Man in the Moon* might be supposed to exhibit, couldn't by any stretch of the imagination be attributed to Turner. Here then was a dilemma; and not being willing to abandon either Turner or the ideal of objectivity, I ended by seeing that Turner was objective in some other fashion than the Man in the Moon. The objectivity of Turner's mind, I found, was a quality he enjoyed in his own right, and not something acquired by training. It wasn't something he had painfully got up in college out of Bernheim — a set of artificially induced and cultivated repressions such as would enable any careful historian

246

to write, let us say, an account of the Battle of Cold Harbor without revealing the fact that his father was an ardent admirer of Grant. That kind of objectivity is common enough, and often pernicious enough, being the best substitute for ideas yet invented. Turner at least didn't need it, having always more ideas than he could perhaps well manage. The objectivity he had seemed rather to spring from that intense and sustained interest which an abundance of ideas can alone generate. A hard truth for me to learn, this was, since I hadn't too many ideas; but I couldn't help seeing that Turner was so wholly absorbed in his work that he hadn't time to think of anything else, not even of the necessity of being objective. He was "disinterested" because he was so interested in the object before him that he forgot, for the time being, to be interested in anything else; he was "objective" because he was so genuinely curious about that object, desired with such singleness of purpose to know it for the sake of knowing it, that his mind was empty, for the time being, of all other objects. This kind of objectivity doesn't come by willing (not that any sane man, living in a world of action, would will to have it); it is a quality of mind, like the sense of absolute pitch, which one is or isn't born with. No doubt it may, if one has it, be cultivated, but at any rate it is inseparable from genuine intellectual curiosity, the lively and irrepressible desire to know merely for the sake of knowing. A rare quality indeed that is, but I think Turner has it.

Another thing about Turner used in those days to strike me as a little odd. I don't know just what to call it. "Independence" isn't quite the word. Of course he was an independent scholar; but then most professors were independent scholars in the ordinary sense of the term. His was a peculiar kind of independence which struck me then, and still strikes me, as relatively uncommon among professors. I might call it a certain obliviousness to professional convention, an almost complete freedom from academic provincialism. I first noticed it indeed because it seemed to me then not quite the thing. For I was then doing what many college boys do—emancipating myself from one form of provincialism by taking on another. Coming fresh, or almost fresh, from the farm into an academic community, the professor's world seemed to me the last word in sophistication. The most obvious form which this sophistication took was a certain smart awareness on the professor's part of belonging to a larger and freer society than the one in which, geographically speaking, he perforce lived. Comfortable enough his ivory tower in Madison was no doubt; but he was likely to be often looking out of it toward the more splendid towers of the east, over-anxiously concerned perhaps to know what the wise men there were thinking and doing. One gathered that there were decencies proper to the academic world, a minor one being that no professor should have too much confidence in himself until he received a call from Yale or Harvard, and even then a lively sense of the fitting, some hangover from colonial days perhaps, would keep him subtly servile and apologetic for being no more than an American scholar who must forever abandon hope of entering the sacred portals of Oxford, Paris, or Berlin. If all this was only a second provincialism worse than the first, I was not yet aware of the fact. It seemed to me then no more than the proper mark of those who had oriented themselves in the intellectual world, quite the attitude in short for a professor to have. Therefore it struck me as a little odd that my admired master Turner didn't have it.

For Turner didn't have it. There was no getting round the fact that he didn't have it at all. I got the distinct impression that he didn't mind living in Wisconsin, seemed to think Portage a jolly good place to come from, as if being born there, even if the fact became known, needn't seriously impair the quality of his scholarship. If he knew that Europe was infinitely richer than the United States in historic remains and traditions, I never heard him mention the fact, at least not with the appropriate air of regret from missed opportunities. He had, on the contrary, every appearance of being contented with his

248

opportunities, seemed indeed to rejoice in his opportunities, quite as a man might who had just discovered a gold mine in his back yard. American history, he seemed to say, is a new lead, never yet properly uncovered, as rich and enticing a mine for the scholar as can anywhere be found, all the better for never having been worked by Waitz or von Ranke. It was as if some rank American flavor, some sturdy strain of backwoods independence, resisting every process of academic refinement, kept the man still proud to be an American citizen, contentedly dwelling in Madison, quite satisfied with the privilege of going every day to the State Historical Society Library where the Draper Manuscripts were.

Even in those days I felt, without quite understanding, this nonprofessional attitude on Turner's part. The time was to come when I found the professional attitude less engaging; and it was probably just because I saw Turner as "different" that these old student day impressions never faded, just because he was never quite the "professor" that his influence was more enduring than that of many professors. His influence was enduring I think because he himself didn't "date." Above all, his ideas about American history didn't date, never struck one as being modeled upon any established authority or cribbed from any school of historians. Something personal there always was in his "point of view," in his "interpretations," as if the subject were being freshly looked at by a mind washed clean of scholastic dust. Not that there was anything aggressive about his independence. He never gave one the impression that, having made up his mind to be original, he was somewhat bellicosely making good. His independence wasn't an achievement. And yet I wonder. Was there not about him too (or did I just imagine it?) some indefinable but quite jolly air of conscious insubordination, just a quick little gesture of the mind impatiently dismissing the solemn snobbery of all that is academically canonized and sacrosanct? I can't be sure, but I like to think so.

That is as it may be. But this I know, that three qualities of the man's mind made upon me a profound and indelible impression. These qualities were: a lively and irrepressible intellectual curiosity; a refreshing freedom from personal preoccupations and didactic motives; a quite unusual ability to look out upon the wide world in a humane, friendly way, in a fresh and strictly independent way, with a vision unobscured by academic inhibitions. These are also the qualities, I think, which have enabled him to make an "original contribution" (not so common a performance as is so often supposed) to the study of American history.

George Lyman Kittredge

»»» 1860 – 1940 «««

AS IN SO MANY OTHER FIELDS, *Harvard has a rich tradition*
of English teaching, whether in rhetoric, philology, or the gen-
eral appreciation of literature. Perhaps no one has equalled the record
of Edward Tyrrel Channing, Professor of Rhetoric and Oratory from
1819 to 1851, but he is now little remembered, for he published
only a few articles and his name has been obscured by that of his famous
brother, the Unitarian clergyman, William Ellery Channing. In
writing of Harvard in that period, Edward Everett Hale said: "Most
of the work of the college was then done in rather dreary recitations,
such as you might expect in a somewhat mechanical school for boys today.
But Edward Tyrrel Channing met his pupils face to face and hand to
hand. He deserves the credit of the English of Emerson, Holmes, Sumner,
Clarke, Bellows, Lowell, Higginson, and other men whom he trained.
Their English did more credit to Harvard College, I think, than any
other of its achievements for those thirty-two years. You sat, physically,
at his side. He read your theme aloud with you,—so loud, if he
pleased, that all the class who were present could hear his remarks of
praise or ridicule."(Edward Everett Hale: James Russell Lowell
and His Friends, *pp. 18–19.) Richard Henry Dana, Jr. characterized*
Channing briefly in this way: "Though severe in his tastes, he was, on
the whole, a wide liker."

In these latter days Harvard has had other extraordinary figures in the
English department, such as the beloved Dean Le Baron Russell Briggs
who taught writing with such success, George Townsend Copeland whose
poetry readings to large classes of students are legendary, and George

251

Lyman Kittredge, militant authority on middle English, witchcraft and farmer's almanacks, on Malory, Chaucer, and above all, Shakespeare.

"Professor Kittredge and the Teaching of English," by a brilliant young professor of the University of Illinois, Stuart P. Sherman, caused considerable turmoil when it appeared in The Nation in 1913 and has possibly helped to widen the horizons of our graduate schools of English. After a vigorous teaching career in the middle west, Sherman edited the New York Herald-Tribune "Books" supplement for two lively years and then drowned in his very prime at the age of forty-five.

The mighty Kittredge, however, lived on to four score and one. In the winter of 1936–37, nearly a year after he had retired from Harvard, he was invited to give a lecture on Hamlet in a course on "The Arts and Their Critics" at the Brooklyn Institute of Arts and Sciences. As I was in charge of that course, I invited him to my home for dinner — but with some trepidation as I had heard many anecdotes of his irascible manner. When it was suggested that he would not want a cocktail before the lecture, he said, "Indeed I would" — and took two, and then held up his beard docilely while my wife retied his bow tie. At the Institute he drew from his pocket a tattered old manuscript, patched and annotated in various inks, and read it with the splendid fire that Gielgud put into his performance of Hamlet. Afterward we chatted over beer, liverwurst sandwiches, and Antony and Cleopatra cigars. It was a cold, starry night and he obviously enjoyed the taxi ride back to Manhattan across the Brooklyn Bridge. He had not made that trip since the Spanish-American War — and I won't soon forget it.

"Kitty"

STUART P. SHERMAN

→≫·≪←

IRST OF ALL, let us declare that Professor Kittredge belongs to that generation of great college teachers which well-informed observers tell us is rapidly giving place to a later undergrowth of special investigators. There are, to be sure, a few small colleges left in the land, which, without much regard for "productive scholarship," still bestow their pudding and praise upon the man who can master his classroom, stab the laggards broad awake, and by the venerable inquisitorial methods discover and develop the young men of parts. But generally nowadays the word is passed round among the rising generation of instructors that the way to get on in the academic walk is not to waste time on one's pupils, but to publish—it matters not what. Whatever indirect responsibility Professor Kittredge may share in the propagation of this notion, it is undeniable that his own example has not sanctioned it. When the "efficiency" experts began last spring their abortive inquiries into the time spent by members of the instructional staff in preparation for each lecture, Professor Kittredge said, as it is reported, "I shall refuse to answer; it is my trade secret." A thoroughly characteristic mot, and it helped reveal the Philistine futility of the investigation. The special flavor of it lay in one's certainty that the questionnaire would, as a matter of fact, be dropped by him summarily and with perfect impunity into the waste basket, and in the universal recognition that as a teacher, pure and simple, Professor Kittredge is, as

253

they say in Cambridge, "one of the glories of the University." We are thinking now particularly of that famous course in Shakespeare which for many years has been one of the good reasons for going to Harvard.

There is a persistent tradition that Professor Kittredge formed what we may call his undergraduate manner in his preliminary pedagogic experiments long ago at the Phillips Exeter Academy. It is a manner primarily adapted to young, resistant, "tough-minded" persons, and it is perhaps not unconsciously reminiscent of Dr. Boyer of immortal memory and of that older schoolmaster at whose hands John Dryden received, as he gratefully testified, the only thrashing that he ever deserved. Exponents of the new style of teaching salute their assembled pupils in the French fashion with a courteous "Gentlemen," deliver an essay spiced with epigrams, or twitter extemporaneously through the hour, bow, and disappear. Or — of another type — enter the lecture room, weary, dreary from their private lucubrations, explain that they are but fellow workers with their pupils in the same vineyard, pull out a sheaf of ill-digested notes, and drone away till the welcome bell. The new style is based not merely on the assumption that the student is "interested in his own intellectual welfare," but also on the far wider assumption that he is interested in his teacher's intricate "special problem." In dealing with undergraduates, Professor Kittredge is an educational realist. He assumes nothing but the general ignorance, indolence, and inattentiveness of undisciplined youth. He sees congregated before him, in that curious mixture fostered by the Harvard system, boys of eighteen and men with hair as white as his own, hard students and loafers from the "Gold Coast," keen-eyed freshmen from the Cambridge and Boston Latin Schools and untrained bachelors from the soft Southern colleges, stiff-necked elderly schoolmasters who wish to "brush up a bit," and opinionated, unlicked cub professors on leave from the exuberant West. He does not cast a farewell glance about the room and dive into a manuscript. He envisages the situation. Before instruction proper can begin this unequal conglomeration of alertness and dullness, humility and conceit, must be subjugated, must be terrorized, must be welded by common apprehension into one homogeneous whole.

Perhaps the technique of terror is a "trade secret," too, but it is also a rich legend recited by every group of men that have studied English at Harvard. After the lapse of a good many years we can call up with perfect distinctness some of the Black Fridays when there was great slaughter of the Innocents. A pretty abrupt hush follows his rapid footsteps up the aisle, deepens as he seats himself sidewise, and menaces us thunderously from behind the formidable blue glasses, becomes painfully intense as he rises to stride to and fro the length of the platform in a kind of tiger tread, and the blackboard pointer, overstrained by his nervous fingers, breaks with an electrifying snap. We are about to enjoy a bad quarter of an hour. "Mr. A! How does a play begin?" "With dialogue," hazards Mr. A. "Mr. B! How does a play begin?" "With the introduction of the characters," stammers Mr. B anxiously. "Mr. C! How does a play begin?" Mr. C, who is from the Gold Coast, quietly mumbles, "I don't know." The hunt is afoot. The next dozen men go down amid derisive snickers — no one dares to laugh aloud — like clay pipes before a crack marksman. Panic spreads. Half of us refuse to answer to our names. The other half, in desperate agitation between an attempt to conjure up any sort of reply and a passionate desire to sink through the floor, shudderingly wait for the next victim, till the pursuer, at last weary of the sport, cries out, "A play begins in *mediis rebus!*" Then we turn to the text. " 'We would not die in that man's company that fears his fellowship to die with us.' Mr. X! Explain 'that fears his fellowship to die with us.' " Mr. X proffers something very elaborate and very confused. "Somebody explain that explanation!" — this with the true Johnsonian shout. "Mr. Y!" Mr. Y moistens his lips, starts, hems, hesitates, fumbles for words. "Come! Come! Mr. Y. Time flies! Hell threats! Heaven invites!" Mr. Y shuns salvation and hangs silent in Limbo. Mr. Z ventures on a surly pleasantry and is greeted with an invitation to "come over and swap jests with me at 2:30 this afternoon." We all envy Mr. Z as we should envy a man invited to take supper in a lion's den. Like many other of the great experiences of life, it was a rigorous ordeal while one was undergoing it, but it was pleasant to look back upon years afterward, and, like Purgatory, it was very salutary.

The instruction proper had, also, as we recall it, a powerful purgatorial quality. What has subsequently seemed to us to be Professor Kittredge's guiding spirit is happily embodied in one of the "golden sayings," to use his own phrase, of Josh Billings: "It ain't the things we don't know that makes such fools of us, but a whole lot of things that we know that ain't so." This, despite the vernacular dress, is the spirit of science, and for at least once in a lifetime it was an entirely wholesome spirit to encounter amid the bogs and fens of Shakespearean "interpretation." "War to the death," was the cry in that course, "on gushing Mrs. Jamesons, moralizing clergymen, and fantastic Teutonic metaphysicians." "There are many ways of studying Shakespeare," he told us, "but the object of this course is to ascertain what Shakespeare said and what he meant when he said it." The session ordinarily began with five or ten minutes during which we called out questions on difficult points in the previous day's reading. These he answered instantly, always without consulting the book, and succinctly or copiously as the case required. For the next ten or fifteen minutes he subjected us in our turn to a grilling examination on whatever we had prepared for the day. For the rest of the hour he commented with racy phrase and startling illustration, and left the room at the last minute, talking all the way down the aisle and halfway down the stairs.

For graduate students there was another manner. Jupiter Tonans gave way to benignant Jove, a being of equal or greater fascination, but with its terrors laid by, alert, omniscient as it seemed, a hawk-eyed critic still, but of princely amenity, tireless helpfulness, and the cordialest interest in one's personal destiny. This is the Kittredge of the disciples — the candidates for the doctorate — who hand down his obiter dicta from year to year, and speak of his chance commendation of some former pupil or pupil's work as one speaks of the conferring of an Order of Merit.

There was nothing lethargic in the atmosphere of those meetings. When the analysis and destruction of a great piece of German interpretation was completed one felt such a glow of satisfaction as must have thrilled the blood of a red-handed Saxon churl when he had assisted good King Alfred in flaying off a Dane skin and nailing it up on a church door. Nor, under that leadership, did one's interest flag when occasion failed for noble rage and cannibalistic enterprise. Fired by that unrelenting ardor, one fixed one's attention with as intense a concern upon a disputed comma in a Canterbuty tale as one could have felt for the most momentous crisis in the affairs of a nation. One could sit for week after week copying down under that dynamic dictation an endless ballad bibliography that one never used, nor ever hoped to use, and yet maintain through it all the spellbound gravity of one hearkening to a seraphic discussion of fate and foreknowledge absolute.

Best of all were the ever memorable individual conferences, when the candidate, now going heavily with his dissertation, visited the arbiter of his fate by special appointment at some hour not far from midnight, and came upon him, in the midst of his study, seated at the center of a great half moon of tomes and treatises, and enveloped and clouded, like a god, in infinite smoke. You began the interview with a half hour of wizardry, during which, while you helped thicken the smoke, he told

257

you of the smoking customs of barbarians or poured out odd stories of witchcraft and alchemy in New England. Then you explained your difficulties and he cleared them up, or you told him what you were hunting for, and he pulled out of some recess or other a box full of references bearing exactly upon the point, and filed away months or years before, when he was working upon the same topic. You returned to your labors with a persuasion that there was no topic which had not, on one occasion or another, engaged his attention. You returned with a feeling, also, that your academic fortune was insured. For it may be said of Professor Kittredge, as it was said of the old Germanic chiefs, who never forgot their friends nor forgave their enemies, he has been a good "Ring-Giver."

We have spoken with some fullness of the more personal side of Professor Kittredge's teaching, because it is only by dwelling upon his daemonic energy, his relentlessly positive temper, and his passion for domination that we can make wholly credible, even to ourselves, the nature and extent of the influence that he has exercised upon the teaching and the study of English at Harvard and throughout the country. For it must be frankly admitted that he has wielded his authority against a good deal of bitter opposition, and that many who have been constrained to submit to it have been rather subjugated than pacified.

There is a current story that a certain student, hankering vaguely in his uncorrected youth for the divine elation and finding himself out of the way of experiencing it, admitted to Professor Kittredge that he was not interested in "mere facts." "I am interested," was the withering response, "in nothing but facts." Doubtless the word "facts" had a wider meaning in the retort than in the provocation, and perhaps the whole incident is apocryphal. It is none the less suggestive. It hints at a type of pitcher, not empty nor entirely worthless, that is not readily filled at that well. It is a curious matter that though

258

for years we have heard witnesses testifying various indebtedness to their guide, philosopher, and friend, we do not recall that anyone has acknowledged indebtedness to him for a "love of good literature." We are inclined to doubt whether he considers it any part of his function to impart to his students a love of literature. We are certain that they receive little encouragement from him to form opinions upon the aesthetic or other merits of the pieces with which they are engaged. Possibly an early abhorrence of elegant lecturers and uninformed enthusiasms has hardened with time into an unconcealed, somewhat contemptuous antipathy for "literary fellows, concerned with the ideas and emotions which constitute the spirit of letters." "What did you learn in those graduate seminars that was permanently useful to you?" the writer once inquired of a favorite pupil, who was teaching modern English literature. "To verify my references," was the reply, "and to transcribe quoted passages with punctilious accuracy." That was, of course, a jest. What the speaker meant was that he had carried away the technique and the ideal of scientific research. That, as we take it, is what Professor Kittredge has principally desired to impart to graduate students.

Now, it is impossible to make the study of literature a rigorously scientific pursuit without terribly impoverishing it. You cannot give it the standing of a science unless you deliberately choose to ignore those scientifically imponderable elements of thought and feeling which essentially and permanently distinguish the field of humane letters from the field of science. In the approach to these elements the scientific spirit is, as everyone would admit, an indispensable lamp to the feet, but in dealing with them one must use a headlight filled with another oil. The moment that you touch upon them, you have passed the boundaries of the unvarnished verifiable fact. You are in the Debatable Land; you are in the moral world. Philosophy and religion lie before you, and ethics and aesthetics — which is not a science outside of Germany — encompass you around. You must proceed with tradition, authority, and a seasoned judgment to guide you, yet walking mainly by the "inner light." You are shoulder to shoulder with the thrice accursed "literary fellows" in the demesne of the man of letters. You are in imminent peril of becoming a literary dilettante, and there is one chance in a thousand that you may become a great critic or literary historian.

Professor Kittredge has taken few chances at making great literary historians or critics. Hating the literary dilettante with a perfect hatred, he has probably never paused to consider whether the odds are not equally heavy against the production of a great philologist, nor whether, for the service to which he is called, the literary dilettante is not on the whole about as useful a kind of humbug or mediocrity as the linguistic dilettante. Pausing, we may suspect, to meditate neither of these important questions, he has squarely turned his back upon the Debatable Land and has led his followers by forced marches into the opposite quarter of the English field, where he has taught them the elements of textual criticism and linguistic science, interested them in the editing of unpublished manuscripts and the collection of folklore, and made them all zealous bibliographers and compilers of card indexes. In short, he has been a potent force in bringing about the present sterilizing divorce of philology from general ideas. If his school has not been very prolific in important books, it should be remembered that one of its maxims is, "Anyone can write a book; the difficult thing is to write an article." This appears to be a veiled way of saying that the digestion of facts, however weighty, sinks into insignificance in comparison with the discovery of facts, however trifling.

The great field for the discovery of facts, memorable chiefly because they have been forgotten, has long been the Middle Ages, and Professor Kittredge is a mediaevalist. To a mind in which the master impulse is a wide-ranging curiosity this tract of literature is endlessly fascinating, by virtue of just those qualities which, to a mind with ulterior purposes like Matthew Arnold's, for example, make it seem almost negligible — its prolixity, its formlessness, its naive superstitions, its lack of high seriousness, its insolidity of substance.

We are not so foolish as to object that an eminent mediaevalist has followed his bent. Our objection is only that he has, in no very indirect way, prevented other men from pursuing their bents. There should certainly be room and following at Harvard for a distinguished scholar in the mediaeval period. But there should also be room and following for men qualified to deal in a really distinguished fashion with the vital ideas and movements of English literature since the Renaissance. We will not speak for the present year of grace — conditions vary somewhat from year to year. But within, say, the last fifteen years, there have been long intervals when, barring the drama, there was almost no instruction in English offered at Harvard that an intelligent graduate student could take seriously in the period from the Sixteenth to the Nineteenth Century. There were popular "snap" lecture courses for miscellaneous good-natured auditors; but for the student who had got beyond that, neither guidance nor encouragement. When, in conformity with the printed invitation, the candidate for the higher degree unfolded to the Department his plans and desires for work in modern literature, a majestic figure waved him to a more removed ground. There was nothing on paper to indicate objection to his enterprise, but after a few weeks he began to perceive that the modern period was not, so to speak, in good odor with those in authority. There was the system which incorporated the leading ideas of the Chairman of the Division of Modern Languages, and which prepared one for research in the Middle Ages. The core of the course was prescribed and the rind very strongly intimated — Germanic Philology, Romance Philology, Historical Grammar, Old Norse, Anglo-Saxon Grammar, Beowulf, Cynewulf, Old Irish perhaps, Ballads and Metrical Romances, Chaucer, Shakespeare, another course in the Drama also desirable. It was notorious that in the grand ordeal of the far-dreaded final examination serious inquisition into your scholarship would, in nine cases out of ten, end with the Fourteenth Century.

Without drawing too closely the links between cause and effect, we may say that the conditions prevailing at Harvard at the period which we have been describing have affected more or less seriously the teaching of English throughout the country. Departments in the older institutions with established and more humane traditions of their own have, of course, been less subject to the influence, and at least one great department has gained in prestige in proportion as it has reacted against it. It is in the small colleges and in the younger universities with rapidly growing faculties that the new generation of English teachers have been planted and have had their way. And it is when you see the newly fledged philologist at work, teaching composition (an art which he has never practised) and Eighteenth Century prose (a sea which for him has never been charted), it is then that you begin to recognize that something is out of joint in the state of Denmark. It is when you have observed half a dozen aspiring instructors publishing in the learned journals first-hand comments on mediaeval syntax, etymology, and beast fable, and uttering in their classrooms third- and fourth-hand comments on Milton, Dryden, and Tennyson — it is then that you understand the vogue of the teachers who "vitalize" literature by the use of the magic lantern. It is when you have attended the annual advertising picnic of the "scientific investigators" and have compared the quality of the papers and discussions at a convention of the Modern Language Association with those of the historical and philosophical societies — it is then that you wonder why it is that, wherever English scholarship is taken seriously, from the Great Lakes to the Gulf of Mexico and from the James River to the Golden Gate, all America mediaevalizes. It is when you have lived for some years in an English department, and have watched your colleagues settling into the role of routine teachers, losing their zest for discovery or taking it as a recreation like golf, abandoning the hunt for subjects and letting the dust gather on their card catalogues — it is then that you feel what Professor Grandgent, in his Anniversary contribution, has described as "the necessity of self-deception regarding the futility of human endeavor." You feel in this "fellowship of scholars" an almost tragical lack of common interests and ideas. You feel as one wandering in an intellectual Sahara in a silence unbroken save by an investigating sparrow chirping from time to time over a kernel of musty wheat in the shroud of Ptolemy the Great.

Sigmund Freud

≫ 1856 – 1939 ≪

WHEN THAT NOW FAMOUS and indispensable magazine of science, Nature, was being planned in 1869, Professor Thomas Henry Huxley was asked to contribute the opening article for the first number, but instead of an original article he translated Goethe's wonderful rhapsody on "nature" which had delighted him from his youth up. "It seemed to me," he said, "that no more fitting preface could be put before a Journal, which aims to mirror the progress of that fashioning by Nature of a picture of herself, in the mind of man, which we call the progress of Science."

Just four years later, at a Gymnasium in Vienna, a youth of seventeen by the name of Sigmund Freud heard an eloquent reading of Goethe's rhapsody and in consequence decided to matriculate in medicine. (As Henry Adams said, "A teacher can never tell where his influence stops.") From 1873 to 1881, he worked his way slowly toward his medical degree while concentrating on the physiology of the nervous system. It was about this time that an older physican and family friend, Dr. Josef Breuer, told him about his strange cure of a woman suffering from hysteria. While in hypnotized state "Dora" had rambled on, endlessly, aimlessly, about her life—but gradually unearthed the forgotten experiences which produced her symptoms, and so recovered.

However, when Freud went to Paris a few years later to study in the clinic of the neurologist, Charcot, he still thought of mental disorders as a result of brain disease and he was not especially interested in the problems of sex. What then was his amazement when he saw Charcot induce in hypnotized patients hysterical symptoms such as paralysis and anesthesia. He rushed back to Vienna to sing the praises of Charcot and to preach to deaf ears the theory of the mental origin of hysteria. But a second visit to France, this time to Nancy, to see the work with hypnotism by Bernheim, convinced Freud of "the possibility of mighty psychic forces which are still hidden from human consciousness." Of course, he now saw in a new light the ingenious method employed by Dr. Breuer in the case of Dora and persuaded Breuer to take up again the "cathartic" treatment while beginning to practice it himself. Together, they collaborated on Studies in Hysteria which was published in 1895, the same year that the discovery of the X-ray was announced by Roentgen.

Such, in a few words, was the beginning of psychoanalysis which has revolutionized psychology and permeated all the social sciences, not to mention literature and the mind of man generally. Breuer quickly withdrew from the collaboration, frightened by the widespread opposition, but younger and bolder men gathered around Freud in his clinic and at his home. In the full sense of the word he was their teacher, and although many of them broke away, to form their own groups, they were all incurably influenced by the master's point of view. Without them that point of view would certainly not have spread through the world in a generation.

After the earliest schism, the seven members of the inner circle, to whom Freud gave identical rings, was composed of Abraham, Witingon, Ferenczi, Jones, Rank, and Sachs. Dr. Sachs moved from Berlin to Boston where he now practices psychoanalysis.

"The voice of the intellect is a soft one, but it does not rest until it has gained a hearing." That remark was made, not by Socrates, or Pascal, or Francis Bacon—but by Sigmund Freud.

Interpreter of Dreams

HANNS SACHS

〈〈〈·〈〈〈

O N A DARK WINTER EVENING in 1904 I walked through the
long courts and narrow doorways of the *Allgemeine
Krankenhaus* (General Hospital) toward the Auditorium
of the Psychiatric Clinic, which was situated at the farther
end of the large cluster of buildings. It was near to the
Narrenturm (Fools' tower), a circular building which still
formed a part of the Psychiatric Clinic, and in which until
the beginning of the nineteenth century the insane were kept
chained to the wall.

This beginning is a bit like the trick by which a novelist
tries to captivate the imagination of his readers and although
this incident tells nothing but the plain truth, I have to pay
the novelist's penalty and to mention a few things that preceded this evening.

By this time I had finished my studies at the law school and
passed, by hook or by crook, the prescribed examinations. The
law did not interest me and I did not feel especially attracted
toward medicine. My interests were centered in literature,
almost to the exclusion of everything else. It seems queer that
my love for literature should land me at the Psychiatric Clinic,
yet this was the perfectly logical, although indirect, outcome.
The connecting link was formed by my boundless admiration
for Dostoevski. I wanted to find, led by the hand of science,
the secrets of the soul which he had almost succeeded revealing
in their nakedness; I hoped to tread in broad daylight the ob-

267

scure and labyrinthine paths of passion which he had traced. I turned first to psychology, at that time under the influence of Wundt, and found it disappointing. It seemed to consist mainly of a long winded terminology, which did not lead anywhere in particular, certainly not nearer to the mysterious springs of human emotions. I began to read about epilepsy which played so conspicuous a part in Dostoevski's life and work, and from there my interest glided over to the neighboring files of psychiatry and psychopathology. What I found looked promising and so I became extremely interested in them. Besides, these sciences held the somber charm of gruesomeness, something like the "occult sciences," which satisfied my youthful longings for the sensational and exotic. All this appealed much more to me than the pedestrian textbooks of "Normal Psychology." At least the facts were stirring, even when the explanations seemed often not sufficiently illuminating and sometimes disappointingly shallow. In the course of these desultory studies a book fell in my hands with the fascinating but bewildering title *Traumdeutung*. From the first I felt strongly aroused by its outstanding originality and I was excited by the entirely new angle under which many trivial, long-known facts assumed a startling significance. No other scientific book had told me about problems that I, like everyone else, always had before my eyes and yet had never seen or tried to understand. No other book made life seem so strange and no other book had explained its riddles and self-contradictions so fully. I said to myself that these stupendous revelations needed and merited the most complete scrutiny; even if it should in the end turn out that every theory advanced in its pages was wrong, I would not regret the loss of time. I was resolved to spend months or even years if the task should require it.

I knew that the author of this electrifying book lived in the same city with me, not far from my home. I heard his name mentioned now and then by people who were acquainted with him and his family. I also knew that he and his science were rejected by the official academic circles but that he had been given the title of a professor extraordinary in recognition of his earlier work in neurology. I found in the catalogue of the University that Professor Freud lectured at the auditorium of the Psychiatric Clinic on Saturday evenings for two hours — an unusual time and not likely to attract a big audience. And now we are back at the starting point.

I knew the lecture hall well because I had been there to listen to the lectures on psychiatry given by the regular professor, Wagner von Jauregg. (He later won the Nobel Prize for his work on the fever-therapy of general paresis; his mind was not open to psychologic subleties, least of all to psychoanalysis. Freud and he had been medical students together and maintained a tenuous relation which was entirely lacking in warmth, but not in mutual respect.) When I had seen the hall before, it was in plain daylight and all the benches had been crowded with students. Now the windows were dark and the only light came from a few bulbs suspended above the table and chair of the lecturer; the ascending rows of empty benches in the dusk gave the room a somewhat sepulchral aspect. Being well aware of my shyness and timidity in the face of any new adventure, even such a modest one, I had persuaded a cousin of mine, who was a medical student, to come with me; I hoped that his presence would give me support. In these unusual and gloomy surroundings I felt more panicky every moment and as a middle-aged gentleman, evidently the professor, entered, I started toward the door, whispering to my cousin a hurried explanation that we were at the wrong place.

What would have happened if my attempt to escape had succeeded? Certainly, my initiation into analysis would have been delayed for a year or more, but it is not impossible that my whole life might have taken another course. Luckily, I did not succeed. The middle-aged gentleman, who wore a short dark-brown beard, was slender and of medium size. He had deep-set and piercing eyes and a finely shaped forehead, remarkably high at the temples. Pointing to a row of eight or ten chairs which stood in a semicircle in front of the benches, close to the table of the lecturer, where a few people were already sitting, he said in the politest way: "Won't you come nearer and be seated, gentlemen?"

We followed his invitation and when he had started his lecture I lost soon every trace of shyness and inhibition. All of it was dissolved in my zealous interest aroused by what he had to say, and in my admiration of the way he said it. This effect widened and deepened the more I listened and learned. My shyness which he had waved aside at our first meeting disappeared and with it went bit by bit many other inhibitions and inner obstacles that had been standing in my way. Of course I attended faithfully every one of the successive lectures.

The chairs had been placed in front of the empty benches because Freud disliked to strain his voice, which was singularly lacking in what is called "metal." A dozen years later when his growing fame attracted big audiences he lectured in another larger, but not amphitheatrical, auditorium and was able to make himself distinctly heard in every part of it. But it meant a great exertion which he disliked, and since in these new audiences serious scientific interest was adulterated by large doses of snobbism and ordinary curiosity, he gave up soon afterwards his academic lectures altogether. After the war he spoke with rare exceptions only at the meetings of the Psychoanalytic Society and at its conventions. His faultless elocution and careful accentuation made him always perfectly audible although his voice had none of the full, rich tones which roll forth and lend to the words a suggestive force. I never heard him raise his voice in anger or excitement.

On these Saturday evenings, which soon became the pivot around which my private universe revolved, the atmosphere was intimate and informal. The number of "afficionados" was six or seven at first and never amounted to more than fifteen. Nearly all of them belonged to the circle which had begun to form itself around Freud and became the nucleus of the first Psychoanalytic Society. All the topics and problems of psycho-analysis which existed then or were just in the process of de-velopment were discussed. Dream-interpretation, the uncon-scious and repression, the structure of neurosis were, of course, the favorite subjects. But the many new vistas opening before our eyes, the unexhausted possibilities for new fields, and new methods of explorations in almost every branch of science added a great deal to the absorbing interest of these hours. We learned something about the nature of transference and began to under-stand the unconscious as the presence of an inner destiny which decrees that the same pattern must be re-lived since the wheel of life turns around a fixed center, and that the oldest ex-periences repeat themselves over and over again under various disguises (repetition-compulsion). We got the first glimpse of "applied analysis" — of using the knowledge of the unconscious and of the analytic technique for interpreting works of art and literature, for the investigation of social problems as well as of those of neurosis and dreams. All this was not preached in a pretentious manner, no great words proclaimed the gran-deur of the new discoveries. Freud did not assume the role of the prophet who tells of the mysteries that were revealed to him. The prevailing tone was a simple conversational one, often interspersed with witty or ironical remarks; his convic-tion of the far reaching consequences of the new truth was too deep to stand in need of emphatic asseveration.

Freud did not lecture on every one of these evenings. We had some periods of seminars when members of the audience were scheduled to give reviews and criticism of a book or an article, which were followed by a general discussion. One occasion I remember particularly well. A newcomer whom I did not know had to give a review of the Association Experi-ment. He started by explaining that the experimenter pronounces a series of words and expects the subject to utter after each of them the word that comes first to his mind. "For instance," he continued, "the experimenter says 'Horse' and the subject reacts with 'Library' (Pferd-Bibliothek)" . . . here Freud interrupted him: "If I am not mistaken, you are a former cavalry officer and have written a book on the psychology of the horse?" "Yes." "Then you have unintentionally given the best proof of the strict determination of associations. With the example which you chose at random, you have presented yourself and your field of interest to the audience."

At another time we had a series of discussions on the right method for interpretation of literary art. Should and could the same technique be used as for the reconstruction of the unconscious content of a dream? The "radical wing," the supporters of the "mother-womb" phantasy, maintained this opinion and tried to exemplify it in *Hamlet*.

I remember one occasion when Freud illustrated a scientific principle by an anecdote from his personal experience which is too characteristic to be omitted. The problem which he he treated was that of "over-determination," that is, of the multiple causality which exists everywhere but is especially important for the products of the unconscious. He warned us not to be easily satisfied even when the known causes seemed perfectly sufficient to produce the effect: "Many years ago," he told us, "an old professor of medicine died who had ordered in his will that his body should be dissected. The autopsy was performed by a renowned pathological anatomist and I functioned as his assistant. 'Look here,' the anatomist said to me, 'these arteries! They are as hard and thick as ropes. Of course the man couldn't live with them.' I answered him: 'All right. But it is a fact that the man did live till yesterday with these blood vessels.' "

When he discussed with us the psychoanalytic therapy of neurosis he used a picture post card of the most ordinary kind for making his point. The picture showed a yokel — we would say a hillbilly—in a hotel bedroom trying to blow out the electric light like a candle. "If you attack the symptom directly, you act in the same way as this man. You must look for the switch."

Freud told us about the past as well as about the future of psychoanalysis and especially of the initial stages of his work, which had led him step by step toward psychoanalysis. He spoke with warmth and gratitude of Charcot as a truly great man and teacher who had encouraged the unknown stranger by admitting him to the circle of intimate disciples. He loved to quote Charcot's answer when anyone tried to contradict an experience by an appeal to an authority *"Cela n'empêche pas d'exister"* (That does not keep it from existing). His favorite was evidently Liébault, the simple provincial doctor who without personal ambition and unaided by the trained staff of a clinic had the courage to help his patients by hypnosis, a method that hitherto had been considered as highly un-scientific and undignified. I remember now, not without a note of sadness, that Freud, who had no trace of any "racial" predilection one way or another, in showing us Liébault's photograph pointed out how un-Latin (today the word would be "Nordic") his face was and how well this was suited to his name which evidently was a variant of the Germanic *Luitpold*.

In later years Freud spoke to me more than once of his student-days in Paris of which he kept a tender reminiscence. Once he told me: "I remember how, on a spring day on the Boulevard Michel, a group of young men and girls walked in front of me. Every now and then they stopped walking and fell spontaneously in a few dance-steps without any apparent cause or motive, just because they were young and in Paris and it was springtime."

While I was listening eagerly to Freud's lectures I studied assiduously his technique of exposition (with a view of model-ing my own after him). I wondered how he succeeded in producing something unexpected and stupendous while his talk moved in simple terms, dispensing with the fireworks of baffling profundity or of glittering paradoxes. I found that he made use of Schopenhauer's recipe for a good style: "Say extraordinary things by using ordinary words." He followed this advice intuitively without being acquainted with it (I know positively that he read Schopenhauer for the first time many years later when he borrowed my handy pocket-edition for the summer). The startling effect of his lectures was based on a peculiar contrast. He gave all the necessary facts, dissected all the basic principles, even those which one would have taken for granted, with the greatest accuracy. He then introduced his conclusions cautiously, on a firm foundation; before he undertook the next step forward he surveyed all possible objections, formulated these clearly and answered them fully, so that when he moved on in an unexpected direction it seemed the most natural thing to do. When he had to leave an argument unfinished or incomplete, he pointed it out and went back to it at the right moment. In this way he led his hearers insensibly on, never giving them the impression that they were participating in a difficult and quite original investigation. They were surprised when they arrived in the end, without mental gymnastics or contortions, at results that contrasted strangely with some of their previously most cherished opinions or prejudices.

César Franck

⋙ 1822 – 1890 ⋘

O UT OF THE PRACTICAL DAILY LIFE, *out of the insecurities and longings of anonymous masses of men, in splendid unrefinement emerged the fine arts — singing and dancing, poetry and painting, sculpture and architecture, to give warmth and direction to every society, for they are the veritable embodiment of its ideals. "The greatest periods of the world's art and literature have been those of expanding horizons when ordinary men found in the arts the model and revelation of their humanity." The decadent period of a culture is marked and measured literally, specifically, by the decadence of the arts, when they grow secret, condescending and excessively self-conscious.*

However slowly and unnoticed the folk arts may evolve, their final flowering in a painting or a symphony is a matter of utmost cultivation, of delicate and desperate thought. Although there has been many a lonely, self-taught genius, for whom training might have been a tragedy, and although the ultimate process of creation must always be lonely, the natural economy of life brings the apprentice to the master, the artist-pupil to the artist-teacher.

It is a long way from Anne Sullivan teaching the spelling of a single word, to César Franck spelling out the structure of a concerto — yet there are the same problems of sympathy, patience and communication.

As most of us listen to the sublime organ music, the oratorios or the single symphony of César Franck, we think of him exclusively as the cloistered composer and do not realize that he was the greatest of modern French music teachers, devoting much of his best energies in sharing, or in trying to share, his exquisite secrets.

275

"Father" Franck

VINCENT D'INDY

->>>·<<<-

To teach an art with fruitful results we must first understand our *craft*, then the *art*, and finally the *pupil* whom we have undertaken to initiate.

It seems a mere commonplace to say that a teacher should himself be well instructed both in his craft and his art — two distinct branches of study, although too often confused — but, as a question of practice, this statement is not remarkable, for in Germany as well as in France (Italy is not to be considered from this point of view) in all the teaching institutions there are very few professors of composition who know how to teach their *art*, because — it must be confessed — they only understand and exercise it empirically.

In my time there were even some teachers of composition at the Paris Conservatoire who did not thoroughly understand their own *craft*, and were therefore totally incapable of imparting it to others.

As to the knowledge of an individual pupil, our entire system of instruction in France being based upon the false principle of reducing all intellects to one level, it is not surprising that our professors of art, acting in agreement with systems adopted elsewhere, are only employed in pouring into young minds that are sometimes widely differentiated the same identical and trivial material, never realising that the pabulum which is good, or at least harmless, for some may be hurtful to others, to whom it should be administered with a

277

corrective or an explanation. Nor do they grasp the fact that precepts necessary to limited minds can become intolerable to students of higher capacity, and may lead to a dangerous or at least premature affranchisement.

It is unnecessary to dwell any further on Franck's skill in the exercise of his craft and on the mastery displayed in his art, but it is important to show clearly one most valuable quality of his teaching — that knowledge of the individual pupil which was wanting in almost all the other professors of composition of his time.

Was he himself aware that he possessed this particular faculty? It seems doubtful; and we might go on to say that Franck was an unconscious philosopher, who studied the psychology of his pupils in spite of himself (I will explain the reason of this later on), and understood how to give each of them the direction and the subject-matter best suited to his temperament. He excelled in his power to penetrate his pupils' thoughts and to take possession of them, while scrupulously respecting their individual aptitudes. This is the reason why all the musicians formed in his school have acquired a solid science of music, while in their works each has preserved a different and personal aspect.

The secret of this essentially wide education lies in the fact that Franck never taught by means of hard and fast rules or dry, ready-made theories, but that his whole teaching was inspired by something stronger than law — by love itself.

Franck loved his art, as we have seen, with a passionate and exclusive ardor, and for this particular reason he loved also the pupil who was to become the depository of this art which he revered above all else; this is why he knew instinctively how to touch the hearts of his pupils and attach them to himself once and for all.

For the entire generation that was so fortunate as to be brought up on his sane and solid principles, César Franck was not merely a farseeing and lucid teacher, but a *father* — and I have no hesitation in using this word to characterise the man who gave birth to the French symphonic school, for we, his pupils, together with many artists who came in contact with him, were drawn instinctively by a unanimous, but independent, agreement to call him "Father" Franck.

While the ordinary run of academic teachers (and especially the professors at the Paris Conservatoire, where their energies are chiefly directed to the production of *premiers prix*) generally succeed in making their pupils rivals — who often end by being enemies — "Father" Franck only set himself to turn out artists truly worthy of this free and noble title; such an atmosphere of love radiated from this pure-minded man that his pupils not only cared for him as for a father, but they were attached to each other in and through him. During the fifteen years which have elapsed since his death his beneficent influence has continued, so that his disciples have kept up their intimacy without the smallest cloud appearing to darken their friendly relations.

But, besides all this, what an admirable professor of composition he was! How sincere and conscientious in examining the sketches we took him! Merciless to all faults of construction, he knew how to put his finger on the mistake without a moment's hesitation; and when in the course of his corrections he came to the passages which we ourselves considered doubtful, although we had been careful not to tell him so, his wide mouth would immediately become serious, his forehead would be puckered up, and his whole attitude expressed suffering. After having played through the unfortunate passage two or three times on the piano, he would raise his eyes to us and let drop the fatal words: "I don't like that!" But when by chance in our first stammering musical utterances we hit upon some new modulation logically brought about, or some attempt at novelty of form which had a certain interest, he would bend over us murmuring: "I like this, I like this!" He was as happy in giving us this sign of his approbation as we were proud to have deserved it.

But let it not be supposed that it was vanity or presumption that caused the master to deduce his judgments from his own likes and dislikes. Nothing could be further from his mind than the arrogant assertions of the *art critic*, announcing sententiously, after a first — and often an absent-minded — hearing, that "this work is sublime, and that one a failure." "Father" Franck never criticised in this free and easy fashion; he listened, re-read, argued for and against, and only formed his opinion when, after attentive self-examination, he felt sure he was in inward communion with the spirit of Beauty and could speak in the name of Truth — not of relative, but of absolute truth.

For — as we who live at the close of the nineteenth century know only too well — Truth is never made manifest through hatred, and the words "I *condemn*," monstrous and frequent though they be, always remain powerless compared with "Father" Franck's simple utterance: "*I like it.*"

"To love, to come out of ourselves, to leave our egotism aside by loving something very superior — almost unknown, perhaps — in which, however, we continue to believe, no matter what name we give it — here is the very basis and essence of a true system such as Plato recommended to the worshippers of the celestial Venus; such as Bossuet taught Christians to regard as the voice of moral perfection. It is the system of all great artists; it was that of César Franck. Through it he came practically into touch with all those masters who have best depicted the ascent of the soul towards God."

I now want my readers to penetrate more deeply into this intuitive manner of teaching, and see how much it differed from the methods employed by the majority of professors in conservatoires and music schools.

The first condition which Franck imposed upon a pupil was not to work *much*, but to work *well*; or, more strictly speaking, not to bring him a great quantity of task-work, but only what had been very carefully prepared.

The student gained greatly by this system, for he acquired the habit, even from his preliminary studies, of neglecting nothing and of bringing up work that was more intelligent than mechanical. This is a thing which too many young people educated in more or less official institutions cannot grasp. Accustomed from their childhood to bring *tasks* to their professors, they cannot conceive that, in Art, such a thing is non-existent. There is no more occasion for task-work in musical composition than there is in painting or architecture; all that is done in the way of art should not be of the nature of a daily imposition, but the result of a struggle in which the young artist has left something of his heart, and for the expression of which he has called into play all his intellectual faculties. The system of making a student produce a quantity of work under the pretext of "getting his hand in" is a very indifferent one of most pupils, since it accustoms them to write any kind of stuff and to be satisfied with everything that flows from their pens, provided the result is copious. Working in this way, they form no notion of the elemental part played by that faculty of the intelligence called *taste*, the mission of which is to determine the choice of materials as well as their symmetrical arrangement; and it is to this error that we must attribute the production of the numerous works — as compendious in thought as they are useless to art — which invade the stage and the concert-room, not only in France, but in Germany and Italy.

"Do not write much, but let it be very good," "Father" Franck used to say, and the strength of his school has been the maintenance of this precept.

When we had finished our study of counterpoint, which he always demanded should be melodic and intelligent, and a course of fugue, in which he advised his students to seek for *expression* rather than mere combination, he was then prepared to initiate us into the mysteries of composition, which, according to him, was entirely based upon tonal construction.

No art, in fact, bears a closer relation to music than that of construction—architecture. In the erection of an edifice it is first of all necessary that the materials should be of good quality and chosen with discernment; in the same way a composer must be very particular in the selection of his musical *ideas* if he wished to create a lasting work. But in building it is not sufficient to have fine materials without the knowledge how to dispose them so that by their cohesion they shall form a strong and harmonious whole. Stones, no matter how carefully hewn, can never form a monumental edifice if they are simply superimposed upon each other without due order; neither will musical phrases, however beautiful in themselves, constitute a great work unless their distribution and concatenation follow some definite and logical order. Only on these conditions can the structure be raised, and if the elements are good and the synthetic order harmoniously contrived the work will be solid and enduring.

Musical composition is just the same. This is what Franck—and perhaps no one else at that time—knew how to make his pupils realise. In practice he adhered essentially to the laws of form, while leaving us complete liberty in the application of them. Thanks to his habit, to which I have already referred, of seeking in each student the special quality to be cultivated for the profit of his art, his instruction was exceedingly liberal-minded; for, while he respected as much as any one the highest laws of our art—the laws of nature and of tradition—he applied them intelligently, reconciling them with those rights of individual initiative which he always left his pupils free to exercise. Severe as he was in pointing out the faults of form and the scamped workmanship which undermine the very foundations of a work of art, he was equally indulgent to faults in detail or failure to observe the letter of the law as laid down by the Schools. When this failure seemed to him justifiable, he would say with a smile that was more genial than ironical: "They would not permit you to do that at the Conservatoire—but I like it very much."

At the same time his courage in admitting everything that seemed to him *good* did not blind him to defects of style. If, after searching investigation, he could not conscientiously approve a disputed passage, he was careful only to say to the student, "That is not good; you must bring it to me again," like any other professor; only Franck went into the reasons for its not being good, and explained them so clearly that the pupil could not fail to be convinced.

One of the most valuable features of Franck's lessons was his demonstration by example. If we were perplexed in the arrangement of our work, involved in some difficulty in the progress of a composition, the master would at once fetch from his library some score by Bach, Beethoven, Schumann, or Wagner. "Look," he would say, "Beethoven (or some other composer) finds himself here just in the same situation as yours. Now see how he gets out of it. Read these passages, and find inspiration to correct your work; but do not imitate—try to find your own solution of the difficulty."

May I be allowed to relate an anecdote bearing upon this? It is of course personal, because it refers to the way in which I became "Father" Franck's pupil, but it gives an idea of his engaging frankness.

After I had played him a movement of my quartet (which I fondly imagined to be of such a nature as to win his approbation), he was silent for a moment; then, turning to me with a melancholy air, he spoke the words which I have never been able to forget, since they had a decisive action upon my life: "There are some good things in it; it shows spirit and a certain instinct for dialogue between the parts; the ideas would not be bad—but—that is not enough; the work is not finished—in fact, *you really know nothing whatever.*" Seeing that I was dreadfully mortified by this opinion, for which I was not at all prepared, he went on to explain his reasons, and wound up by saying: "Come to see me, if you want us to work together. I could teach you composition."

When I got home — the interview took place very late in the evening — I lay awake at night, rebelling against the severity of this sentence, but agitated in the depths of my heart, and I said to myself that Franck was an old-fashioned musician who knew nothing of a young and progressive art. Nevertheless, the next day, having calmed down, I took up my unfortunate quartet and went over, one by one, the observations which the master had made, emphasising his words the while, according to his custom, by innumerable arabesques scrawled in pencil over the manuscript, and I was obliged to own to myself that he was perfectly right — I knew nothing. I went to him, almost in fear and trembling, to ask if he would be good enough to take me as a pupil, and he admitted me to the organ class at the Conservatoire, of which he had just been appointed professor.

This class, which I always remember with emotion, was for a long time the true centre for the study of composition at the Conservatoire. At that period (I am speaking of the far-away years from 1872 onward) the three courses of *advanced composition* were taken by the following masters: Victor Massé, composer of comic operas, who had no notion of symphonic music, and who, being constantly ill, was in the habit of passing on his duties to one of his pupils; Henri Reber, an elderly musician of narrow and old-fashioned views; finally François Bazin, who had no idea of what musical composition meant. It is not astonishing, therefore, that César Franck's lofty teaching, based upon Bach and Beethoven, but admitting all new and generous impulses and aspirations, should have attracted all the young spirits endowed with noble ideas and really enamoured of their art. In this way the master almost unconsciously drew off all the truly artistic forces scattered through the various classes in the Conservatoire, not to mention the pupils outside who went for their lessons to his quiet room in the Boulevard Saint-Michael, the high windows of which gave out upon a shady garden—a rare occurrence in Paris. Here we gathered once a week; for "Father" Franck was not contented with instructing us at his organ class, in fugue, counterpoint, and improvisation; he invited to his house such of his pupils as seemed worthy of some special teaching, and this was done in an entirely disinterested spirit, which is not usual among professors of public institutions, in which the gratuitous instruction announced in the prospectus is, alas! far from being a reality.

Such was Franck's affection for his disciples that he never neglected any opportunity of proving it, or even of giving them any information which he thought would interest them. When, after the fatigues of the day, he had said good-by to those he was in the habit of receiving in the evening, he frequently sat down at his writing-table, not to compose or orchestrate, but to write—often at great length—to his pupils in the provinces, drawing up, with the greatest care, instructions and advice for their benefit.

I cannot refrain from quoting one example of this affectionate solicitude, although it concerns me personally.

Having been summoned to Antwerp, on the occasion of the exhibition of 1885, in order to conduct some of his works at a festival concert, the programme of which included a little composition by his pupil, he still found time, amid all his occupations, to write me this letter, wherein he speaks far more of others than of himself:

Antwerp, Friday, August 14.

"My dear Vincent,

"A thousand thanks for your kind and affectionate letter. I need hardly say that it is one of those that gave me the greatest pleasure.

"I will write you a longer letter another time, but I want

285

to tell you that at a concert here your 'Chevauchée du Cid' was played *perfectly*, and had a great success. Fontaine sang the solo. You were in the same company as your master, whose march and ballet music from 'Hulda' were warmly applauded.

"I must say good-bye, my dear Vincent. Give my kindest remembrances to your dear wife.

"A kiss to the charming children.

"Duparc is *established* near Pau. He has *bought* a property.

"Your old friend,

"César Franck."

In spite of his natural affability, Franck was regarded with suspicion by most of the musicians of his day, and as, notwithstanding his modesty, he could never bring himself to cringe to the powers that be, any more than he would conform in a flabby way to the sacrosanct regulations of the Conservatoire when it seemed to him necessary that they should be broken, he was, throughout his career, the object of the envy and hatred of his colleagues, who evidently misunderstood him, because his mind was in every way the exact opposite of theirs.

This hatred sometimes extended to his pupils—a more serious matter, since I have known competitions in which prizes were withheld from those who most deserved them, merely in order to spite the professor. The next day our good "Father" Franck, who never suspected an injustice, would be so far from blaming the jury that he innocently helped us to seek out all the faults that might have brought about this adverse decision.

It is not within the limits of my subject to find fault with the lack of culture among the students of the Conservatoire at this time, a deficiency which, it must be confessed, was due to their teachers. It will be sufficient to say that while they were completely ignorant of all the music of the sixteenth and seventeenth centuries, and of a great part of the work of the eighteenth, they usually regarded Bach as a bore, and Gluck's style was the butt of their wittiest jokes. They found consecutive fifths in "Armide," and—*proh pudor!*—declared they had discovered them also in a fugue sent up for competition by Franck himself! At the present moment a change has come over the spirit of the Conservatoire, and every student of composition would consider himself dishonoured unless he embellished his efforts with a multitude of more or less conspicuous consecutive fifths. At the time of which I am speaking Bizet's "Carmen," which had just been performed, found no grace in the sight of these critics, and I knew students of composition who then accused this work of excessive Wagnerism, while others turned away their eyes from so coarse a subject and cried "Fie!" at the top of their voices. Finally there were some who deliberately refused to read any music, even the greatest masterpieces, for fear, so they said, of "weakening their individuality"!

Of all this Franck knew nothing, and in spite of the conventional errors of the schools, he continued to exhort his pupils to read a great deal of fine music, old and new. He himself was as enthusiastic as any youth over the absolute beauty of Bach's works, which he taught us to interpret on the organ.

Neither could he have understood—and would have been very much surprised to hear it proclaimed as a discovery—that Art ought to be the expression of Life—as though Art ever had been or could be anything else! As though the frescoes of Giotto or Gozzoli, Rembrandt's Syndics, the west door of Amiens Cathedral, Beethoven's sonatas, and Gluck's music dramas were not just as admirable "slices of life" as the most modern works of art—I mean, of course, those that spring from the artist's heart. But, according to the naïve partisans of this aphorism, the word "life" dispenses us from all preliminary study; we can all be born architects and raise up a monumental edifice without having learnt to balance the weight of our material; every one of us guided by "inspiration" could write a symphony straight away. These are things that the mind of Franck was incapable of grasping; his art, the outcome of long study and creative suffering, is the antithesis of the theories described above.

At the same time, how truly vital, throbbing with a sane and intense vitality, is the work of César Franck! How ardently he expresses the joys and griefs which he sees around him. Not merely does he interpret in music the life and emotions of others, but he expresses himself. What does it matter that the characters in *The Beatitudes* are not represented in modern dress, if we, men and women of to-day, are profoundly touched by the sublime invocation to eternal justice; if we ourselves suffer with the persecuted, and if we discern the soul of our beloved master in the melodies he devoted with such tenderness to the description of meekness and purity?

Undoubtedly Franck's art was all compounded of goodness and absolute sincerity, just as his teaching was all love and charity, and on this account it will live; for Doubt and Hatred, although they may have sometimes destroyed useful things, have never constructed anything endurable. Love and Faith can alone conceive and bring forth an immortal work.

Theodor Leschetizky

⤜ 1830–1915 ⤛

THE PIECE IS COMPOSED. *What shall be done with it? How shall it be rendered? Always there may be the case of the shaggy self-taught virtuoso who makes his way against infinite odds. But we cannot be at all sure that there would have been an Elman, a Zimbalist or a Heifetz without a Leopold Auer, whose pupils, according to Jacques Barzun, "can be recognized at forty paces by their posture and even in a dark room by the sound they make."*

Each November the Leschetizky Association of America holds its Paderewski Birthday Dinner, in commemoration of a great teacher and his greatest pupil. Among the concert-artist members, all Association alumni, listed last year were Eleanor Spencer, Alexander Brailowsky, Richard Buhlig, Heinrich Gebhard, Miecyslav Horszowski, Edwin Hughes, Frank LaForge, Artur Schnabel, Arthur Shattuck, and John Powell. And many of these have their pupils who will pass on the Leschetizky spirit if not his "method."

The son of a Bohemian music master and a Polish mother, Theodor Leschetizky was born in Poland and brought up in Russia where he taught for a few years at the St. Petersburg Conservatory. But in 1845 he settled in Vienna and there entered on one of the longest and most fruitful of teaching careers. He was a fine concert pianist and made occasional tours, and he was a composer of ability but teaching was his profession and his passion. Books were written about his "method" at the very moment he was shouting that he had none!

"Don't have a method," he said to Ethel Newcomb. "It is far better to leave your mind a blank for the pupil to fill in. You will

289

discover more easily, in this way, what he needs. Even in technique it is impossible to have a method, for every hand is different. I have no method and I will have no method. Go to concerts and be sharp-witted, and if you are observing, you will learn tremendously from the ways that are successful and also from those that are not. Adopt with your pupils the ways that succeed with them, and get away as far as possible from the idea of a method. Write over your music room door the motto: 'No Method'!"

Ethel Newcomb was a talented American girl who studied for years with Leschetizky and finally became one of his chief assistants — a rare distinction in the light of the general Continental suspicion of American art and artists.

A Typical Lesson

ETHEL NEWCOMB

≫≫·≪≪

THERE WERE SOME LESSONS that might be called typical lessons and this is one of my own that I well remember. "Well, what have we to play to-day?"

"The Schumann *Carnaval*, Herr Professor."

"Really, the Schumann *Carnaval*! Learn the Schütt *Carnaval* sometime too. That is also a real Carnaval. People don't play it enough—there is a very good reason why; it has to be played well, as the Schumann has to be. Nowadays it must be *more* than well played. You know, I have been talking about you to-day; Martha Schmidt was here, and we spoke of you. She says she met you in the Prater the other day, and her account of the conversation with you is not quite satisfactory." This he says laughingly, and I begin to be a little disturbed. "Oh, don't take it too seriously, or I shall think she was right. She says you were offended because she made some criticism of your technique. You were not offended, were you?"

"No, I was very much obliged to her."

"Well, she thinks you resented it, but Martha is probably right—she knows a great deal. You must remember, too, that she expresses herself more freely than you do. When you are really serious you are quiet and uncommunicative. You should be more expressive and say what you think. People should give the correct impression of themselves. There is generally no reason for being misunderstood in this world. Of course, that is not the Viennese temperament. Now, there is Schütt, for instance. He is expressive, and sometimes might be a little less so in public. In the Bösendorfer Hall, for instance, if something delights him he begins to make love to the performer. No one is expressive enough for him. But he has written many beautiful pieces, and his *Carnaval* is one of them. Perhaps I say too much, but parts of it to me are more beautiful than the Schumann *Carnaval*. And how I wish I myself had written that little *Prelude in D Major* of his! Learn to play Schütt's music as it really is, and you will become more expressive at the piano, perhaps too much so. Americans might go too far if they really got started; but I think there is not much danger of that."

This I find ambiguous, and he smiles at my confusion. Leschetizky has often said that our Puritan background has stamped us all with too much rigidity in our bearing as well as in our souls.

"But Martha told me other things, too. Martha says you have now in your repertoire three ballades of Chopin and only one Bach fugue. If I can ever find your specialty in music, I shall thank Heaven, but up to now I have not found it, and we must not become unbalanced. Better one Chopin ballade and three Bach fugues. And then, my dear child, you never learn things like the *Entincelles* of Moszkowski. Don't be too scornful of that sort of piece. You need those pieces to complete your repertoire. You know a dinner must have the accessories. That is a piece you hand out to your audience like sweets wrapped in silver paper and served on a silver plate. There must be nothing about it that isn't perfect to the last detail. Study like Fannie Bloomfield Zeisler, who, when she has something like that to learn, extracts everything from it; she presses everything out of it — like juice from a lemon. She misses nothing. And you must also take pleasure in studying such things. They are not thick with music as is the Schumann *Carnaval*. There is nothing special there, you understand. *You* must make them interesting and beautiful yourself. — Well, now the Schumann *Carnaval*; we must not talk too much, some one is coming afterward.

"Do you know, this life is really killing me. I suffer so in some of the lessons. I give my heart's blood. They say 'yes,' but they play 'no.' Perhaps you will brighten me up now with the *Carnaval* of Schumann well played. You are going to play it in the class surely."

I have just noticed a little unusual disorder in the room. Leschetizky always smokes a great deal during the lessons, and to-day there are many cigar ashes around the pianos. The chairs on one side of the room are pushed away from their usual places, which all means to me that Leschetizky has been giving a difficult and tiring lesson before mine, or perhaps more than one. He has evidently been walking also, as he often does, to indicate graceful tempos, or to show the pupil what awkward ones he is using; or he has been correcting bad pauses; or showing by suddenly plunging ahead, or drawing back, the way the pupil is playing. A glass of water near by makes me suspect that he has been tiring his voice and has probably been shouting. If a pupil played unrhythmically he generally did stop him with shouts. This is not all conducive to my happiness at the moment, but I get myself together as well as I can, and begin the Schumann *Carnaval*.

"Ho, ho," he says, "well now, a little more courage to begin with! More festive than that! I was very much pleased the other night on entering the house of a friend of yours to hear a piece very well played, which I didn't know at all. A waltz of Moszkowski, you say. Well, I apologize — you *do* learn the side pieces, since it was you who were playing it. Very good — sentimental; well, the *Carnaval* of Schumann is sentimental in places. Where one learns the true spirit of the *Carnaval* is here, in Vienna."

I try again to make the opening chords like his. When I say I cannot, I receive a long lecture on the changes that have taken place in my tone and touch lately, especially about the fingers, which Leschetizky thinks are not now strong enough to "temper" the muscular force that my arms have acquired. He has noticed this before, he says, and I would give anything I possessed if I had not been slighting my finger technique so that my chords could roll out in the smooth way that his do without any apparent effort.

"You see, Martha Schmidt was perfectly right," he goes on. "Martha is now the best in the class." Again Leschetizky launches forth in a description of the things she has just accomplished. "She has a real interpretation for everything she plays. She goes to every concert, and comes away with an intelligent criticism. Why don't I accept a position as critic on some small newspaper in Austria or in France? Write as correspondent for Viennese concerts? Excellent practice," Leschetizky says. I begin to think that we shall not be able to play much of the *Carnaval* to-day, if we get so far afield, and I put my hands on the keys again.

"There you are, in a hurry — always in a hurry," he says. "You play hurriedly sometimes, too. And your pauses are not good." Here he compares relaxing all the muscles to the deep breathing of the singer. "And take long breaths," he says, "you will relax the muscles better then." He tells me what deep breaths Rubinstein used to take at the beginning of long phrases, and also what repose he had and what dramatic pauses. "There is more rhythm between the notes than in the notes themselves." He reminded me that Liszt used to say this. "Paul Szalit is the only one who ever asked me to tell how Rubinstein breathed. No one else ever seemed interested to know.

"Well, now once more, and go on."

I get to the second page when Leschetizky's posture at the piano attracts my attention. He sits there forlornly and really looks as if he were going to weep.

"I thought you were going to make me happy to-day," he says. And then, most dejectedly, "Really, to-day, if you do not play that part with warmth, I cannot bear to hear it. If you knew how often lately I have heard the Schumann *Carnaval*. Play me the Schütt *Carnaval* instead — that's fresh — that's new. I am tired of the Schumann *Carnaval*."

I hardly know what to do myself at this point, so I ask him if I may try it once more. The pedal is wrong.

"My dear child," he says, "God won't help you. You have to hear that yourself." This makes me laugh, and my laugh for the moment saves the situation.

"There is great charm in this part, but with you it is all lost. I admit this first part is also the most difficult. In the rest of the *Carnaval* the expression is given, so to speak. With understanding one can play the rest better."

We proceed to the Pierrot, but I have not succeeded in dispelling his depression. Some moments of a lesson with him are very long, and he has stopped me at the first chord, and shakes his head mournfully.

"You ought to know better than that," he says. "You did the same thing at your last lesson — you do not even know what," he says. "That must not be told you twice. You must *hear* it! If a stranger heard you play that way he would say that you were a very talented person, but you had a bad teacher. It isn't your strength at all, it is your ear! Why the bass so loud?" he says, coming over to my piano. "Never cover up the top when it has anything to say. Yes, that one note one calls bad, really bad," he says. I try again.

"Stop!" he calls. "Wait! You do not have to catch any trains, have you, or *have* you, perhaps?" he said, going back to his piano. "I haven't any to catch, and here I sit, waiting to hear a plain A flat played with tone. I tell you, you would be the first to criticize if you heard some one else play like that! You go to a concert to have pleasure in the music, don't you? Well, it is no pleasure hearing it played that way. Now, I notice that you can learn a piece quite perfectly at first, but then you let it go, and sometimes in the end, it does not

295

sound as you think it sounds, or the way you mean it to sound, and believe that it does sound. The right sound must be kept, and also brought out. Yes, you smile, but you should not smile just this minute. Don't you think that Mr. Sauer would have studied a whole hour on these two or three bars to bring out clearly the meaning of the notes, if he was not satisfied with them? You are not always clear, besides sometimes you must even underscore. For you it is clear, of course, because you know it, but not every one does know. Besides there will be some who know it so well that they suspect you do not. You have a brain for this purpose, and you must not be satisfied because you understand the notes yourself. The other one must understand them, too. On occasions one uses the brain, you see."

"Yes," I say, and try to smile.

"Until you learn to think an hour for every hour you play, you have not learned to study.

"We have come to the end of the Pierrot. You mustn't distort him," he says. "Just the same Pierrot had some noble instincts; he was a loving creature, too."

We get over to the Eusebius, and I cannot please him. Every phrase seems to depend on the way one plays the one preceding, and every time Leschetizky plays the whole so differently that I am discouraged, and beg to be allowed to leave it until another time.

"Not at all. Not at all," he says. "You will go home, and think and think, and come no nearer to it. This is a question of touch and tempo, and if you will only listen better! Why, some people learn a language by listening, and never see a book. The grammar will not teach you how to play this part. Stop thinking now, for a moment, and listen." Leschetizky plays this part again, but still very differently.

"It cannot be the same every time," he says. "Don't try so hard, but let your good ear direct you." In the second half

296

he jumps impatiently from his chair and shows me by stiff and jerky motions what my rhythm has been.

"I would like to let it go as well as you would," he says, "but we must not leave it this way. It must be richer and fuller. There are no bare branches here. You must have the leaves on the trees. One does not become an artist in a day," he remarks. "There are so many qualities that go toward the playing of this one part: warmth, abandon, and fine shading, and intense listening, and will power—all those things besides the notes."

I have not even followed the marks of shading in the good Peter's edition. "It would be so much easier to be more attentive to those marks," he said, "unless, indeed, one could make better marks oneself, and some do not even take the trouble to find out the meaning of the names—Estrella, Florestan, etc."

Leschetizky hates nothing more than dejection on the part of a pupil. I start out as bravely as I can with the next, and also finish the one called Coquette.

"Deceiver!" is his one word when I finish. A smile or a laugh or a pleasantry always made everything better in the lessons and, when he reiterates "Deceiver," I think the best thing I can say is, "I believe you are right," which brings a smile to his face.

"Of course," he says, "you know the meaning of coquette as well as any one. Well, then, since you have understood me, let us go on."

I realize now that I must play and not be stupid, and that if I have studied the piece well at all, I must at least do something that will show a little spirit and initiative.

"Yes, I know you can do it," he remarks, "but then, why so timid in the beginning? Timidity in feeling is no good. The tempos are the manners, in one sense, and your manners in playing are too timid."

In another place I have tried to make a difficult technical passage easier by playing some of the notes with the left hand, which belong to the right. The change is too conspicuous and makes it appear that my technique is not adequate.

"Play it as it is written," he tells me. "This is a General's piece, and you must play it like a General."

I ask him if it is good at another place.

"No," he sings out. "You lost some of the tones there. Begin at the eleventh bar."

At my failure to do this instantly he laughs at some thought of his own.

"Must you begin back at the stove?" he says.

"Stove?" I repeat. He only laughs the more.

"You do not want to be like the dancer. — Yes, there was a dancer once who always had to begin back at the stove when he broke down, because he had always started at the stove."

I see the application of this, as I am unable to begin at any bar, and have to go back to the first.

"You must be able to begin at any measure," he says, "or you will always be nervous over slips of memory. When you make a mistake, study it. The mistake makes the right way clearer."

"Why did you stop?" he questions me at another place. "It was good. Go on, go on! Play ideally, child, *ideally*. That is all that is required of one."

We now have a long conversation about the differences in interpretations that have been given the Reconnaissance. Paderewski had once played it so, Rosenthal and D'Albert in another way, and one or two of the pupils had actually done something unusual and beautiful. The fingering made some difference in interpretation. As we proceed, he criticizes my pianissimo. It is not singing enough. One place should be piously played. He turns to me with a sly twinkle in his eye, and asks if I do not know what it is to be pious.

"Well," he goes on, "I am not afraid of the Davidsbündler. Your rhythm is all right. Those are the easy things for you, but there is the danger. They must be well finished, too, or else you will disappoint your good friends. You must surprise rather than disappoint. Never disappoint an audience. You have studied well this week," he says, "and learning to study well is the main thing. It is half the battle."

I am overjoyed to hear this from him, as my last lesson was rather a mystery to me.

Someone comes in to ask if the pupils who have waited so long shall continue to wait. Leschetizky apologizes and says, "No, I cannot do any more today."

We go into the dining room, and I am invited to have dinner with him, all the conversation turning toward Schumann and Schütt and the various artists who have interpreted the Schumann *Carnaval* to please great audiences.

Auguste Rodin

⋙ 1840 – 1917 ⋘

F<small>AMILIARITY</small> with works of art does not necessarily breed contempt but it often breeds that casual take-it-for-granted attitude
that we bestow on an old shoe. The sense of wonder is entirely supplanted
by a sense of recognition and the work in question appears obvious, easy,
simple. This can happen to Beethoven's Fifth Symphony or Tschai-
kowski's Pathetique, not to mention the delicate melodies of Stephen
Foster when played constantly on the radio. Jaded aesthetes and professional critics, in their desperate search for novelty, naturally grow insensitive to threadbare masterpieces and sometimes say foolish things
about them. It might be well to make a fresh study of those threadbare
masterpieces and then put them away for a decade.

Does this not all apply to Rodin who, to many people, is the only
sculptor and whose only work was The Thinker? We are so familiar
with that figure in reproductions in plaster and the rotogravure of advertising pages that we do not stop to look at him. As a matter of fact
he is hardly a "thinker" at all but is primitive man just beginning to
think and was designed to sit, contemplative, above the gates of Dante's
Hell!

Pictures of sculpture are certainly no substitute for the originals but
a fine collection published by the Phaidon Press gives us a real feeling
for the mighty range of Rodin's chisel.

In 1910 Rodin was a triumphant world figure with his battles all
behind him. At that time he could have scarcely been considering another
pupil or apprentice in his studio, but even at seventy, one may become
a teacher again, in spite of himself, if the would-be pupil is sufficiently
persevering.

301

Old Master

MALVINA HOFFMAN

->>>·<<<-

*"Vivre c'est rien, mais sacrifier sa vie pour un idéal est la
seule chose qui donne sa véritable qualité à l'homme."* —
RODIN, *in conversation.*

WITHIN A YEAR, my mother decided to give up her life
in America and devote herself to helping me in my
artistic studies abroad. I had worked day and night
trying to collect enough funds to pay for the steamer tickets,
designing covers for sheet-music and patterns for wallpapers
and linoleums, and making pastel portraits of babies and young
children. We sailed away with a letter of credit for one
thousand dollars left to my mother in legacy by a thoughtful
friend. In the good old days of 1910 we were able to travel
through Italy and Switzerland, to Paris and London, establish
ourselves in various studio and alcove apartments, and live in
the student quarters of the *rive gauche* for fifteen months, on
this thousand dollars.

To anyone who has had the good fortune of being an art
student in Paris and who has been poor enough to know the
joys of a Sunday lunch on the Boulevard Montparnasse, after
a week of home cooking and dishwashing, when *dessert et café*
were added to the menu as a real spree, it would be unnecessary
to state that there were no obstacles ominous enough to dim
the promise of even a distant horizon. Reading the menus from
right to left during the lean years made everything edible seem
precious and worth fighting for. Many were the laughs in-

303

dulged in, when the inevitable *gateau de riz* would be suggested as a means of satisfying any stray hunger pangs that might still be lurking in the mind or body of a passionate young art student.

It was my determined intention to become a pupil of Rodin. While still in America I had studied his work from books and photographs, and from the varied and interesting collection of his clay studies, bronzes, and marbles owned by Mrs. John Simpson in New York.

When I had tried five times in vain to present a letter of introduction at Rodin's studio, Rue de l'Université, my hopes were almost frustrated and the situation had become pretty desperate for me. His concierge gave me little encouragement, but some last grain of hope drove me to extreme action on my fifth visit, and I said:

"Tell Monsieur Rodin that if he does not see me today I must return to America, but that I came to Paris to study with him, and that I must deliver a message to him from his friend Madame Simpson. I shall not leave, he must admit me today."

The surprised guardian seemed to sense my adamant determination, and in a few moments came back smiling.

"Well, at last I have permission to admit you," she said, and I followed her past the many studios until she knocked at Rodin's door.

I found myself in a room crowded with marbles and covered clay models on stands. There were four or five Frenchmen with black coats and red rosettes in their lapels, talking to Rodin, who looked me over with a hooded searching gaze that made me feel rooted to the spot and unable to move. He came forward slowly, and put out his hand. As I gave him the messages, in my unconjugated French, from his friend across the seas, his grip tightened and he asked me why I had not mentioned her name at my first visit. I began to feel my blood move again in my veins. "So you were determined not to leave without seeing me," he said. I nodded. "What have you under your arm in that envelope?" he asked. "Oh, just two photographs of the only sculpture I have ever done—I am just a beginner but I find I cannot escape it. Sculpture seems to have taken possession of me and my desire is to be your pupil if you will be willing to guide me and criticize my work."

"Let me see the photographs," he said. "Who are these two men?"

"Well, the marble is of my father," I replied. "He was a musician who, after a long life, was serenely meditative. The other is of a young violinist who is just making his début in America as a soloist."

Rodin looked at the photographs for some minutes, put them back into the envelope, and handed them to me. "Character seems to interest you. You have studied these men well. One is the mature artist with his life battles behind him, the other is the young dreamer with his battles ahead of him. Wait here a few moments. I am just describing this marble of mine to these gentlemen and then I am lunching with them." Rodin went back to the visitors and started to tell them that the figure represented a fallen angel that had broken his wings on a rock and that the idea had been conceived after reading a certain poem. He began reciting the lines in a deep monotone, but his memory failed him and he grew violent trying to recall the ending of the sonnet. He strode up and down before the great marble group.

By some extraordinary coincidence, I happened to know the poem, and when I saw that he could not recall the lines, I walked towards him. "Maître," I ventured, "I know that poem, shall I recite it?" He turned on me almost savagely— "What—you know it?—let me see if you do—recite it!" My blood was pounding, but I began the lines in a slow, quavering voice:

"*J'ai perdu ma force et ma vie,*
Et mes amis et ma gaîté;
J'ai perdu jusqu'à la fierté
Qui faisait croire à mon génie.

"*Quand j'ai connu la Vérité,*
J'ai cru que c'était une amie;
Quand je l'ai comprise et sentie,
J'en étais déjà dégoûté.

"*Et pourtant elle est éternelle,*
Et ceux qui se sont passés d'elle
Ici-bas ont tout ignoré.

"*Dieu parle, il faut qu'on lui réponde.*
Le seul bien qui me reste au monde
Est d'avoir quelquefois pleuré."

I stepped back once more to my place at the door, not daring to raise my eyes.

There was a murmur of surprise from the group of men. Rodin's voice suddenly rose in a tone of almost brutal abruptness—"*Allons, au déjeuner, mes amis*—*il est tard.*" He showed his friends out of the door, turned toward me—"Here," he said. "This is where my keys hang," and he lifted an old rag from a nail on the wall, on which hung two keys. "You may use them to open the other studios. Uncover all the work and examine the trays of plaster studies and I will see you when I return." He went out, closed the door and locked it from the outside. I had certainly not only been admitted at last to his studio, I was locked into it—for better or worse— and I wasted no time wondering what it all meant, but started in at once to pull the linen shrouds off the marbles. A new world seemed suddenly to engulf my imagination. When I had examined one room I went to the next and then to another and finally returned to where I had started and began making drawings of the small plaster hands of which there were thirty or forty in various positions lying in wooden trays. I worked so intently that I did not notice that the fire in the stove had gone out and that the studio had grown icy cold. I did realize quite definitely, however, that I was very hungry, for I had not had anything to eat since my cup of coffee at 7:30 A.M. and I suddenly noticed that it must be well into the afternoon as the winter light had begun to fade. I recovered all the marbles, and as I went over to try the door, hoping to be able to open it from the inside, I heard a knock. Wondering what I should do, I made no response — for if it were some visitor what would he think if I said I could not open the door? The knocking became louder and then a key turned in the lock and the door opened. Rodin came in and looked about. He caught sight of me behind one of the marble blocks. "Well," he said. "What have you done all this time? Why is everything covered over? Did you not examine the work or did you not like it, that you have covered everything again?"

I explained hastily that the sight of so many of his groups was too much for me to cope with at one time, and that although I had examined them all, I had re-covered them carefully and had concentrated my attention on the little plaster hand which seemed to be more my size. I had made a few drawings of this and he examined my sketch book. After looking through it he said, "My child, do you think these are all drawings?"

"Why, yes," I answered naively, "I *did* think so, what are they?" for I could see he was not of my opinion.

"They are sketches," he said. "Michelangelo *never* made sketches, everything he drew was a study, a real drawing. See that you never make any more sketches. Beware of the weakness of your American artists," pointing his finger at me very threateningly.

307

"What is their weakness?" I asked.

"*C'est leur sacrée facilité,*" he said, and then, going over to the stove, he realized how cold it had grown. The fire was out, and we were in semidarkness. He came back and felt my hands; they were cold. He took off his heavy cloth cape and wrapped it about me and went to work remaking the fire. "Why did you let it go out?" he asked, and "Why do you look so pale and tired? By the way, did you have any lunch before coming to me at noon?"

"No, I had my coffee early but did not expect to be able to stay here so long today—it has been a great feast for a hungry artist, I shall never forget it."

He sat down beside me, drawing the little stools near the stove. "You forgot the fire, my child, because of the inner fire that burns you, but you cannot neglect hunger—nature is a stern mistress, and if you play tricks with her she will punish you every time. When I locked you in today, I never thought about food, I just wanted to make sure that you would be alone with my work, and that I would find you on my return." He rubbed my hands and held them near the glowing stove. "Now you must go home and take the little hand with you and make careful drawings for a week. Every day you must go to the Louvre and study and make copies of the old masters— Leonardo Da Vinci and Michelangelo and Raphael—not to copy their technique only but to understand it, and develop a technique of your own, and each week come back here and bring me what you have done—and be sure to eat plenty of beefsteak and potatoes"—at this point he encircled my absurdly small wrist with his strong sensitive fingers—"you are too thin and sculpture needs plenty of fuel for the fires of art burn fiercely. When you come back, I may be drawing from a model, if so you may draw with me. You know where the keys hang, from now on you may feel at home in my studio."

And so it was that my studies with Rodin began. They continued for over a year, until I returned to America in 1911.

As I was leaving for America, Rodin urged me to study anatomy by dissection. "We have no facilities for such study in Paris but through your doctor friends you may be able to find a way in America to make your own dissections." I asked Doctor George S. Huntington at the College of Physicians and Surgeons in New York to admit me to the laboratories as a student. The sights and smells so shocked me that my determination was almost destroyed. One day as I stood wavering, Doctor Huntington suddenly appeared, scalpel in hand, and said smiling, "Well, well, Malvina, you look pretty green this morning—can it be that you regret having asked me to teach you how to dissect and learn the principles of anatomy?" His kindly blue eyes challenged me—"Remember you are the only woman up here and medical students are likely to jeer at you if you give any signs of funking."

My blood rushed up into my head again and I could feel the color come back into my cheeks. Doctor Huntington led me to the operating table; I put on my rubber gloves, and he said, "Now watch me closely, as I reveal to you the beautiful mechanism God built into our knees for you to see here the basic principles on which all bridges and levers are constructed."

The delicate accuracy of his technique (in spite of the fact that he had lost two or three of his fingers) was amazing. He turned his instruments over to me, and said he would return in two hours to see what progress I had made. "Be careful," he said as he left, "these scalpel blades are sharp; don't cut those tissue-paper sheaths that hold all our muscles in place. Remember everything you will discover is beautiful and wonderful, then you'll be all right." What a teacher! What sensibility and understanding he had for a cringing pupil—this man who spent his life searching for the hidden wonders of comparative anatomy and wading about in a gory laboratory from morning until evening!

After my first year, and by request of a group of artist friends, he was able to persuade Columbia University to open a special department of dissection and anatomy for artists. At first all the class attended enthusiastically, but gradually the numbers dwindled; the formaldehyde and grim surroundings were too repugnant for their eyes and nostrils.

A year later Mother and I went back to Paris and I continued my studies, dividing my time between night classes at the academy and working in my own studio. Each week I had a searching and constructive criticism from Rodin, sometimes drawing and sometimes watching him carve marble.

On Sunday morning I often went to the great studio of Rodin's home at Meudon, near Paris. He would show me the series of portrait heads in plaster, which he made while he was studying his sitters. Sometimes he would make six or seven different studies of the same person — varying slightly the pose of the head or the expression of the face. Frequently I knew him to start a portrait, and after a few sittings, to call in a plaster caster and have a mold made as a record; then he would make a "squeeze," that is, the fresh clay would be pressed into the negative of the piece mold and with this stage of the portrait safely registered, he would feel more free to make bold changes or experiments, without the fear of losing what had been achieved up to that point. The first plaster was a guide to which he could always refer if he felt himself in doubt during the subsequent sittings. He would hand me little plaster figures and ask me to cut off the arms and legs; then with white wax he would rearrange the groups, changing a gesture and adding action or some new suggestion of composition.

One incident which made a great impression upon me took place at the entrance to the Rue de Varenne studio. I was kept waiting a long time for Rodin to arrive. I took two small bits of clay and rolled them absent-mindedly into two pieces about five inches long. These I pressed together in my closed hand, and studying the result was amazed to find that the pressure of my fingers had clearly suggested the forms of two standing figures. I added the two heads and was tapping the base on the stone step to make it stand up, when Rodin appeared. He asked me what I was doing and I showed him the little group. "Just an accident," I said, "made while I was waiting for you."

After carefully examining it from all sides, he said very seriously, "There is more in this than you understand at present. An accident, you say? Well, it is one of those accidents which one must catch and transform into science. You will keep this, and model this group one half life size and cut it in marble—but before you do it, you must study for five years. Will you promise to do this?"

"Yes," I answered, and wondered deeply how Rodin could see so clearly and decisively into the future. Eventually I carried out the idea and called it the "Column of Life."

Sometimes Sam would go to Meudon with me, taking his violin. Rodin would invite Rose Beuret to sit with him in the studio and listen to the music, after which she would bring us bowls of fruit, and milk and bread and butter. He told me, before presenting me to Rose, that she was "a violent nature, jealous, suspicious, but able to discriminate between falsehood and truth, like the primitives, and possessed of the power of eternal devotion . . . You will be good friends, I know, but remember what I have said about her." His eyes glowed fiercely under his shaggy brows and then his face changed into a friendly smile.

It was years later, almost at the end of her life, that she became his wife—she who had been the "shadow of the sun" as she described herself to me, since her eighteenth year. Her love of music was almost pathetic; tears often ran down her thin cheeks while she was listening, so starved was she for any such emotional relaxation—her life had been completely devoted to the service of her beloved master, first as his model, then as his cook and housekeeper, and as the mother of his son. At the end of her long life he finally decided to marry her legally. After a few weeks of supreme pride and happiness, Rose Beuret Rodin died, and now the great bronze figure of *The Thinker* broods over the tomb in the Meudon garden where Rodin and Rose lie side by side under a common slab of granite.

While studying the first stages of my profession from the practical point of view in Paris, I became increasingly aware of the importance of understanding the *craft* as well as the *art* of sculpture.

Under the guidance of Emanuel Rosales, the Italian sculptor, I was introduced to the complexities of chasing and finishing my own bronzes. I watched for many hours how his deft fingers controlled the metal tools and how he was able to clean the surface of a freshly cast statuette, never harming in any way the modelling or texture of the forms.

During my first visit to a French foundry, I was quite over-whelmed by all the stages of handling through which every piece of sculpture has to pass. I listened to the remarks of the workmen and became friendly with the foreman of each de-partment, and these men very patiently explained to me just what the workmen were doing and how to hold the tools myself and control them without damaging the metal. They would give me old pieces of twisted bronze to practice on, and I found it very exciting to be able to restore the surface to a smooth, even finish and have it approved by the founders.

The casual remarks of these master craftsmen concerning other sculptors were a revelation to me. It seemed that very few of the artists ever took the trouble to visit the foundry and in fact during the years that I have visited foundries so frequently, I have seldom encountered a sculptor who showed any active interest in how his sculpture was reproduced in bronze.

It was about this time that I began to realize what a serious handicap it was for a woman to attempt competition with the men in the field of sculpture. There was absolutely no traditional credit given to a woman in this field of activity, and I felt convinced of the necessity of learning my profession from the very beginning, so as to be able to control the workmanship of the great number of craftsmen with whom I was obliged to come in contact, both in France and in America.

I remember very well that Mestrovic, the Yugoslav sculptor, said to me when I first met him, that the first thing I must do as a woman was to learn the principles and technical side of my work better than most men, before I could start *even*, without the handicap of a preconceived idea that women were amateurs in art and generally took up sculpture as a diversion or a pastime. I wonder if the women in other professions, such as music and literature, have ever realized what a serious obstacle this femininity becomes in the field of sculpture — and with good reason, for the work itself demands that we stand on our feet from morning until night, lifting heavy weights, bending iron, sawing wood, and building armatures; we must know how to use carpenters' tools and plumbers' tools, and be able to calculate the strains and necessary supports to build up the clay figures. These last are often treacherous and collapse at just the moment when we are enthusiastically bringing them to completion.

Robert Henri

⇒ 1865 – 1929 ⇐

ONE CAN GET UP A CONTROVERSY *if not a quarrel on almost any issue in a group of American artists and critics but they seem to be unanimous about the unsurpassed teaching ability of Robert Henri. Whatever they may think of his paintings, they will still enthuse about his rich and lively influence. "Why," said one of them, "there isn't an important American artist over fifty today who wasn't at one time a pupil of Henri's."*

Forbes Watson, in an editorial devoted to Henri the teacher, not the artist, pointed out that older men such as William Henry Chase and John Henry Twachtman, shared some of Henri's views but lacked his teaching skill: "It required his extraordinary personal magnetism, his fervor, his passion for the verbal communication of his ideas to place before a vast succession of eager youth, the new world of vision and to make general, knowledge which before had been too special to be effective."

Everyone agrees on Henri's extraordinary command of language which is so necessary unless the teacher is to do the students' work for them or hold up his own for imitation. In wandering about a studio he could not interrupt with a lecture but he could startle, arouse, with an aphorism or clear away a fog with a phrase. As Rose Henderson put it, "He had a remarkable gift for words, for achieving crisp arresting sentences that stuck in your mind like bright bits of color."

Following Helen Appleton Read's article on Henri are a few pages of selections from his classroom remarks, as taken down by Margery Ryerson.

Word Painter

HELEN APPLETON READ

>>>·<<<

EVEN DURING HIS LIFETIME a legend had sprung up about Robert Henri. A legend, as is so often the case with legends, depending as much upon the effect of a magnetic personality as upon actual accomplishment — but differing in one important respect from the orbit followed by legend-making personalities, it reached its height while he was a young man and commenced waning while he was still at the height of his productive powers. Now that the time has come to estimate Henri's contribution to American art the factors which contributed to the creating of the legend and those which tended to dispel it must be taken into consideration. Furthermore, estimating Henri's contribution to American art is not merely assigning him the proper niche in the American Hall of Fame, it resolves itself quite as much in recognizing the influence that his personality and aesthetic philosophy had upon the development of art in this country.

Robert Henri was a great teacher. A man with enormous personal magnetism. He was probably the greatest single influence in American art. If one concedes the controversial existence of an American school — then Henri founded it. His teaching was not merely a case of passing on to his pupils such technical facts as he believed were essential to a painter's equipment, it embodied a philosophy of life as well whose basic tenets were humanity and liberalism. Their observance paved the way for the independent idea in this country and the acceptance of modern art.

In that extraordinary personal compilation of Henri's say-ings collected by Margery Ryerson under the title, "The Art Spirit," there are aphorisms which belong in any glossary of American philosophy. When he said "The distinguishing mark of all great men is their humanity," he was voicing his own distinguishing characteristic, the characteristic which was also the common denominator of his painting and philosophy of life — the quality that inspired such ardent devotion in all those who sought his advice or came within the circle of his friend-ship. Once a Henri pupil always a Henri pupil. Which is to say that the point of view with which he imbued his pupils has not grown stale or been superseded by succeeding cults and movements since humanity continues to be one of the verities.

George Bellows, Rockwell Kent, Edward Hopper, Guy Péne du Bois, and Glenn Coleman were among his pupils and continued, each according to his personal interpretation, the aesthetic philosophy that he taught them. And he accomplished this, not through the imposition of a technique or through a conscious effort to found an American school, but by revealing art as a medium with which to express life. To understand why relating art to life was epochal, why it became a cause and why those who followed the leadership of the man who preached this aesthetic gospel were classed as radicals, it is necessary to reconstruct the point of view that prevailed when Henri first established his reputation as trail blazer and liberal.

In the early 1900's, when Henri was first widely acclaimed as the bad boy of American art, American taste and production were at their lowest ebb. Sentimental landscapes, studio models posed in period costumes, sweetened puritanized nudes, deleted of every vestige of sensuous allure that at least gave their Salon prototypes a *raison d'etre*, were the pictures that took prizes and were bought by collectors. The schools fol-lowed the lead set by current standards of taste.

When Henri returned from Europe he brought with him a new set of values. His own tendency to regard painting as an

318

interpretation of life had been strengthened by his admiration for Courbet's warm humanity and Manet's interest in the contemporary scene. In the nineties and early 1900's Manet and Courbet were still regarded as radicals, their pictures were collected by only a few connoisseurs. The salonniers and academicians held sway in France as in this country. Henri's affiliation with the left wing evinced itself as early as 1888 when he made his first trip to Paris and where he found prevailing standards of teaching unsympathetic to his ideals. In between European visits he had already commenced establishing his reputation for liberalism in painting as well as teaching. The Philadelphia School of Design for Women was his first vehicle for expounding his ideas on art and life. His association with such kindred spirits as George Luks, John Sloan, Everett Shinn, and William Glackens in the Philadelphia group was the nucleus from which developed the independent idea. It was not, however, until he returned to this country in 1901 after his third trip to Paris and settled in New York that his reputation as archradical and leader of a new school was firmly established.

What was the magic that gave these glamorous portraits of dark-haired women in white — sometimes they were red-haired women — their power to stir the imagination of the younger generation to the extent that they did? Why did they arouse a crusading spirit such as has only been paralleled in the battle over modern art? As we look at them now they seem inherently conservative, savoring more of Whistler and Manet's refinements than Courbet's exuberant humanism. And it was their too warm-blooded realism it must be remembered that caused the schism between the academic conservatives and the radicals. Even then, I suspect, it was the aura of Henri's personality and the ideals he was battling for that lent them a radicalism that they did not in actuality possess. Liberalism, down with corrupt officialdom, relating art to life, were concepts which came to be synonymous with his painting. It is true that when contrasted with the insipidities which passed as portraits of human beings in current academies the frankness of their appeal as women was startling. They reflected what was always Henri's major aim, getting the essential quality of his sitter's personality. Throughout his long and prolific career, in which portrait painting was his typical expression, this effort to isolate the quality that makes people themselves remains a constant factor.

In the matter of teaching Henri's radicalism was largely a matter of point of view. He did not introduce startling new aesthetic formulas except insomuch as he advised his pupils to paint directly without making a preliminary drawing and filling it in with color as was the then prevailing method of academic instruction. But he had the priceless pedagogical gift of stirring the imagination of his pupils — of making them excited about their work. There was far less talk of brushwork, as it was called then, than in the Chase and Mora classes at The Art Students' League. And this despite the fact that Henri himself was an exponent of brushwork and possessed an amazing technical facility which was a distinct detriment in an aesthetic code that emphasized an interpretation of life rather than an exposition of virtuosity.

In the Henri classes painting was revealed to the prewar generation for the first time as only another medium whereby the emotions of everyday life could be expressed. All the arts were discovered as kindred and relevant to painting. Isadora Duncan, Wagner, Dostoievski were discussed with Manet, Daumier, Eakins, and Courbet. While he brought to our attention the great names of the nineteenth century European painting — the men who had been the graphic historians of their day — still to win recognition abroad and practically unknown in this country — he also taught us to appreciate the native genius. He was the first teacher to point out Eakins's rugged integrity and Ryder's romanticism as being distinctly American in quality. In the Henri class I heard Walt Whitman for the first time unblushingly discussed in a mixed gathering. Advising his pupils to go to the life about them for subject — advocating the axiom that it is not the subject but what you feel about it that counts — was heady theory to the youth of the first decade of this century brought up on the T-square method of instruction and to whom subject had been more or less a peg on which to hang technique. The Henri class became the rallying ground for eager youth. When we packed our paintboxes and journeyed north from the then conservative classes of the League to the Henri School in the old Lincoln Arcade, it was tantamount to throwing our gauntlets in the face of the old order.

Living fully, as a necessary ingredient to the production of vital work, brought about a reaction from Victorian conservatism in manners and morals, as well as in art. This Tolstoyan point of view, which advocated all life as subject matter for art, brought in its wake the belief that the working classes and the slums were nearer the realities and, therefore, more fitting subjects for art. This induced a species of socialism, and the Henri School came to stand for all forms of radicalism and independence. Self-conscious and naive as much of this may now seem, nevertheless, it fostered the spirit of independence and tolerance without which subsequent liberal movements would have been impeded.

John Sloan, in his foreword to the Henri Memorial Exhibition which was held at the Metropolitan Museum in the spring of 1931, said of this preparation, "His thirty years of teaching were devoted to the emancipation of the art spirit in the United States, his work and inspiration as a teacher were factors in preparing the way for the earnest and growing interest in art which is so clearly evidenced in this young country today."

The first concrete group expression of the new liberalism was in 1910 when an Independent Exhibition was held in a loft building on Thirty-fourth Street. This had no relation except in spirit to the Society of Independent Artists formed six years later. Henri's portrait of Mrs. Henri was given the place of honor, one of those vivid character studies which give reality to his reputation of relating art to life. Rockwell Kent, George Bellows, Randall Davey, Homer Boss, Glenn Coleman, and Dorothy Rice were among the exhibitors. Bellows showed one of his prize-fight series, the Johnson-Dempsey Fight, which called forth more violent excoriations than did *The Nude Descending the Stairs* when it was exhibited at The Armory Show three years later.

Difficult as it must have been to cede his place as radical and trail blazer to the new order which even overlooked his contribution in preparing the way for the new trails, he never ceased to give his sympathetic support to any sincere expression of opinion whether or not it coincided with his point of view.

Of the so-called modern movement inaugurated by the Armory Show in this country Henri commented with characteristic liberality:

"There always has been a new movement and there always will be a new movement. It is strange that a thing which comes as regularly as clockwork should be a surprise.

"In new movements, the pendulum takes a great swing, charlatans crowd in, innocent apes follow, the masters make their successes, and they make their mistakes as all pioneers must do. It is necessary to pierce to the core, to get at the value of a movement, and not be confused by its sensational exterior."

He believed that the most vital of art of all time has its roots firmly planted in the soil of life. Furthermore, that the American temperament was fundamentally opposed to the cerebral formalization of art with its almost complete nullification of human and emotional elements which was one of the basic tenets of the modern European school. The growing tendency of the more gifted young American painters to return to human experiences for their inspiration demonstrates this.

Emerson had the same thought in mind when he said, "The fine arts have nothing casual but spring from the deepest instincts of the people who created them."

But with the liberal idea firmly entrenched Henri retired from the scene of action except insofar as he supported the independent idea by sending faithfully to the Independent's Annual Exhibition. His productivity did not, however, abate. He continued to paint "my people" as he called the types who stirred a responsive chord in him, whether they were Spanish gypsies, Irish peasants, Japanese, Indians, or Americans.

The strong family resemblance found in any representative collection of his work is due to his being unable to do good work unless his subject possessed a quality of inner intensity to which he responded. Dignity, he called it, and by dignity he meant poise and harmony between the inner and the outer being.

When he painted a portrait commission, with its inevitable limitations and where the response so necessary for him to do his best work was frequently absent, the result became an impersonal demonstration of his amazing virtuosity. Conscious of this he tended away from portrait painting and during the later years of his life dedicated his talent almost exclusively to painting types which interested him primarily from the human angle, notably the series of sympathetic and tender portraits of children.

Even now when it is still difficult to weigh and balance the relative merits of his pictures these portraits and the earlier full length portraits of women would seem to be the summation of his skill as a painter and sensitive recorder of personality. In the story of American painting they are outstanding contributions in realistic portrait painting.

Notes Taken by Margery Ryerson from Robert Henri's Criticisms and Class Talks

Art is the giving by each man of his evidence to the world. Those who wish to give, love to give, discover the pleasure of giving. Those who give are tremendously strong.

Be always looking for the thing you like and not afraid of overstating it. We want the simple vision of one who sees and enjoys. Suppose all people try to declare the things they like.

Study to appreciate.

Your painting is the marking of your progression into nature, a sensation of something you see way beyond the two pretty colors over there. Don't stop to paint the material, but push on to give the spirit. We do not enjoy or admire the material in life, for we hate a miser or a *merely* business man. So why should we draw like a miser? Rather, we should work like a person who sees beyond the objects we draw. We should draw with this spiritual sight. Thus the measure of a painting is the conception of the artist. The value of a work of art depends on the flight the observer takes from it. The cause of revolutions in art is, that, at times, feeling drops out of the work and it must fight to get back in again.

The artist should have a powerful will. He should be powerfully possessed by one idea. He should be intoxicated with the idea of the thing he wants to express. If his will is not strong he will see all kinds of unessential things.

A picture should be the expression of the will of the painter.

There is a joy in the pursuit of anything.

Life is finding yourself. It is a spirit development.

You will never draw the sense of a thing unless you are feeling it at the time you work.

324

Search for the simple constructive forces, like the lines of a suspension bridge.

If painting is painting, it is drawing. You do not stop drawing when you begin to paint, for painting *is* drawing.

Originality can be halted but not stamped out or taken away.

Don't demonstrate measure but demonstrate the results you may get from the employment of measure. There is geometry in all good expression.

The model is not to be copied, but to be realized. The painting is the result of the effect of the model on the artist. It is not the model we need but the vision. Thus when a great artist, as Isadora Duncan, affects us, that is when we realize her, we are great as well as she. Thus the observer can be great as he looks at a picture; that is, to the extent to which he sees it as wonderful. The greatness of the picture as it hangs on the wall is up to the observer.

There has never been a painting that was more beautiful than nature. The model does not unfold herself to you, you must rise to her. She should be the inspiration for your painting. No man has ever over-appreciated a human being.

Energy, vitality and unity are the essential things about man. The strength of a wild horse lies in its unity. The thing that makes the artist is a gigantic individual development.

Is your painting in accord with the big scheme in nature? Anyone who desires to make a thing in large, simple terms is in a healthy state.

Self education, only, produces expression of self.

Don't ask for a criticism until you are sure you can't give it to yourself. Then you will be in a fine state to receive it.

You can't impose education on anyone.

By my teaching I hope to inspire you to personal activity and to present your vision.

I am interested in the size of your intention. It is better to overstate the important than to understate it.

Things should all be moving toward the expression of a great idea.

Fight with yourself when you paint, not with the model. A student is one who struggles with himself, struggles for order.

Positiveness makes for good art. Don't work flatly, softly, roundly and negatively.

All concession is lying.

You will never get form till you *want* it. And wanting to want it is not wanting it.

Think of solidity as you work.

Think of values as giving form, not as spots of light and dark.

Learn giving and receiving in giving.

That which is worth while in a landscape is the expression of human emotion in it.

The sympathetic painting of a still life has more humanity in it than a head, unsympathetically painted.

Do whatever you do intensely.

The artist is the man who leaves the crowd and goes pioneering. With him there is an idea which is his life.

The strong make-up of the human body is beauty and refinement. The human body is terrific. Beauty is a terrific thing, as great as structure. Very few life studies are strong enough to live.

If you work from memory, you are most likely to put in your real feeling.

A great painter will know a great deal about how he did it, but still he will say, "How did I do it?"

The real artist's work is a surprise to himself.

The big painter is one who has something to say. He thus does not paint men, landscape or furniture, but an idea.

A worker or painter should enjoy his work, else the observer will not enjoy it.

All real works of art look as though they were done in joy.

326

Reveal the spirit you have about the thing, not the materials you are going to paint. Reality does not exist in material things. Rather paint the flying spirit of the bird than its feathers.

The coming into the presence of a piece of art you truly love causes a tremendous revolution to occur in you.

Feel the dignity of a child. Do not feel superior to him, for you are not.

A work of art is the trace of a magnificent struggle.

In great art there is no beginning and end in point of time. All time is comprehended.

The paintings of such masters as Titian, Velasquez and Whistler are like great documents hurled down. Each is a great decision. They are records of the thought and struggle of the artist. The picture stands as a record of how much and how little the artist knows, as rough as he was and as capable as he was. The mistakes left in a drawing are the record of the artist's struggle.

Ralph Waldo Emerson

⋙ 1803 – 1882 ⋘

THERE IS NEVER *a really good excuse for a bad lecture; and in an age of cheap paper, linotype and mimeographing machines there is very little excuse for a lecture that merely imparts factual information. But a lecture may also arouse, stimulate, give perspective on a subject, prepare the way for discussion, exhibit a mode of thought, present dramatically a movement of ideas, in a way that no other method of teaching can do. In the house of education there are many rooms—and intimate face to face colloquy need not be held in all of them.*

What the American people would have been in the Nineteenth Century, what they would be now, if Ralph Waldo Emerson had not given hundreds upon hundreds of lectures through four decades, from the Atlantic coast to the Mississippi valley, no one in his right mind would try to say; but certainly some notion of their great value is indicated by the references to them in countless letters, diaries and articles. It was by no means an easy life for Emerson but he kept at it almost to the end.

In that wonderful journal out of which his lectures and later his essays grew, he once summed up his conception of the platform: "Here is all the true orator will ask, for here is a convertible audience, and here are no stiff conventions that prescribe a method, a style, a limited quotation of books and an exact respect to certain books, persons or opinions. No, here everything is admissible, philosophy, ethics, divinity, criticism, poetry, humor, fun, mimicry, anecdotes, jokes, ventriloquism, all the breadth and versatility of the most liberal conversation; highest, lowest, personal, local topics, all are permitted, and all may be combined in one speech;—it is a panharmonicon."

Years later, when the mercury was twenty below zero at Beloit, Wisconsin, Emerson jotted down in the ever-present journal these words: "This climate and people are a new test for the wares of a man of letters. All his thin, watery matter freezes; 'tis only the smallest portion of alcohol that remains good. At the lyceum, the stout Illinoian, after a short trial, walks out of the hall. The Committee tells you that the people want a hearty laugh, and those who give them that, are heard with joy. Well, I think the people are always right (in a sense), and that the man of letters is to say, These are the new conditions to which I must conform. The architect who is asked to build a house to go upon the seas, must not build a Parthenon, or a square house, but a ship. And Shakespeare, or Franklin, or Aesop, coming to Illinois, would say, I must give my wisdom a comic form, instead of tragics or elegiacs, and well I know to do it, and he is no master who cannot vary his forms, and carry his own end triumphantly through the most difficult."

In February, 1849, a young novelist who had not yet started on his masterpiece, Moby Dick, was visiting in Boston and wrote to an editor friend in New York: "I have heard Emerson since I have been here. Say what you will, he's a great man." And a week later: "I was very agreeably disappointed in Mr. Emerson. I had heard of him as full of transcendentalisms, myths & oracular gibberish; I had only glanced at a book of his once in Putnam's store—that was all I knew of him, till I heard him lecture.—To my surprise, I found him quite intelligible, tho' to say truth, they told me that that night he was unusually plain.—Now, there is something about every man elevated above mediocrity, which is, for the most part, instinctively perceptible. This I see in Mr. Emerson. And, frankly, for the sake of argument, let us call him a fool;—then I had rather be a fool than a wise man.—I love all men who dive. Any fish can swim near the surface, but it takes a great whale to go downstairs five miles or more; & if he don't attain the bottom, why, all the lead in Galena can't fashion the plummet that will. I'm not talking of Mr. Emerson now—but of the whole corps of thought-divers, that have been diving & coming up with blood-shot eyes since the world began."

330

Emerson the Lecturer

JAMES RUSSELL LOWELL

->>>·<<<-

T IS A SINGULAR FACT that Mr. Emerson is the most steadily
attractive lecturer in America. Into that somewhat cold-
waterish region adventurers of the sensational kind come
down now and then with a splash, to become disregarded
King Logs before the next season. But Mr. Emerson always
draws. A lecturer now for something like a third of a century,
one of the pioneers of the lecturing system, the charm of his
voice, his manner, and his matter has never lost its power over
his earlier hearers, and continually winds new ones in its
enchanting meshes. What they do not fully understand they
take on trust, and listen, saying to themselves, as the old poet
of Sir Philip Sidney —

> "A sweet, attractive, kind of grace,
> A full assurance given by looks,
> Continual comfort in a face,
> The lineaments of gospel books."

We call it a singular fact, because we Yankees are thought
to be fond of the spread-eagle style, and nothing can be more
remote from that than his. We are reckoned a practical folk,
who would rather hear about a new airtight stove than about
Plato; yet our favorite teacher's practicality is not in the least
of the Poor Richard variety. If he have any Buncombe con-
stituency, it is that unrealized commonwealth of philosophers

331

which Plotinus proposed to establish; and if he were to make an almanac, his directions to farmers would be something like this: "OCTOBER: Indian Summer; now is the time to get in your early Vedas." What, then, is his secret? Is it not that he out-Yankees us all? that his range includes us all? that he is equally at home with the potato-disease and original sin, with pegging shoes and the Over-soul? that, as we try all trades, so has he tried all cultures? and above all, that his mysticism gives us a counter-poise to our super-practicality?

There is no man living to whom, as a writer, so many of us feel and thankfully acknowledge so great an indebtedness for ennobling impulses — none whom so many cannot abide. What does he mean? ask these last. Where is his system? What is the use of it all? What the deuce have we to do with Brahma? I do not propose to write an essay on Emerson at this time. I will only say that one may find grandeur and consolation in a starlit night without caring to ask what it means, save grandeur and consolation; one may like Montaigne, as some ten generations before us have done, without thinking him so systematic as some more eminently tedious (or shall we say tediously eminent?) authors; one may think roses as good in their way as cabbages, though the latter would make a better show in the witness box, if cross-examined as to their usefulness; and as for Brahma, why, he can take care of himself, and won't bite us at any rate.

The bother with Mr. Emerson is, that, though he writes in prose, he is essentially a poet. If you undertake to paraphrase what he says, and to reduce it to words of one syllable for infant minds, you will make as sad work of it as the good monk with his analysis of Homer in the *Epistolae Obscurorum Virorum*. We look upon him as one of the few men of genius whom our age has produced, and there needs no better proof of it than his masculine faculty of fecundating other minds. Search for his eloquence in his books and you will perchance miss it, but meanwhile you will find that it has kindled all your thoughts. For choice and pith of language he belongs to a better age than ours, and might rub shoulders with Fuller and Browne, — though he does use that abominable word *reliable*. His eye for a fine, telling phrase that will carry true is like that of a backwoodsman for a rifle; and he will dredge you up a choice word from the mud of Cotton Mather himself. A diction at once so rich and so homely as his I know not where to match in these days of writing by the page; it is like homespun cloth of gold. The many cannot miss his meaning, and only the few can find it. It is the open secret of all true genius. It is wholesome to angle in those profound pools, though one be rewarded with nothing more than the leap of a fish that flashes his freckled side in the sun and as suddenly absconds in the dark and dreamy waters again. There is keen excitement, though there be no ponderable acquisition. If we carry nothing home in our baskets, there is ample gain in dilated lungs and stimulated blood. What does he mean, quotha? He means inspiring hints, a divining-rod to your deeper nature. No doubt, Emerson, like all original men, has his peculiar audience, and yet I know none that can hold a promiscuous crowd in pleased attention so long as he. As in all original men, there is something for every palate. "Would you know," says Goethe, "the ripest cherries? Ask the boys and the blackbirds."

The announcement that such a pleasure as a new course of lectures by him is coming, to people as old as I am, is something like those forebodings of spring that prepare us every year for a familiar novelty, none the less novel, when it arrives, because it is familiar. We know perfectly well what we are to expect from Mr. Emerson, and yet what he says always penetrates and stirs us, as is apt to be the case with genius, in a very unlooked-for fashion. Perhaps genius is one of the few things which we gladly allow to repeat itself — one of the few that multiply rather than weaken the force of their impression by iteration? Perhaps some of us hear more than the mere words, are moved by something deeper than the thoughts? If it be so, we are quite right, for it is thirty years and more of "plain living and high thinking" that speak to us in this altogether unique lay-preacher. We have shared in the beneficence of this varied culture, this fearless impartiality in criticism and speculation, this masculine sincerity, this sweetness of nature which rather stimulates than cloys, for a generation long. If ever there was a standing testimonial to the cumulative power and value of Character, (and we need it sadly in these days,) we have it in this gracious and dignified presence. What an antiseptic is a pure life! At sixty-five (or two years beyond his grand climacteric, as he would prefer to call it) he has that privilege of soul which abolishes the calendar, and presents him to us always the unwasted contemporary of his own prime. I do not know if he seem old to his younger hearers, but we who have known him so long wonder at the tenacity with which he maintains himself even in the outposts of youth. I suppose it is not the Emerson of 1868 to whom we listen. For us the whole life of the man is distilled in the clear drop of every sentence, and behind each word we divine the force of a noble character, the weight of a large capital of thinking and being. We do not go to hear what Emerson says so much as to hear Emerson. Not that we perceive any falling-off in anything that ever was essential to the charm of Mr. Emerson's peculiar style of thought or phrase. The first lecture, to be sure, was more disjointed even than common. It was as if, after vainly trying to get his paragraphs into sequence and order, he had at last tried the desperate expedient of shuffling them. It was chaos come again, but it was a chaos full of shooting-stars, a jumble of creative forces. The second lecture, on "Criticism and Poetry," was quite up to the level of old times, full of that power of strangely-subtle association whose indirect approaches startle the mind into almost painful attention, of those flashes of mutual understanding between speaker and hearer that are gone ere one can say it lightens. The vice of Emerson's criticism seems to be, that while no man is so sensitive to what is poetical, few men are less sensible than he of what makes a poem. He values the solid meaning of thought above the subtler meaning of style. He would prefer Donne, I suspect, to Spenser, and sometimes mistakes the queer for the original.

To be young is surely the best, if the most precarious, gift of life; yet there are some of us who would hardly consent to be young again, if it were at the cost of our recollection of Mr. Emerson's first lectures during the consulate of Van Buren. We used to walk in from the country to the Masonic Temple (I think it was), through the crisp winter night, and listen to that thrilling voice of his, so charged with subtle meaning and subtle music, as shipwrecked men on a raft to the hail of a ship that came with unhoped-for food and rescue. Cynics might say what they liked. Did our own imaginations transfigure dry remainder-biscuit into ambrosia? At any rate, he brought us life, which, on the whole, is no bad thing. Was it all transcendentalism? Magic-lantern pictures on mist? As you will. Those, then, were just what we wanted. But it was not so. The delight and the benefit were that he put us in communication with a larger style of thought, sharpened our wits with a more pungent phrase, gave us ravishing glimpses of an ideal under the dry husk of our New England; made us conscious of the supreme and everlasting originality of whatever bit of soul might be in any of us; freed us, in short, from the stocks of prose in which we had sat so long that we had grown wellnigh contented in our cramps. And who that saw the audience will ever forget it, where every one still capable of fire, or longing to renew in himself the half-forgotten sense of it, was gathered? Those faces, young and old, agleam with pale intellectual light, eager with pleased attention, flash upon me once more from the deep recesses of the years with an exquisite pathos. Ah, beautiful young eyes, brimming with love and hope, wholly vanished now in that other world we

335

call the Past, or peering doubtfully through the pensive gloam-
ing of memory, your light impoverishes these cheaper days! I
hear again that rustle of sensation, as they turned to exchange
glances over some pithier thought, some keener flash of that
humor which always played about the horizon of his mind like
heat-lightning, and it seems now like the sad whisper of the
autumn leaves that are whirling around me. But would my
picture be complete if I forgot that ample and vegete countenance of Mr. R—— of W——, how, from its regular post at
the corner of the front bench, it turned in ruddy triumph to
the profaner audience as if he were the inexplicably appointed
fugleman of appreciation? I was reminded of him by those
hearty cherubs in Titian's Assumption that look at you as who
should say, "Did you ever see a Madonna like that? Did you
ever behold one hundred and fifty pounds of womanhood
mount heavenward before like a rocket?"

To some of us that long-past experience remains as the most
marvellous and fruitful we have ever had. Emerson awakened
us, saved us from the body of this death. It is the sound of the
trumpet that the young soul longs for, careless what breath
may fill it. Sidney heard it in the ballad of "Chevy Chase,"
and we in Emerson. Nor did it blow retreat, but called to
us with assurance of victory. Did they say he was discon-
nected? So were the stars, that seemed larger to our eyes, still
keen with that excitement, as we walked homeward with
prouder stride over the creaking snow. And were they not
knit together by a higher logic than our mere sense could
master? Were we enthusiasts? I hope and believe we were,
and am thankful to the man who made us worth something
for once in our lives. If asked what was left? what we carried
home? we should not have been careful for an answer. It
would have been enough if we had said that something beautiful had passed that way. Or we might have asked in return
what one brought away from a symphony of Beethoven? Enough
that he had set that ferment of wholesome discontent at work

336

in us. There is one, at least, of those old hearers, so many of whom are now in the fruition of that intellectual beauty of which Emerson gave them both the desire and the foretaste, who will always love to repeat:

> *"Che in la mente m'è fitta, ed or m'accuora*
> *La cara e buona immagine paterna*
> *Di voi, quando nel mondo ad ora ad ora*
> *M'insegnavaste come l'uom s'eterna."*

I am unconsciously thinking, as I write, of the third lecture of the present course, in which Mr. Emerson gave some delightful reminiscences of the intellectual influences in whose movement he had shared. It was like hearing Goethe read some passages of the *Wahrheit aus seinem Leben.* Not that there was not a little *Dichtung,* too, here and there, as the lecturer built up so lofty a pedestal under certain figures as to lift them into a prominence of obscurity, and seem to masthead them there. Everybody was asking his neighbor who this or that recondite great man was, in the faint hope that somebody might once have heard of him. There are those who call Mr. Emerson cold. Let them revise their judgment in presence of this loyalty of his that can keep warm for half a century, that never forgets a friendship, or fails to pay even a fancied obligation to the uttermost farthing. This substantiation of shadows was but incidental, and pleasantly characteristic of the man to those who know and love him. The greater part of the lecture was devoted to reminiscences of things substantial in themselves. He spoke of Everett, fresh from Greece and Germany; of Channing; of the translations of Margaret Fuller, Ripley, and Dwight; of the Dial and Brook Farm. To what he said of the latter an undertone of good-humored irony gave special zest. But what every one of his hearers felt was that the protagonist in the drama was left out. The lecturer was no Æneas to babble the *quorum magna pars fui,* and, as one of his listeners, I cannot help wishing to say how each of them was commenting the story as it went along, and filling up the necessary gaps in it from his own private store of memories. His younger hearers could not know how much they owed to the benign impersonality, the quiet scorn of everything ignoble, the never-sated hunger of self-culture, that were personified in the man before them. But the older knew how much the country's intellectual emancipation was due to the stimulus of his teaching and example, how constantly he had kept burning the beacon of an ideal life above our lower region of turmoil. To him more than to all other causes together did the young martyrs of our civil war owe the sustaining strength of thoughtful heroism that is so touching in every record of their lives. Those who are grateful to Mr. Emerson, as many of us are, for what they feel to be most valuable in their culture, or perhaps I should say their impulse, are grateful not so much for any direct teachings of his as for that inspiring lift which only genius can give, and without which all doctrine is chaff.

This was something like the *caret* which some of us older boys wished to fill up on the margin of the master's lecture. Few men have been so much to so many, and through so large a range of aptitudes and temperaments, and this simply because all of us value manhood beyond any or all other qualities of character. We may suspect in him, here and there, a certain thinness and vagueness of quality, but let the waters go over him as they list, this masculine fibre of his will keep its lively color and its toughness of texture. I have heard some great speakers and some accomplished orators, but never any that so moved and persuaded men as he. There is a kind of undertow in that rich baritone of his that sweeps our minds from their foothold into deeper waters with a drift we cannot and would not resist. And how artfully (for Emerson is a long-studied artist in these things) does the deliberate utterance, that seems waiting for the fit word, appear to admit us partners in the labor of thought and make us feel as if the glance of humor were

338

a sudden suggestion, as if the perfect phrase lying written there on the desk were as unexpected to him as to us! In that closely-filed speech of his at the Burns centenary dinner, every word seemed to have just dropped down to him from the clouds. He looked far away over the heads of his hearers, with a vague kind of expectation, as into some private heaven of invention, and the winged period came at last obedient to his spell. "My dainty Ariel!" he seemed murmuring to himself as he cast down his eyes as if in deprecation of the frenzy of approval and caught another sentence from the Sibylline leaves that lay before him, ambushed behind a dish of fruit and seen only by nearest neighbors. Every sentence brought down the house, as I never saw one brought down before — and it is not so easy to hit Scotsmen with a sentiment that has no hint of native brogue in it. I watched, for it was an interesting study, how the quick sympathy ran flashing from face to face down the long tables, like an electric spark thrilling as it went, and then exploded in a thunder of plaudits. I watched till tables and faces vanished, for I, too, found myself caught up in the common enthusiasm, and my excited fancy set me under the *bema* listening to him who fulmined over Greece. I can never help applying to him what Ben Jonson said of Bacon: "There happened in my time one noble speaker, who was full of gravity in his speaking. His language was nobly censorious. No man ever spake more neatly, more pressly, more weightily, or suffered less emptiness, less idleness, in what he uttered. No member of his speech but consisted of his own graces. His hearers could not cough, or look aside from him, without loss. He commanded where he spoke." Those who heard him while their natures were yet plastic, and their mental nerves trembled under the slightest breath of divine air, will never cease to feel and say:

> "*Was never eye did see that face,*
> *Was never ear did hear that tongue,*

339

Was never mind did mind his grace,
  That ever thought the travail long;
But eyes, and ears, and every thought,
Were with his sweet perfections caught."

Epilogue

WHILE A LECTURE was going on before a large class, a student in the back row fell unquietly asleep. The professor noticed the defection but continued with his remarks, more in sorrow than in anger. A few minutes later the boy recovered consciousness, and blurted out an apology. "No," said the professor, "it is I who should apologize to you—for not keeping you awake." An obvious confession of duty, perhaps, but one so unusual that it caused a small furor within those ivy-clad walls.

Whatever else the teacher may do for his students, he must first of all awaken, arouse, startle into thought; he cannot assume that they have his interest in the subject, or that his presence automatically eliminates boredom and daydreaming. Socrates was a gadfly before he was a midwife of ideas and so to some extent is every good teacher, ranging from use of the playful question and gentle irony to the sweeping assertion and the harsh demand. And the first meeting between teacher and students is often crucial: If a vital contact is not established then, it may never be. "At last a Man," young Louis Sullivan's inner cry after his first class with Moses Woolson, would be more common, if more teachers had a sense of dedication—and of drama. "While good teaching will differ widely in its methods, there is at least one thing in which all good teaching will be alike; no teaching is good which does not arouse and 'dephlegmatize' the students—to borrow an expression attributed to Novalis—which does not engage as its allies their awakened, sympathetic, and co-operating faculties." (James Bradley Thayer: Introduction to *Cases on Constitutional Law*)

Unfortunately the initial awakening of the students does not necessarily involve their prolonged co-operation. That depends largely on the "contagious enthusiasm" of the teacher which is the most needed trait of all. The very words run through the literature of education. "But there he was; a strong man talking with knowledge and a sort of dark enthusiasm: and, sentence by sentence, he enforced the high contagion." "There was always the abiding note of contagious enthusiasm and generous encouragement." "The teacher has a double function. It is for him to elicit the enthusiasm by resonance from his own personality and to create the environment of a larger knowledge and a firmer purpose."

This enthusiasm need not be blatant or theatrical but it is continuously present, like air for a wing. The fine teacher has no fear of feeling and does not attempt to achieve that specious academic objectivity which freezes a class. Rather he knows that it is actually impossible to separate thought from emotion and that it is dangerous to try, for the apparent split leads to private neuroses and public explosions. "The most useful investigator, because the most sensitive observer," said William James, "is always he whose eager interest in one side of the question is balanced by an equally keen nervousness lest he become deceived." "Be passionate in your work and your searchings," said Pavlov, at eighty-seven, to the academic youth of Soviet Russia. He never recommended what Nietzsche sneeringly called "immaculate perception."

It may not be difficult for the teacher to sustain enthusiasm at the higher levels of education where the horizon is always receding but what of the teacher at the lower levels restricted to the same routine courses, term after term? Why, here is the chance of a lifetime, or rather an early chance at many lives and the responsibility is enormous! Only a relatively small number of young Americans go beyond high school, and those who do, are already marked, for better or for worse; and that is why the longest chapter of the Harvard Report on *General Education in a Free Society* is devoted to secondary education. The primary or secondary school teachers may know their materials so well that they can devote their best energies to the ever changing problems of their art and the ever changing individualities of their pupils.

Of course, contagious enthusiasm should go along with thorough knowledge of the subject, so that it can be presented not only warmly but accurately and coherently. Whether "thorough knowledge" means scholarship or original research is a question. It is true that many an outstanding teacher has no interest in the ink that brings promotion or professional recognition. But at least at the college or university level the teacher who does not want to go deeply into his subject, or advance its boundaries, or put his views into some definitive form, usually lacks zeal — and sometimes the respect of his colleagues and students. (Of the college and university teachers we have studied, Charles Edward Garman is the only one who did not write some significant articles or books.)

Yet, paradoxically, the fine teacher, who knows his subject thoroughly and has the power to excite interest in it, always carries his students beyond its boundaries. Any subject can be liberal if it is taught by a liberating mind. Any so-called liberal subject such as English, history, or philosophy can be and often is taught in a dry, deadening, way. There are Rutgers alumni who still think that their best course was first year Greek with the aging Professor Kirk, just as Dean Donham still remembers the broadening effect of Shaler's Geology 4 at Harvard. Yet Geology and first year Greek do not often arouse nostalgic memories.

In *Lanterns on the Levee,* William Alexander Percy spoke of old Judge Griffin with whom he "browsed and ranged and broke every law of pedagogy" while they read Shakespeare, Dante, and Milton together. "As with all great teachers, his curriculum

343

was an insignificant part of what he communicated. From him
you didn't learn a subject, but life. I suspect anyway that the
important thing we learn we never remember because they become part of us, we absorb them. We don't absorb the multi-
plication table (at least not the seventh and the eleventh), but
those things that are vitamins and calories to the spirit, the
spirit seizes on and transmutes into its own strength, wholly
and forgetfully. Tolerance and justice, fearlessness and pride,
reverence and pity, are learned in a course on long division if the
teacher has those qualities, as Judge Griffin had."

At a time of much talk about semantics, it might be well to
touch for a moment on the basic matter of communication. The
teacher is apt to be sceptical of the student who says that he
knows the answer to a question but cannot quite put it into
words. But so the student might be suspicious of the teacher,
who seems to possess the apparatus of learning, but cannot convey it clearly. The difficulty may lie in a poor vocabulary or
simply in verbal timidity. The same point can always be made
in several ways and indeed should be, for a class of any size,
but the teacher often sticks to a single phrasing and shies from a
sharp use of the vernacular or a resounding piece of resplendent
rhetoric, original or quoted. However, young people are delighted to have their lessons brightened up with linguistic local
color and they like to jot in their notebooks a memorable
aphorism. But if winged words are lacking, so are winged illustrations which go to the heart of an issue. Mere obvious,
plodding illustrations help, of course, but remote, fantastic
examples startle and stretch the mind. As the poet must be "a
master of metaphor," according to Aristotle, so the teacher
needs a rich fund of analogy and metaphor, not only to make the
complex appear more simple, but to make meaning meaningful,
emotion warm and real. When one thinks of the way in which
Anne Mansfield Sullivan communicated a whole world to the
blind and deaf Helen Keller, those who deal with normal stu-

344

dents must blush a little at their own feeble range of imagery.

No doubt some "psychological distance" between teacher and student is inevitable and desirable. It is a little foolish and certainly inaccurate to say that they are just friends, just equals, studying the same problem. But too often the distance between them is enormous and their voices can hardly be heard across the gulf. Dr. Oliver Wendell Holmes, who lectured to a rough-and-tumble class of several hundred medical students for thirty-six years (at one in the afternoon!) and held them with his minute information and his rippling humor, knew a thing or two about teaching. "The professor's chair," he said, "is an insulating stool, so to speak; his age, his knowledge, real or supposed, his official station, are like the glass legs which support the electrician's piece of furniture, and cut it off from the common currents of the floor upon which it stands."

The degree of this insulation chiefly depends on the temperament of the professor himself, but it can be reduced in many specific ways, when dignity is not confused with pomposity. We may recall Patten's breakfasts, Burr's dinners and excursions, Kittredge's late evening conferences in his study at home. But numberless informal contacts would be possible if that wretched ten minute interval between classes were widened. After a lecture or a discussion, a group of interested students frequently wants to gather around the teacher's desk but they or he has to dash off to another class — and lively ideas are sacrificed to a mechanical schedule. Similarly with the fixed office hour, it is ideal for a prolonged conversation but both the proud and the shy students often fail to take advantage of it. They may seem to be "apple polishing" or they may be intruding on the professor's time. But if they felt free to approach him at a chance meeting on a path, there could be hundreds of brief, peripatetic discussions that would be more spontaneous than most specific office appointments. It was no mean compliment when one professor said to another: "I have never seen you

alone on the campus." For that colleague was accessible to any
student who passed by.

Beyond the campus, however, there is the world and no ivy
walls will ever again be high enough to keep them separate.
There is charm in the cloistered scholar but he becomes more
and more of an anachronism and indeed a danger when he fails
to give his students a sense of what is going on outside. There is
no academic subject now, be it physics or politics, economics
or history, philosophy, or psychology, that can be treated in
isolation without considering its far-reaching implications.
Wild winds, remote winds blow through every class room
and no one can keep them out. "The characteristic that distinguished Prof. Patton from most of the other teachers at the
University of Pennsylvania was that while he always had one
eye on the class room, the other eye was forever on the community," said Scott Nearing. But that was forty years ago.
More and more teachers have that double vision today, to their
glory and their deeper happiness.

In discussing this question of great teachers with many
people, I found that a number of them distinguish between
their most "finished" teacher and their "best" teacher. It
seems that the finished teacher would always start at a very
specific point in a lecture or discussion and proceed in an
orderly fashion to a definite conclusion. There were no apparent
doubts in his mind and no hesitations in his manner. Indeed he
often talked "like a book." When he finished a point, it was
clear and simple. When he finished a subject, it was closed—
and one hardly ever wanted to return to it again.

On the other hand, the best teacher often started at the
wrong point and made several false starts. He was tentative in
his inferences and often hesitant in his manner. He would get off
on a tangent and then ask the students how they got there. He
frankly and frequently confessed his ignorance. His eyes would
often be fixed on a distant point as he thought out loud, often

346

to the dismay of the students. At the end of a discussion he would leave at least some loose ends — which were live ends. He made few things completely clear and simple. But he made his students think and he opened windows and he pointed to the horizon beyond.

Index of Names

349

INDEX